D1268868

The
Church
as
Counterculture

SUNY series in Popular Culture and Political Change
Larry Bennett and Ronald Edsforth, editors

The
Church
as
Counterculture

Michael L. Budde and
Robert W. Brimlow, editors

State University of New York Press

"Practicing the Politics of Jesus" is reprinted from *A Peculiar People*, by Rodney Clapp. Used with permission from InterVarsity Press, P.O. Box 1400, Downers Grove, IL 60515.

Published by
State University of New York Press, Albany

For information, address State University of New York Press,
90 State Street, Suite 700, Albany, NY 12207

Production by Michael Haggett
Marketing by Anne M. Valentine

Library of Congress Cataloging-in-Publication Data

The church as counterculture / edited by Michael L. Budde and Robert W. Brimlow.
      p. cm. — (SUNY series in popular culture and political change)
    Includes bibliographical references and index.
    ISBN 0-7914-4607-7 (alk. paper) — ISBN 0-7914-4608-5 (pbk. : alk. paper)
    1. Christianity and culture—United States. I. Budde, Michael L. II. Brimlow,
    Robert
  W., 1954–   III. Series.

  BR115.C8 C49 2000
  261'.0973—dc21
                                                                    99-043439

10   9   8   7   6   5   4   3   2

For Joan and Terri

Contents

The
Church
as
Counterculture

Introduction

The third-grade teacher approached one of us in the parking lot after school a while back. "We have a situation I need to discuss with you," she said. "Your daughter Rachel hasn't been saying the Pledge of Allegiance with the rest of the class."

"And?" said the dad.

"Well, I talked with her, and she said your wife told her that Mom and Dad don't say the Pledge of Allegiance because people use that to justify going off to war and killing people. But I explained to her that patriotism is about love of country and being proud of your country."

"You need to know," said the dad, "that I don't consider my daughter's refusal to say the Pledge of Allegiance to be a problem at all."

"Yes well," said the teacher, "it's just something we do together as a class. Like saying prayers."

"You say prayers, which I support, because this is a Christian school," said the dad. "When did nationalism become part of the curriculum?"

The teacher was surprised by the question, and not at all interested in answering it. "Well, I just wanted you to know about my talk with Rachel. Good bye."

Neither Mom nor Dad have ever suggested to their kids that they should boycott nation-worship via the Pledge of Allegiance, the Battle Hymn of the Republic, or other civil religion rituals. Sometimes the kids participate on their own, sometimes they don't. Since that conversation in the parking lot, Rachel reports that the teacher has stopped ordering her to say the Pledge of Allegiance. Instead, a band of eight-year-old stormtroopers took up the cause.

1

"They draw pictures of the flag and wave them in front of me, Dad," she said. "They say, "Why don't you love our country? What's the matter with you?" I tell them that the Pledge is about killing and war and I don't believe in that. But they keep on teasing me."

"Welcome to the club, kiddo," said the dad. "Some people would rather do what other people tell them than think for themselves. Like sheep."

"I have a *lot* of sheep around my desk," she said. Although Rachel no longer sits while the rest of the class stands for the Pledge of Allegiance (no need always to dramatize your refusal, offers the dad), she still won't make promises to Caesar. Maybe she's learning important things at that school after all—just not what they had in mind.

As far as we know, Bill Keane has never visited Rachel's elementary school. But there's not much doubt that he's seen—and probably experienced—the sort of Christian-citizen formation nurtured there and in countless other contexts in which the churches proclaim their compatibility with existing systems and ideologies of power.

Keane, a product of the Philadelphia Catholic school system, is the creator of what his syndicate calls the most widely carried newspaper cartoon strip in the world (more than fifteen hundred daily newspapers). His "Family Circus" comic strip is a warm, uplifting world where cute kids say cute things, parents learn to find joy in the little things of life, and the spirits of departed loved ones remain part of the family. The "Family Circus" celebrates and uplifts the middle-American picture of the ideal family, seven days a week, all across the country.

We found ourselves thinking of Rachel's showdown with her school's patriotic front when we read Keane's February 7, 1998, offering. A little girl, kneeling on her bed with her hands folded in prayer, looks up at her mommy and says, "I couldn't remember the Lord's Prayer, so I said the Pledge of Allegiance."

Keane hoped his readers would find the vignette cute, with a warm sense of recognition. We experienced the sense of recognition, all right, but it made us sad instead.

Neither Rachel nor Bill Keane (we presume) have much experience in international diplomacy. But the notion of church they have observed—as grease in the machine of order, worship of the national collective—is in full display in debates over what may be the primary foreign policy concern of the American establishment: economic and political relations with the People's Republic of China. When President Clinton honored

President Jiang Zemin of China with a full state dinner in October 1997, he was joined by a boatload of transnational CEOs (the list included the heads of Xerox, AT&T, Atlantic Richfield, Boeing, Pepsico, Eastman Kodak, Motorola, IBM, Westinghouse, Time-Warner, Mobil, Proctor & Gamble, General Motors, Bell Atlantic, General Electric, and Walt Disney Company)[1] eager to pursue profitable opportunities provided by the authoritarian capitalism that is post-Maoist China.

The harmony of that secular table fellowship convened by Clinton was threatened by yet another upwelling of protest concerning China's repression of human rights. Much of that protest has focused on the Chinese government's persecution of religious groups that refuse to submit to control and supervision by the state. Many members of Congress, human rights advocacy groups, and a coalition of religious organizations (from the right and left) have demanded that the U.S. government revoke most-favored-nation trade status for China over the issue of religious persecution and human rights abuses—a position opposed by the Clinton administration and the transnational corporate sector.

It is not surprising that Clinton and Jiang would try to defuse the issue by engineering a three-week tour by three U.S. clergy to China with instructions to "dialogue" with the regime's leaders on religious liberty. Nor were the selections for the February 1998 trip especially remarkable; on the contrary, in many ways they epitomized the broad middle of the American religious landscape: Archbishop Theodore McCarrick, head of the International Policy Committee of the National Conference of Catholic Bishops; Rabbi Arthur Schneier, president of the Appeal to Conscience Foundation, a New York–based group that works worldwide for religious liberty; and the Reverend Don Argue, president of the National Association of Evangelicals. McCarrick and Argue are also members of the State Department's Advisory Committee on Religious Freedom Abroad.

Most remarkable, at least in how clearly they reveal the mainstream church's sense of its role in contemporary society, were some of the arguments the clergy offered their Chinese hosts in defense of religious freedom. Political leaders need not view Christians and other believers as threats to order—on the contrary, the state's order and stability can more effectively be enhanced by adopting the same religion-and-society pattern prevalent in the United States.

"We have stressed that people of faith are good citizens, honest people, who do their jobs and pay taxes," said Rev. Argue after the visit. "It's to China's advantage to work with such people. . . . They serve in the military, they are volunteers in their communities."[2]

Why persecute, in other words, when you can gain the same outcomes—persons willing to kill, die, and pay for the state—through gentler forms of co-optation, assimilation, and domesticated faith? Even before meeting with their hosts, Argue described his goal as "help[ing] the Chinese government understand that Christians are good citizens. They show up for work on time. They pay their bills. They're honest."[3]

One can perhaps forgive the dictators in Beijing for misunderstanding the political implications of Christianity. After all, in their internal dealings they have had to contend with an underground Catholic Church whose members would sooner risk decades of imprisonment than subordinate the gospel to tyrants. The regime reads the New Testament and becomes uneasy; it becomes unnerving to read about the risen Lord leading people to step across the borders of nationality, class, and gender in the service of a Kingdom no government can control.

The rulers in Beijing can be forgiven their lack of experience with churches that join their religious and political loyalties, that are almost entirely at peace with militarism, economic exploitation, and national idolatry. While the state-sponsored Patriotic Association churches (Catholic and Protestant) claim more members than the persecuted underground church, the regime's leaders have yet to gain the peace of mind that rulers enjoy when the gospel is safely marginalized, minimized, and melded with lesser loyalties.

It's good that the Reverend Argue is there to help them understand the American way. Perhaps he will organize an American visit for his dialogue partners in the Chinese government's religious bureaucracy. For our part, we can direct them to Christian schools where children learn the Our Father, the story of Jesus, and some other prayers—while also memorizing and devoutly reciting the Pledge of Allegiance, the Star-Spangled Banner, and all the sacramentals associated with Veterans Day and the Fourth of July. No doubt they will like what they see, and hurry home excited about still another American practice useful in their rush toward superpower status.

Too many volumes of edited essays have their genesis, it seems, in bad academic conferences. Usually the editors collect all the papers—good, bad, and ugly—polish them a bit and ensure uniformity in the footnotes. These volumes are then offered for sale to all those academic specialists who were fortunate enough to miss the live proceedings. While the idea for this book also originated at an academic conference, its development followed a significantly different path.

In 1995, we attended a ten-day conference designed to explore Catholicism and higher education. It didn't take us long to figure out that we were out of step with those who organized the program. Nearly all of the primary speakers and most of the workshop facilitators were steeped in a view of the church in which one's religious convictions and loyalties meshed easily with the roles of citizen, scholar, American, and middle-class professional. In a variety of contexts, we were told that the "incarnational" nature of the Catholic tradition requires us to embrace—critically at times, but always embrace—the cultures, identities, and loyalties of our non-Christian surroundings. That being a Christian, or a Catholic, might put people at odds with some of those roles was a largely unexplored possibility. Rather than seeing Christian identity as a distinctive way of being in the world, one that necessarily involves the willingness to live differently in service to the gospel, we were counseled against being "exclusive," "particularistic," or—God forbid—"sectarian." What we had hoped would be a challenging dialogue on what it might mean to be the church in a post-Christian environment, instead turned out to be a monologue on behaving as "responsible" scholars, citizens, and Americans—with "responsibility" defined by communities for whom Christianity is just another "preference" to be tolerated when possible, and marginalized when necessary.

So the two of us talked and drank a lot of coffee. When we could no longer stand the conference speakers' countless references to Robert Putnam's "bowling alone" metaphor (intending to draw attention to the collapse of civic community and the rise of individualism in the United States), we skipped a session and went bowling—together. We drank more coffee and talked about the ways in which Christianity should be the *defining* identity against which all others—nationalism, class, race, gender, kinship, and the rest—should be measured. We talked about the currents within the churches—not at all represented at the conference—calling for a more radical Christianity, one that calls the church back to its roots as an alternative community committed to Christian discipleship and the Way of the Cross.

This book is one product of those conversations and all that coffee. It is part of larger movements of the Spirit within the churches that call into question the dominant notions of church, vocation, and ways of living in the world. It challenges the sterile frameworks of "church versus sect," and the stagnant polemics about whether Christians should be for or against the "world" or "culture." Rather, this radical reform impulse within the Christian world challenges the legitimacy of such categories as conventionally understood and employed; it suggests that they have been most commonly used as tools in the Constantinian (and later, the modernist) effort to make the gospel conform to the preferences, priorities, and structures of worldly power.

To persons steeped in the radical traditions of Christianity, baptism signifies a decisive break with one's previous desires and priorities (1 Pet 1:14). It calls people to reconfigure prior allegiances to caste and kin, country and gender, as part of what it means to join the Body of Christ, the symbolic prefiguration of forgiveness, mutual assistance, service, and worship that the Creator will bring to fruition in the promised Kingdom of God. The vocation that comes to Christians is inseparable from the church, the material and sacramental reality that testifies to Jesus' commitment to a new way of being in the world, one that does not rely upon domination and killing as the firmament of human association. Discipleship—making the priorities, practices, and affections of Jesus one's guide to the Christian life—is an intrinsically ecclesiocentric proposition, for it is only as a community of faith that the necessary processes of discernment, disagreement, and reconciliation become a real part of our world.

As noted by theologian Miroslav Volf:

> Christians do not come into their social world from outside seeking either to accommodate to their new home (like second generation immigrants would), shape it in the image of the one they left behind (like colonizers would), or establish a little haven in the strange new world reminiscent of the old (as resident aliens would). They are not outsiders who either seek to become insiders or maintain strenuously the status of outsiders. Christians are the insiders who have diverted from their culture by being born again. They are by definition those who are not what they used to be, those who do not live like they used to live. Christian difference is therefore not an insertion of something new into the old from outside, but a bursting out of the new precisely within the proper space of the old.[4]

Volf also expresses the inescapably collective nature of the Christian vocation, in which baptism and difference make sense:

> No one can baptize himself or herself; everyone must be baptized into a given Christian community. Baptism is an incorporation into the Body of Christ, a doorway into a Christian community. Baptism will not do the distancing for you, but it will

tell you that genuine Christian distance has ecclesial shape. It is lived in a community that lives as "aliens" in a larger social environment.[5]

The radical discipleship movement within the churches is delightfully hard to stereotype. It includes conventional scholars and academics, as well as local congregations and leaders not burdened by years of academic socialization. It is relentlessly transdenominational: mainline Protestants and Catholics learn from (and critique) Anabaptists; Jews and Christians struggle together to read and pray the Hebrew Bible; pentecostals dialogue with evangelicals, and both learn from neglected parts of the Catholic tradition. Its theological and social literature is extraordinarily interdisciplinary, with theologians, social scientists, philosophers, historians, and humanists reading one another's work, combining approaches, and trying to orient their scholarship to the upbuilding of the Christian community and not merely the pursuit of academic career objectives. And best of all, it confounds conventional notions of liberal and conservative, left and right, and church and sect.

Given the minimalist ecclesiology in play at the conference we attended—where it was hard to discern how or why being Christian would make any difference in one's way of life (except to "be nice")—we decided to produce a book that gives voice to a view of Christian life and practice that makes more sense to us. The contributors here all have something important to say about taking seriously our relations to Jesus, the gospel, the body of Christ, and the Kingdom of God.

In inviting their participation in this book, our instructions to contributors were open-ended: write on whatever you want regarding radical Christianity and the church. We offered the image of the church as among the primary "paths that lead to life," a popular translation of Acts 2:28, which in turn quotes Ps. 16: 8–11. We like how the image joins the New Testament to the Old, and its sense that God intends the gathered community to blaze a trail that others might follow in moving from darkness to light, from death to life. It ties the fate of the church to the legacy of the Jews. The Christian community is not immune from sin and failure—no purity of groups is required or evident here—but at its best the church knows itself as called to be different. We think that God intends the church to be an ongoing human experiment—infused with grace and Spirit—in the world, a continuous trial-and-error of fellowship built on love, reconciliation, and sacrifice. To do so, it must stay true to the Way of Jesus and others who have set their hearts on the Kingdom of God before all else (Lk. 12:21). To be that kind of church, it must be countercultural (hence our title, *The Church as Countercul-ture*), an alternative community, in the midst of cultures and powers that operate on assumptions and priorities not centered on the Kingdom.

The point of this book was not to lay out a party line, nor to pro-vide a beginning-to-end strategy for church renewal. We intended instead to construct a constellation of ideas, arguments, and resources that might inspire others as the movement advances. One piece of evi-dence pointing to the vitality of this movement is its ability to elicit sympathetic challenges and engagements "within the family" of schol-ars and believers committed to this vision of church and mission to the world. While the contributors agree on many things, they do not (as you will see) agree on everything; we have not attempted to force a false consensus on the strong and effective voices presented here. In fact, we think the variations among the contributors—in focus, tone, and analy-ses—is itself a good thing to be celebrated and encouraged. Persons looking for a tight and rigid editorial hand in this volume will be dis-appointed. We sought chapters that would provide resources (from scripture and church history, theology, social theory, and the like) and exemplars of how theology, philosophy, and social analysis are con-ducted under the formative commitments of discipleship and the King-dom of God. We are not troubled that some might consider our edito-rial framework "too light" a yoke for a book like this. We have seen countless edited volumes where the most directive of editorial frame-works do not protect against the curse of chapters of "uneven quality." Like planets in a solar system, the chapters here move in profoundly different orbits, but they all revolve around a common sun. We think their quality is uniformly strong, even if they don't march in a thematic or organizational lockstep.

Given all that, Rodney Clapp's "Practicing the Politics of Jesus" does what every good first chapter does—it lays a broad foundation informed by diverse sources and themes. He provides a useful explo-ration of the "Constantinian" ecclesiology criticized by many other con-tributors. He also develops many New Testament themes and narratives central to the "politics of Jesus," which he and others (famously the late John Howard Yoder, whose 1972 book of the same title remains impor-tant) see as an alternative to Christian theology and practices cut to fit the needs of imperial power.

According to Clapp, the church is faithful to its origins when it views itself as a community distinct from larger social forces; the church remains "eminently Jewish" in this and similar matters. The continuities between Israel and the young Christian communities—a mainstay in many recent Pauline studies—suggests that efforts to reclaim the radical nature of the church must remain rooted in dialogue with Judaism and the Hebrew Bible.

Noted Old Testament scholar Walter Brueggemann provides just this sort of anchor with his chapter, "Always in the Shadow of the Empire." As he does in his magisterial *Theology of the Old Testament* (Fortress Press, 1997), Brueggemann works like a craftsman, shaping linguistic, social-historic, and theological materials in ways that illustrate how the failures, triumphs, and experiences of the Israelites remain our own and continue to teach us about God's plan for the church and the world.

Among other things, Brueggemann and Clapp demonstrate the theological and scriptural inadequacy of Christian self-understandings that privilege a false or cheap universality over the scandal of particularity that is the vocation of the Jews as the chosen people and the church as sharers in that legacy.

Judaism, Christianity, and the Roman Empire meet—*collide* might be a better word—in Marianne Sawicki's contribution. In "Salt and Leaven: Resistances to Empire in the Street-Smart Paleochurch," Sawicki brings her unusual combination of talents to bear on a close study of the practices and ecclesiology of the precanonical churches of occupied Palestine. Sawicki blends her expertise in biblical archaeology, history, philosophy, and social theory to present a provocative picture of the earliest churches as inconspicuous subversives whose life patterns and discourse denied legitimacy to Roman pretensions and claims. While she is sympathetic to the social and ecclesial agenda of many of her fellow feminist and liberation theologians, Sawicki counsels against reading the present-day ecclesial objectives of those groups (a "discipleship of equals," or an "exodus" people, for example) into the first-century churches. Doing so is not only bad theological and historical practice, in her view, it also hides from us first-century ecclesial strategies that might help the church resist and subvert the dominant order in our "post-Constantinian" environment.

When it comes to highlighting the contemporary implications of being a church that takes itself seriously, few people have done so more effectively than Stanley Hauerwas. In "The Nonviolent Terrorist: In Defense of Christian Fanaticism," Hauerwas challenges the presumed value neutrality that undergirds societal consensus on matters like terrorism. Turning the tables further on conventional discussion of social ethics, Hauerwas argues for a quality of Christian witness serious enough about nonviolence that it appears as "terroristic" or "fanatical" to the reigning powers, for whom war and killing are indispensable tools of the trade. When the church allows itself to be different, a community formed by the power of the Christian narrative, it "can be understood as an international conspiracy against all politics based on 'self-preservation.'" And that, says Hauerwas, is all to the good.

The most common charge hurled against Hauerwas, Yoder, and other theologians of radical Christianity is that they are "sectarian"—and being a sectarian is a bad thing. Sectarianism, say the critics, forces an ethic of perfection on the Christian community, presumes to shrink God's grace to cover only the self-selected few of the sect, and abandons the poor and needy of the world by creating an insular Christianity separate from the world. Philosopher Robert W. Brimlow enters the discussion in "Solomon's Porch: The Church as Sectarian Ghetto," with a novel perspective.

Unlike liberal critics, Brimlow is persuaded by Hauerwas' emphasis on the particularity of Christian discourse and the church. In fact, Brimlow invites Hauerwas to be *more*, not less, sectarian. Such a move seems justified, argues Brimlow, when one moves toward greater specificity in usage of terms such as "coercion," "public policy," and "society." Considering the implications for Christian witness and practice, it may be worthwhile to reappropriate some of the negative labels—Brimlow even defends the value of a "Christian ghetto"—and recast them as positive manifestations of the faith.

Church practices are also central to the concerns of Michael Warren, who asks what significance Christian congregations have had in relation to the "social and cultural horrors" of the twentieth century. In "Decisions That Inscribe Life's Patterns," Warren argues that if the church has failed to be the body of Christ in our era, the practices and patterns of real-life congregations must be interrogated for inadequacies and distortions.

Warren explores the sociological processes and structures that form practices and attitudes in society, and that impact on whether or how the church works to embody "Jesus' view of the human." And while much in the church's attempts to live the gospel in the twentieth century has served to "disaffirm or deny" the gospel, he is able to point to more promising examples of what he calls "communities of renegotiated discipleship." Such communities do not respect denominational lines, and appear in varying cultural environments. They are among ongoing efforts to "re-specify the specifics of the Gospel in a way suited for a particular time"—and the church needs many more such efforts if it is to remain credible and faithful in the years ahead.

One of the most studied—and hyped—expressions of Warren's "communities of renegotiated discipleship" is the base Christian community movement. In "Legion and the Believing Community: Discipleship in an Imperial Age," Curt Cadorette draws upon his years of pastoral experience in Peru and reflects upon the "preferential option for the poor," liberation theology, and the church in the era of neoliberal capitalism. Significantly, Cadorette joins his treatment of base communities in poor countries with an examination of middle-class "intentional communities" of Christians in wealthy ones. Both represent real-life attempts to construct lives of Christian purpose in the face of empire—the base communities in the provinces, the intentional communities in the imperial center. While their immediate problems and approaches differ, both innovations "explain the gospel and the catholic way of being in a dehumanized and oppressive world. . . . They open up [people's] eyes so they can see who they really are without the distorting effect of the imperial lens . . . that invariably makes us too large or too small, grandiose or self-loathing in unreal ways."

Roberto Goizueta's chapter on the popular religion of Hispanic/Latino Catholics in the United States parallels Cadorette's discussion of base and intentional communities as enabling the church to amplify its "incarnation vision" within "diverse cultures, humanity, and historical experience." In "'There You Will See Him': Christianity beyond the Frontier Myth," Goizueta examines the negative consequences of the U.S. "frontier myth," freighted as it is with notions of power, superiority, fear, and exclusion.

In contrast, Latino faith and practice in many respects manifests a "border" consciousness that is more open to ambiguity, adaptation, and to welcoming the outsider. "Latino Christian communities," suggests Goizueta, "are living witnesses to the truth of the Gospel claim that Galilee, or 'the other side of the border,' is not merely a heathen wilderness in need of evangelization but a privileged locus of God's self-revelation." Far from being merely a realm of superstition and privatized religion, popular religion contains much that sustains the radical, countercultural nature of the gospel in a United States that still privileges control, power, and "purity."

While Goizueta delves into one countercultural stream within Catholicism in the United States, Michael Baxter explores another. In "'Blowing the Dynamite of the Church': Catholic Radicalism from a Catholic Radicalist Perspective," Baxter examines how the separation of theology and social theory by Catholic scholars (in the 1930s and continuing into our time) helped to make the gospel a "socially impotent" force in the culture.

Baxter contrasts the integration of theology and social theory by Catholic Worker cofounders Peter Maurin and Dorothy Day with the disintegrated scholarship of John Courtney Murray, George Weigel, Charles Curran, and other leading figures in Catholic social ethics. While the work of Maurin and Day encouraged experiments in living the gospel in more complete ways (e.g., personal responsibility for feeding the hungry, giving hospitality to strangers, teaching others about oppression and injustice, life in community), the discourse of the Americanists ends up "privileg[ing] the ethical agenda of the nation-state" instead of the gospel of Christ. The "public theology" that most American Catholic theologians prefer to the Catholic Worker legacy remains unwilling or unable to take seriously the Worker's contention that "the modern nation-state is a fundamentally unjust and corrupt set of institutions whose primary function is to preserve the interests of the ruling class, by coercive and violent means if necessary—and there will always come a time when it is necessary." The separation of theology and social theory practiced by most "public theologians" robs them and the church of any way of impacting public life *except* by supporting and influencing the state.

Like Baxter, Michael Budde explores what happens when the Cross is trimmed to fit the prerogatives of the powerful. In "Pledging Allegiance: Reflections on Discipleship and the Church after Rwanda," Budde ponders "the irrelevance of Christianity as a category having any purchase on human loyalties or obligations." He does so by looking closely at the genocidal slaughter in Rwanda (1994), in which more than 800,000 (overwhelmingly Catholic) Tutsi Rwandans were murdered by (overwhelmingly Catholic) Hutu Rwandans. Budde lists Rwanda's genocide as "one of this century's most recent, world-class failures of Christianity," an example of "what can happen *in extremis* when Christian formation is shallow and weak, easily bent to the purposes of groups who worship secular power instead of Yahweh."

Although he explores how and why the Catholic Church in Rwanda subordinated the imperatives of the gospel to political and tribal ideologies, Budde gives no support to those "Africa-bashers" who see the region as peculiarly backward, barbaric, or ruthless. In fact, according to Budde, "if Rwandan Christians deduced that Christians could kill one another (and everyone else) in the service of 'more important' obligations, that is a lesson they learned from the white European churches." To him, returning the church to its proper vocation "requires us to refuse the rituals of obedience and allegiance that states and similar institutions demand." That proper vocation of the church is to "explore new possibilities of [creating] human community that are *not* built upon an order entailing the right to kill or command death on [its] behalf." Such is the obligation and challenge of the church in Rwanda and everywhere else.

We offer these essays to the church as a "straining forward to what lies ahead" (Phil 3:13) and as an invitation to continued prayer and discussion about what it means to be disciples.

NOTES

1. Tom Strode, "Jiang, Amid Protests & Questions, Defends China on Human Rights." *Baptist Press News Service*. October 31, 1997, p. 4. Available at www.erlc.com/Rliberty/Persecution/1977/1031/jiang.htm.

2. Steven Mufson, "U.S. Religious Leaders Tread Softly in China: Panel Meets Only with State-Approved Groups," *Washington Post*, February 19, 1998, p. A-21.

3. Associated Press. "U.S. Clergy Starts Mission to China, Seeks to Show That the Faithful Will Aid the State," February 10, 1998.

4. Miroslav Volf, "Soft Difference: Theological Reflections on the Relation between Church and Culture in 1 Peter." *Ex Auditu* 10 (1994): 4. Available at www.northpark.edu/sem/exauditu/papers/volf.html. Pagination from website.

5. Ibid., p. 5.

1

Practicing the Politics of Jesus

Rodney Clapp

Summing up the ambiguity of the Roman emperor Constantine, and what has come to be called Constantinianism, the classical scholar Charles Norris Cochrane writes that Constantine may be unique, "the one human being to have enjoyed the distinction of being deified as a pagan god, while, at the same time, he was popularly venerated as a Christian saint."[1] Allegedly seeing a vision of Christ's cross in the sky as he rode into battle, Constantine was the first emperor to convert (at least ostensibly) to what had been a despised and dismissed "slave religion." For better and for worse, this conversion changed history.

What might be called the Constantinian shift began around the year 200 and took over two hundred years to grow and unfold in full bloom.[2] Thus it began before Constantine's birth and matured after his death. Yet this monumental shift well deserves his name. Not only was he the first emperor to convert, he made his aim the legislation of Christ's millennial kingdom in a generation.[3] And indeed, he enacted a number of laws that no doubt pleased the church of his day—making divorce difficult, aiding the poor, and ending the gladiatorial games, for instance. Less grandiosely but more lastingly, Constantine was the first in what would be a long line of emperors, princes, and presidents who saw Christianity as the unifying force that might bind and discipline their otherwise diverse subjects.

I do not want to pretend that the pre-Constantinian church was all good and the church after Constantine all bad. From Pentecost onward, the church has always lived in tension, never, as even a cursory reading of 1 Corinthians reminds us, being more than comparatively faithful. "Constantinianism," then, is not an excuse for ignoring or despising the

15

history of the church beyond the New Testament. The significance of the symbol or concept of Constantinianism is to indicate that the pre-Constantinian church did not see itself as the sponsor of the world, with "world" here meaning the fallen and rebellious creation.

Sponsorship is a tricky affair, as soda pop and automobile makers nervously demonstrate when their celebrity commits a crime or loses the national championship. Etymologically, the word springs from the Latin *sponsus*, which has to do with guaranteeing and taking responsibility for the achievement of a desired outcome. The guarantor warrants, pledges, or promises for that which is guaranteed. So guarantors are re*spons*ible for payment on a loan if the debtor defaults on it. Here is where sponsorship gets tricky. Whose identity and purpose is more determinant, the sponsor's or the sponsored's?

In baptismal sponsorship, the sponsor's identity and purposes are more fundamental and determinant than those of the baptismal candidate—often, as in my Anglican tradition, an infant with only the most nascent identity and purposes of its own. Here the candidate is sponsored into the Christian community and faith, on that community's and faith's terms. The sponsor will, in *The Book of Common Prayer*'s words, "be responsible for seeing that the child you present is brought up in the Christian faith and life."[4]

But there are other kinds of sponsorship. Surely the most pervasive in our time is commercial sponsorship. In the commercial realm a sponsor wants to associate with an athlete, movie star, television program, or celebrated event in order to gain prominence and favorability through the sponsored's visibility and popularity. So Nike sponsored Michael Jordan, one of the most famous athletes in the history of any game. No one seriously believed Nike shoes enabled him to defy gravity, to slip Houdini-like through three defenders for the score, to consistently slacken spectators' jaws with amazement. In this case, the sponsor's identity and purposes are clearly less fundamental than the sponsored's. Visit Chicago's Niketown—a five-story shrine disguised as a department store—and you will find encased for adoration not only Jordan's footwear and jerseys, but a wall-sized poster of the shoe-god soaring through the sky. Nike quite successfully wants people to associate their goods with basketball magic; Michael Jordan Just Does It.

Similarly, it is with the Constantinian shift that the church decides to derive its significance through association with the identity and purposes of the state. In the pre-Constantinian setting, the church saw the state as having a preservative function. It was "to serve God by encouraging the good and restraining evil, i.e., to serve peace, to preserve the social cohesion in which the leaven of the gospel can build the church" and render the present age more tolerable.[5] All this made the state important, but hardly central. The church considered itself, not the state, to be carrying the meaning of history. In the words of the Letter to the Ephesians, it is "through the church" that "the wisdom of God in its rich variety" is made known "to the rulers and authorities" (Eph 3:10).

As theologian John Howard Yoder observes, the most "pertinent fact" of the Constantinian shift was not that the church was no longer persecuted, but that the two visible realities of church and world were fused. There was, in a sense, no longer anything to call "world"—state, economy, art, rhetoric, superstition, and war were all baptized.[6] Yoder summarizes the reversal neatly. Before Constantine, "Christians had known as a fact of experience that the Church existed, but had to believe against appearances that Christ ruled over the world. After Constantine one knew as a fact of experience that Christ was ruling over the world, but had to believe against the evidence that there existed a believing Church."[7]

Several important corollaries followed. With Constantine, Christian history begins to be told as the story of dynasties. The ruler, not the ordinary person, is made the model for ethical deliberations. The question is no longer, "How can we survive and remain faithful Christians under Caesar?" but "How can we adjust the church's expectations so that Caesar can consider himself a faithful Christian?" Thus the ethical requirements of the church were adapted to the level of what might be called "respectable unbelief."[8] The statesman must be seen as Christian, but without significantly changing his statecraft. The morality of a statement or action is tested on the basis of whether or not the ruler can meet such standards (say, telling the truth, or not killing). As Yoder writes, "The place of the church or of persons speaking for Christian morality . . . is that of 'chaplaincy,' i.e., a part of the power structure itself. The *content* of ethical guidance is not the teaching of Jesus but the duties of 'station,' 'office' or 'vocation.'"[9] Lawyers will play by the rules of the guild of lawyers, doctors by the guild of doctors, bankers by the guild of bankers, and so forth. Christian lawyers, doctors, and bankers may be different in some ways from their non-Christian colleagues, but they accept their professions as basically defined and regulated apart from the radical formative power of the Christian story.

In a real sense, then, it becomes fine and commendable for professing Christians to participate in the state and other realms of culture *as if* the lordship of Christ makes no concrete difference. Even for Christians, culture begins to be seen as autonomous, as holding its own key to its establishment, maintenance, and true purposes. The church, in other words, created secularism, a secularism that even Christians must laud and obey.[10]

PRIVATIZING THE CHURCH

After creating secularism, the church steadily but all too surely depoliticized and privatized the faith and mission of Jesus Christ. In his famous book *Christ and Culture,* H. Richard Niebuhr approvingly quotes the observation of Rabbi Joseph Klausner about just such a Jesus:

> Though Jesus was a product of [Jewish] culture, . . . he endangered it by abstracting religion and ethics from the rest of social life, and by looking for the establishment by divine power only of a "kingdom not of this world." Judaism, however, is not only religion and it is not only ethics: it is the sum-total of all the needs of the nation, placed on a religious basis. . . . Judaism is a national life. . . . Jesus came and thrust aside all requirements of national life. . . . In their stead, he set up nothing but an ethico-religious system bound up with his conception of the Godhead.[11]

But such a rendering of Jesus and his mission is only possible through a Constantinian grid. Now, as the Christian church's sponsorship of Western secular culture is less and less desired—and increasingly actively dismissed—it is not too much to say that a new consensus has evolved in scholarship on Jesus. What this consensus suggests is a conclusion opposite to that of Klausner and Niebuhr. Though Constantinian Christians all too quickly forgot how to be good Jews, the new consensus recognizes that Jesus and the earliest, New Testament Christians did not. They were all (even the Gentiles) good Jews in the sense that Klausner thought they were not. That is, they saw themselves embodying a national, or social and political, way of life. Israel's story was, in a profound sense, their story—and they did not privatize, psychologize, and etherealize it to make it theirs.

Now that the long Constantinian age has all but passed, we Christians find ourselves in a situation much more closely analogous to that of New Testament Christians than the Christendom for which some nostalgically long. The Bible, it turns out, offers abundant resources for living in a wildly diverse and contested world. With Constantine finally buried, theologians and biblical scholars find themselves able to reclaim, and present again to the church, the politics of Jesus.[12]

JESUS' WORLD

Perhaps the main reason that the Bible has, at least in recent centuries, seemed to offer scarce political or cultural guidance is that Christians have read a "rank anachronism" back into its text. The strict split between "religion" and "politics" belongs to centuries much later than the first. As N. T. Wright remarks, "No first-century Jew . . . could imagine that the worship of their god and the organization of human society were matters related only at a tangent."[13]

Even the most rank anachronizer will not deny that there is much of the political, the physical, the social, and economical throughout the Old Testament. Israel, after all, is a nation, an irrefutably political entity. And it is a political entity born of social, not merely psychological, rebellion—the revolt of slaves against what was then the world's most powerful empire, Egypt. The story of the nation Israel is, like that of all nations, one of conquest (the vanquishing of Canaan), of hierarchy and its powerplays (the kingdom of David), of hope and striving for justice as well as security. Israel's story, furthermore, does not become apolitical the moment it loses its capital and its land, and is sent into exile. The nation is scattered, but still a nation, and now a nation whose prophets hope strenuously for the restoration of that capital and land. Isaiah, Jeremiah, Joel, Micah, and Zechariah all cite Zion as the place of God's climactic (and clearly political) saving act.[14] So: "Hear the word of the LORD, O nations, and declare it in the coastlands far away; say, 'He who scattered Israel will gather him, and will keep him as a shepherd of a flock'" (Jer 31:10).

Yet even if all this is recognized, there remains a strong tendency to imagine that the political and social dimensions of faith fell away at, or with, the birth of the church. A moment's pause reveals how untenable this assumption is. To make the earliest church asocial and apolitical is to suppose that suddenly the Jews of Jesus' day ceased worshiping a God that, for hundreds of years, their people had considered eminently involved with history and politics. In fact, Jesus proclaimed his message and gathered his disciples in a politically charged context. His was a society grinding under the oppression of a distant, colonizing empire, that of Rome. The Jews of Jesus' day and place, although they were regathered in Palestine and had rebuilt the Temple in Jerusalem, considered themselves still in exile, "since the return from Babylon had not brought that independence and prosperity which the prophets foretold."[15] The Pharisees and other parties vying for control were in no sense "religious" in such a manner that their aims excluded the political, the social, and the economic. Their political agendas ranged from the most "conservative" (the Sadducees, most nearly allied with the occupying Romans and so least desirous of significant change) to the most radical (the dispossessed Zealots, who advocated violent revolution).[16]

To make good, faithful, and biblical sense of Jesus, we simply must take into account the world in which he lived and the problems he (or any other religious figure) was expected to address. Wright summarizes the situation: "Jewish society faced major external threats and major internal problems. The question, what it might mean to be a good and loyal Jew, had pressing social, economic and political dimensions as well as cultural and theological ones."[17] As various explorations of the psychologization of America have suggested, it is perhaps only the most affluent, socially stable people who can ignore social, economic, and political questions and concentrate on their abstracted inner well-being. Christian Science and other mind-cure groups so popular in the nineteenth century made no converts in Naples or Calcutta. Outside the United States, they appealed only to the English upper middle class. I doubt that Christian Science, or, for that matter, Christianity as it is now severely psychologized by many liberals and evangelicals alike, would have found many converts—or even had made any sense—to first-century Palestinian Jews. You might just as well have entered into an argument with them that the world was really round or that the earth was not the center of the cosmos. The anachronism, whether drawn from our physical sciences or our preoccupation with individualistic psychology, is equally rank.

Wright emphasizes that "the pressing needs of most Jews of the period had to do with liberation—from oppression, from debt, from Rome." None of this is to suggest for a moment that Jewish (and Jesus') faith was purely political, whatever that might mean. But it does suggest that other issues "were regularly seen in this [political] light." This context—the actual context of Jesus' life and work—renders incredible Troeltsch's confident assertion that the "values of redemption" preached by Jesus were "purely inward" and led "naturally to a sphere of painless bliss."[18] The hope of Israel was, as Wright puts it, not for "disembodied bliss" after death, "but for a national liberation that would fulfill the expectations aroused by the memory, and regular celebration, of the exodus. . . . Hope focused on the coming of the kingdom of Israel's God."[19]

LANGUAGE MATTERS

Indeed, given such blatantly political language as "exodus" and "kingdom," it can be difficult to comprehend how we have managed to so thoroughly privatize the New Testament faith. Of no less political provenance than "kingdom" is the term gospel, or *evangel*. In the Greco-Roman world from which the early church adopted it, "gospel" was a public proclamation of, say, a war won, borne by a herald who ran back to the city and, with his welcome political news, occasioned public celebration.[20] Christian ethicist Allen Verhey suggests that Mark, in calling what he had written a "Gospel," was meaning to evoke *evangel* as it was used within the Roman cult of emperor to refer to the announcements of the birth of an heir to the throne, of the heir's coming of age, accession to the throne, and so forth. If so, the writer of the Gospel is comparing the Kingdom of God come in Jesus to the quite this-worldly and political kingdom of Caesar.[21] It would not be amiss to translate "The Gospel According to Mark" as "The Political Tidings According to Mark." In short, if Mark in his world had wanted to convey a privatistic and individualistic account of Jesus' life and death, he could have thought of many better things to call it than a Gospel (Mk 1:1).

No less political is the language used to describe the church's worship. Our word "liturgy" comes from the Greek meaning "work of the people," or, as we might put it now, a "public work." In Roman society, "to build a bridge for a public road across a stream on one's private property would constitute a liturgy." Military service at one's own expense was an act of liturgy. The wealthy sought favor by sponsoring lavish "liturgies"—huge dramas for the entertainment of the citizenry. *Leitourgoi,* or, very roughly, "liturgists," in the secular Greek usage of the times referred to government officials.[22] "Worship," to modern, privatized Christian ears, too easily connotes escape from the world (we worship, after all, in a "sanctuary"), a removal from the political and the social. Yet inasmuch as we read these connotations onto the word in its New Testament context we are saying something oxymoronic like the "private public work" of the church. The New Testament Christians themselves, I submit, were not so confused.

No less cultural and political is the very word used to describe the new community of God. "Church" (the Greek *ekklēsia*) from the fifth century B.C. onward referred to the assembly of citizens called to decide matters affecting the common welfare.[23] The Hebrew *qahal* denotes a solemn, deliberative assembly of Israel's tribes. The assembly par excellence, for example, was at Mount Sinai, where the Law was received (Deut 9:10, 18:16). When the ancient Jews translated the Old Testament into Greek, *qahal* was rendered *ekklēsia*. This is the term Christians seized on to describe their own assemblies. Thus the *"Ekklēsia* of God" means roughly the same thing as what New Englanders might call the "town meeting of God."[24]

Given all this, it is unsurprising that early observers of Christianity were not struck by its "religious" (in our privatized sense) qualities. What struck outsiders, says Wright, was the church's "total way of life"—or in my terms, its culture.[25] The Romans called Christians "atheists" (they refused cultic emperor worship) and classified Christianity as a political society. So classifying Christianity meant that it was under a ban on corporate ritual meals, much as many governments down to the present ban the "free assembly" of those considered subversive. Christians, says Wright, "were seen not just as a religious grouping, but one whose religion made them a subversive presence within the wider Roman society."[26] There can be no doubt that Rome consistently saw Jews and early Christians as a social and political problem and took action against them accordingly.

Of course, we know that the Romans misunderstood both Jews and Christians on many counts. Did they also grossly misconstrue their intentions here? The thoroughly political language adopted by the church suggests otherwise. The clincher is that if the early church had wanted itself and its purpose to be construed in privatistic and individualistic terms, there were abundant cultural and legal resources at hand for it to do just that. The early church could easily have escaped Roman persecution by suing for status as a *cultus privatus,* or "private cult" dedicated to "the pursuit of a purely personal and otherworldly salvation for its members" like so many other religious groups in that world.[27] Yet instead of adopting the language of the privatized mystery religions, the church confronted Caesar, not exactly *on* his own terms, but *with* his own terms. As Wayne Meeks summarizes the matter, early Christian moral practices

> are essentially communal. Even those practices that are urged upon individuals in the privacy of their homes . . . are extensions of the community's practice—indeed they are means of reminding individuals even when alone that they are not merely devotees of the Christians' God, they are members of Christ's body, the people of God. That was how the Christian movement differed most visibly from the other cults that fit more easily

into the normal expectations of "religion" in the Roman world. The Christians' practices were not confined to sacred occasions and sacred locations—shrines, sacrifices, processions—but were integral to the formation of communities with a distinctive self-awareness.[28]

The original Christians, in short, were about creating and sustaining a unique culture—a way of life that would shape character in the image of their God. And they were determined to be a culture, a quite public and political culture, even if it killed them and their children.

BIBLICAL FAITH ON THE GROUND

What I am suggesting is that the Constantinian church, for many centuries, responded to the world in such a manner that it lost a sense of itself as an alternative way of life. Most immediately, the late Constantinian modern belief in some truths (preeminently scientific truths) as acultural and ahistorical truths made it seem as if there was a neutral, nonperspectival viewpoint available to anyone, anywhere who was rational and well-meaning. In that atmosphere, much of the church thought it necessary to divide Christianity into (1) private truths, or values, to be confirmed by individuals apart from any communal and political context, and (2) public truths, or facts, which consisted of Christianity translated into acultural and ahistorical truths, "essences" more or less instantiated in all viable cultures.

But this was distorting, since Christianity, like Judaism, is historically based. It concerns what has happened with a particular people, namely ancient Israel, and through a particular man who lived and died in a specific time and place, namely Jesus the Nazarene, "crucified under Pontius Pilate." It is true that most religions posit a god who in no way can be pinned down or identified by time and place. But not so the religion of the Israelites. As Robert Jenson observes,

> Other ancient peoples piled up divine names; the comprehensiveness of a god's authority was achieved by blurring his particularity, by identification of initially distinct numina with one another, leading to a grandly vague deity-in-general. Israel made the opposite move. Israel's salvation depended precisely on unambiguous identification of her God over against the generality of the numinous.[29]

The God of Israel simply is he who led Israel out of Egypt, established it in the Promised Land, abandoned it to exile and promised some day, somehow, to end that exile. Thus Israel's God can only be identified narratively, by the telling of this story. That is why, "In the Bible the name of God and the narration of his works . . . belong together. The descriptions that make the name work are items of the narrative. And conversely, identifying God, backing up the name, is the very function of the biblical narrative."[30]

Accordingly, when those not born into the heritage of Israel later come to know and worship Israel's singular God, they can only do so through this same story—but now extended and made more encompassing by the life, teachings, death and resurrection of the Jew Jesus. Put bluntly, Christians *"know how* to pray to the Father, daring to call him 'Father,' because they pray with Jesus his Son."[31]

In modernity, this particularity was such a scandal that many Christians acted as if (and sometimes outright argued that) everyone of all and sundry faiths worshiped the same "God" and that the story of Israel and Jesus was secondary to knowing this "God." Now in post-Constantinian postmodernity, all communities and traditions (including the scientific) are called back to their inescapable and particular histories.[32] Christianity no longer need worry about its "scandal of particularity," since it is recognized that particularity "scandalizes" everyone. The upshot for Christians is that the church does not have to aspire any more to a supposedly neutral language and story; now we can freely speak our own language and tell our own story.

To phrase it only slightly differently, we can now embrace, more wholeheartedly than we could under the modern regime, what might be called the Bible's narrative logic. Modernity pushed us toward a logic, or way of seeing and thinking, concerned to find "universal" and "reasonable" principles that could be embraced apart from any historical tradition. Modern "logic" is at work in Matthew Arnold's eagerness to think that Greek philosophy, Jewish faith, and indeed "all great spiritual disciplines" move toward the same goal. All alike, says Arnold, now quoting Christian scripture, aim for the final end "that we might be partakers of the divine nature."[33] Yet there have been and are many divinities worshiped and admired by humanity. What divine nature do we aspire to? Will we partake of Zeus's caprice? The Mayan god's lust for human blood? And how do "great spiritual disciplines" that claim no divinity (such as Buddhism) then partake of this selfsame divine nature?

Biblical logic, by contrast, does not search for disembodied, abstracted essences. It is historical through and through. It deals with particular characters and events unfolding over time, and as such it is narrative, or story-based. Hence the God who will later elect Israel creates the heavens and the earth, then suffers its rebellion (Gn 1–3). Spiritual, political, familial, and economic division and alienation ensue (Gn 4–11). Now this specific Creator God decides to reclaim the world. Yet this God is not a very good modernist, and so aims to reclaim the world not by calling the divided peoples to "principles" or "essences" that somehow reside within all of them. Instead God chooses a particular man, Abraham, and promises to make of him a "great nation" through which "all the families of the earth shall be blessed" (Gn 12:2–3).

The rest of the Old Testament is the story of this God's refusal to give up on a chosen, if often fickle and unfaithful, people. Israel is that strange and great nation elected to wrestle with the strange and great God Yahweh down through the centuries. This election is often not such an appealing privilege, since the God who has chosen Israel will judge Israel when it departs from its covenant (Is 7:9). Yet God, even if God sometimes judges, will not relinquish a sure grip on the descendants of Abraham and Jacob. As Ben Meyer writes, "Though any generation in Israel might fall victim to catastrophic judgment, Israel itself will never go under."[34] Once again biblical narrative logic is relentlessly particular. Thus most of Israel may stray, but God will snatch a remnant from the lion's mouth (Am 3:12) and make it "the new locus of election and the seed of national restoration."[35] Ultimately confident in God's election, Israel suffers its national ups and downs, but persists in looking ahead to a new reign like glorious David's (Am 9:11–15; Is 11:1–9; Jer 30:8–9). It hopes in a new and paradisal Zion (Is 2:2–4, 28:16), a new covenant (Jer 31:31–34), and vindication in the teeth of its national enemies (Ps 137). So:

> Listen to me, my people,
> and give heed to me, my nation;
> for a teaching will go out from me,
> and my justice for a light to the peoples.
> I will bring near my deliverance swiftly,
> my salvation has gone out
> and my arms will rule the peoples. (Is 51:4–5)

As N. T. Wright memorably puts it,

> This is what Jewish monotheism looked like on the ground. It was not a philosophical or metaphysical analysis of the inner

being of a god, or the god. It was the unshakable belief that the one god who made the world was Israel's god, and that he would defend his hill against all attackers or usurpers. To the extent that Israel thought of her god in "universal" terms, this universal was from the beginning made known in and through the particular, the material, the historical.[36]

THE NEW TESTAMENT IN THE LIGHT OF JEWISH POLITICS

It is according to the rules of this narrative logic that Jesus understood his mission and the early church interpreted its Lord and its life.[37] Exactly twelve disciples, one for each of the tribes of ancient Israel, are chosen. This is but one sign that the church saw itself as Israel's seed restored, and that a crucial aspect of its early mission was to call on all Israel to claim its heritage.[38] The disciples were a flock (Lk 12:32) destined to be scattered (Mk 14:27; Jn 16:32) much as Israel had been scattered. But like Israel they would be regathered (Mk 14:28; Jn 16:17, 22) and enjoy kingly rule when God drew the world's drama to its end (Lk 12:32; Mt 19:28).[39]

Following the Bible's narrative logic, Israel and the disciple remnant within it is saved in even more specific terms. Everything depends on the single man, Jesus, who takes onto himself the history and destiny of Israel. Thus, like Israel, Jesus was the one called out of Egypt (Mt 2:15). Like Israel, Jesus wanders, is tempted and fed by God in the wilderness. Like Israel, Jesus cares for the poor, the orphaned, and the stranger.

Jesus of Nazareth, as he apparently understood himself and certainly as he is interpreted by the New Testament documents, was a living recapitulation of Israel's history. More precisely, Jesus did not merely copy the history of Israel, but realized it afresh in terms of his own life and obedience. By so doing, he re-presented not only Israel's past but its future, what it would come to be through Yahweh's mighty consummating works.[40] Hence Jesus (with and through his disciples) will build a new and unsurpassable temple.

Now it is crucial to recall how important the temple was to the biblical story. Within Israel, the temple bore manifold social, spiritual, political, economic, and cultural importance. In contemporary America, it would be the equivalent of the entire range of our iconic political and cultural institutions: the White House, Capitol Hill, the National

Cathedral, Wall Street, and Hollywood.[41] More than this, Jerusalem, in a profound theological sense, was considered the center of the earth—the hill Yahweh would defend against all attackers. And at the center of Jerusalem was the temple, in whose inner chambers the King of the Universe was known to dwell with an especially awesome presence. To this temple's courts all the world would someday stream, bearing offerings and worshiping the earth's one true God—Israel's Lord (Ps 96:8–10).[42]

In this light it is hard to overstate the significance of Jesus' climactic few days in Jerusalem. His entry on a donkey identifies him with the lowly and peaceable king of Zec 9:9. His attack on the temple, if so it may be called, simultaneously critiques Israel theologically, culturally, politically, socially, and economically. And since the temple was the center not only of Israel but the universe, the cleansing of the temple purifies not only of Israel but the entire cosmos.[43] Jesus and the church together, furthermore, are the new temple, a temple whose splendor will exceed that of any built with human hands (Mk 14:58; cf. 2 Sm 7:4–17 and Hg 2:9).

But the new temple will be built in three days—the span of time between Jesus' crucifixion and his resurrection—which means it can be built only through Jesus' death. So Jesus proceeds to his death. Under covenantal dynamics, Israel is blessed when it responds obediently to God and cursed when it strays. Roman-occupied Israel, as I have noted, still considered itself in exile, under the curse. But Jesus the Christ (Messiah-King) represents Israel, so can take on himself Israel's curse and exhaust it.[44] He perishes as King of the Jews, at the hand of the Romans, whose oppression is "the present, and climactic, form of the curse of exile itself. The crucifixion of the Messiah is, one might say, the *quintessence* of the curse of the exile, and its climactic act."[45]

Narrative logic, then, reveals the significance of Jesus' resurrection. As David Hume was to observe many centuries later in impeccable modern terms, if Jesus was raised from the dead that *in and of itself* proves nothing except that a first-century man in a backwater country somehow survived death. It is only within the context of Israel's story that Jesus' resurrection assumes its supreme significance. For this was not just any man who died, but a man who took onto himself Israel's story. And within Israel's story, resurrection had long functioned as a symbol for the reconstitution of Israel, the return from exile, and the crowning redemption. In the Israel of Jesus' day, resurrection was seen as the divine reward for martyrs, particularly those who died in the great and final tribulation and brought Israel to its own divine reward. The prophet Ezekiel, for instance, saw the return of Israel in the figure of bones rising and taking flesh (37: 1–14). Since at least Ezekiel, the symbol of corpses returning to life not only denoted Israel's return from exile, but implied a renewal of the covenant and all creation. So Jesus' resurrection was nothing less than the monumental vindication (or justification) of Israel's hopes and claims. Israel has claimed throughout its history that its God is the single Creator God, and Jesus' resurrection at last redeems that claim.[46]

Recall one more time the Bible's narrative logic. Israel's God is universal, but known as such only through the particular, the material, the historical. God elects Abraham, and from Abraham a nation, and from that nation Jesus. Now from Israel and Jesus flows God's blessings on all the world. God restores Israel then, building on this event, God seeks the Gentiles. As Meyer writes, "This scheme is recurrent in Acts. First, the word is offered to the Jews, who split into camps of believers and unbelievers. The believers by their faith constitute restored Israel, heir of the covenant and promises. Now and only now may gentiles find salvation, precisely by assimilation to restored Israel."[47]

The early Christians saw themselves as continuing Israel's story under new circumstances. The church "understood itself now as messianic Israel covenanted with her risen Lord" (Acts 2:38, 5:30–32).[48] It, with Jesus' headship, is the new temple, the sanctuary of the living God. It in fact is nothing less than the first fruits of a new humanity, reborn in the last Adam named Jesus. Thus the church was seen, by itself and others, as a "third race," neither Jew nor Gentile but a new and holy nation or people (*hagios ethnoi*—1 Pt 2:9). Narrative logic drives home to a theological conclusion that is unavoidably cultural and political.

Consider Eph 2:11–22. Here the Gentile addressees of the letter are reminded that before Christ they existed in the political status of "aliens from the commonwealth of Israel," and as a consequence "strangers to the covenants of promise, having no home and without God in the world" (v. 12). But now "by the blood of Christ" the Gentiles—we members of disparate nations among whom Israel was sent as a light and an example—have been made part of the same humanity as Israel (vv. 13–15). Christ has broken down the dividing wall between the Hebrews and the Gentiles, for "he is our peace" (v. 14). This is not a peace of mere inner, psychological tranquility: it is the peace of two reconciled peoples, a peace made possible by the change wrought "through the cross" (v. 16), a change of nothing less than the political and cultural status of the Gentiles from "aliens" to "*citizens* with the saints" (v. 19).

Thus Christian faith, far from being a matter solely between the individual and God, amounts to being grafted into a new people. For the writer to the Ephesians, those who are justified are justified because they believe the gospel and through it become God's covenant people. Gentiles, through baptism, are incorporated into the body and life of God's particular, historical people. Baptism is initiation into a new culture, a culture called church that now, exactly as a political and social entity, is poised at the pivot point of world history. As theologian John Milbank puts it, "The *logic* of Christianity involves the claim that the 'interruption' of history by Christ and his bride, the Church, is the most fundamental of events, interpreting all other events." The church claims to "exhibit the exemplary form of human community" and as such "it is *most especially* a social event, able to interpret other social formations, because it compares them with its own new social practice."[49]

In short, the church understands itself as a new and unique culture. The church is at once a community and a history—a history still unfolding and developing, embodying and passing along a story that provides the symbols through which its people gain their identity and their way of seeing the world. The church as a culture has its own language and grammar, in which words such as *love* and *service* are crucial and are used correctly only according to certain "rules." The church as a culture carries and sustains its own way of life, which includes:

- a particular way of eating, learned in and through the Eucharist.
- a particular way of handling conflict, the peculiar politics called "forgiveness" and learned through the example and practice of Jesus and his cross.
- a particular way of perpetuating itself, through evangelism rather than biological propagation.

In its existence as a culture, the church is eminently Jewish. Only in certain Constantinian, and peculiarly modern, terms could it regard its mission as acultural, its gospel as ahistorical, its existence as apolitical. Instead, what political scientist Gordon Lafer says of the Jewish nation and its witness is true as well of the church:

> [The Jewish emphasis on] social solidarity . . . helps to make sense of the concept of a "chosen people," which will be a "light unto the nations." The example that Jewish law seeks to set is one aimed not at individuals but specifically at other "nations." The institutions of solidarity that mark off Jews' commitments to one another from their more minimal obligations to outsiders are not designed to be applied as universal law governing rela-

tions among all people, but rather to be reiterated within each particular nation. This, then, is the universalist mission of Judaism: not to be "a light to all individuals," . . . , but *rather to teach specific nations how to live as nations.*[50]

THE INDIVIDUAL: A MODERN MYSTIFICATION

So: The church as what I am calling a culture is a manner and mode of church that is, as George Lindbeck says, "more Jewish than anything else. . . . It is above all by the character of its communal life that it witnesses, that it proclaims the gospel and serves the world." And such is why "An invisible church is as biblically odd as an invisible Israel."[51] Biblical narrative logic simply demands a specific, visible people, a society or societal remnant, a *polis*.

I realize all this will strike many readers as exceedingly strange. I too, after all, have been reared and shaped in late modernity, taught to conceive of persons and Christianity in liberal, individualistic terms. So I understand that what I am calling for is an arduous retraining of the imagination, the learning and practice of a new grammar or logic. But perhaps it will ease the difficulty to remember that much of this grammar is new only to us. In historical perspective, it is our individuated, isolated self that is exceedingly strange.

As rhetorician Wayne Booth notes, the self as "in-dividual" (literally "un-divided one") is barely more than two centuries old. The in-dividual was invented by a succession of Enlightenment thinkers and became, in its most extreme but perhaps also its most widespread interpretations, a view of the self as "a single atomic isolate, bounded by the skin, its chief value residing precisely in some core of in-dividuality, of difference." Thus it remains popular—almost second nature—to think we get at our "true self" by peeling away social ties like the skin of an onion. The "real me" is not my membership in the worldwide church, my shared kin with Clapps around the country, not my connection—with three million other people—to the geography and culture of Chicago. The "real me" is my unique, in-dividual, core self. The in-dividual self values itself most for what is supposedly utterly different and unconnected about it. But, objects Booth, such an understanding of self is incoherent. Can we really believe that we are not, to the core, who we are because of our kin, our occupations, our political and social situations, our faith or philosophical associations, our friendships? And if our "true self" is whatever stands apart from those around us and is altogether unique about us, most of us are in trouble. The bizarre modern, liberal notion of the self means that even the greatest geniuses have only minimal worth. "Goethe," says Booth, "was fond of saying that only about 2 percent of his thought was original."[52] Truly, as Philip Slater remarks, "The notion that people begin as separate individuals, who then march out and connect themselves with others, is one of the most dazzling bits of self-mystification in the history of the species."[53]

In fact, Booth continues, "People in all previous cultures were not seen as *essentially* independent, isolated units with totally independent values; rather, they were mysteriously complex persons overlapping with other persons in ways that made it legitimate to enforce certain kinds of responsibility to the community." In these settings, persons were not "'individuals' at all but overlapping members one of another. Anyone in those cultures thinking words like 'I' and 'mine' thought them as inescapably loaded with plurality: 'I' could not even think of 'my' self as separated from my multiple affiliations: my family, my tribe, my city-state, my feudal domain, my people."[54]

Are the biblical cultures part of the "previous cultures" Booth here remarks on? Scholars have again and again noted the Hebrew conception of "corporate personality," the understanding that families, cities, tribes, and nations possess distinctive personalities and that individuals derive identity from and so might represent these social bodies.[55] We need no new frame when we extend this picture. Writing on the concept of personhood in New Testament times, Bruce J. Malina notes, "the first-century Mediterranean person did not share or comprehend our idea of an 'individual' at all." Rather, "our first-century person would perceive himself as a distinctive whole *set in relation* to other such wholes and *set within* a given social and natural background."[56]

So when Paul spoke of the church as a "body," he borrowed the metaphor from a fable widely used in several cultures of antiquity. Just as "Israel" could serve as the name either of an individual (Jacob) or a community (the nation), so could Paul use "Christ" to refer to an individual (Jesus of Nazareth) or a community (the church). In the words of New Testament scholar Charles Talbert, "'Members' . . . is Paul's term for the parts of the body through which the life of the body is expressed (cf. 1 Cor 12:12, 14–26; Rom 6:13). Paul is saying then that individual Christians in their corporeal existence are the various body parts of the corporate personality of Christ through which the life of Christ is expressed."[57]

It is no simple matter to "translate" ancient understandings of self (or anything else) into our later, quite different setting. Yet I think this is another task that is made more feasible by our post-Constantinian, post-modern setting. As Booth comments, the in-dividuated self has been crit-icized from its beginning, and "it has been torn to pieces and stomped on by almost every major thinker in this century."[58] Furthermore, freed from its distorting Constantinian "responsibility," the church no longer must support a view of the self as in-dividuated and able to determine the good apart from all "accidental" ties of history or community. We can reaffirm that, just as there can be no individual Americans apart from the nation America, so can there be no Christians apart from the church. We can be like the apostle Peter, who "did not learn God's will by Socratic questioning and rational reflection, but as the member of a group who had been with Jesus 'from the beginning in Galilee.'"[59] We can be like the early followers of Christ the Way, who trained fresh imaginations and became a new humanity by devoting themselves "to the apostles' teaching and fellowship, to the breaking of bread and the prayers" (Acts 2:42). After Constantine, on the other side of modernity, we can regard and embrace the church as a way of life.

NOTES

1. Charles Norris Cochrane, *Christianity and Classical Culture* (London: Oxford University Press, 1944), p. 12. It is now, in fact, debated whether or not Constantine was genuinely a Christian. Some suggest he simply used Christian-ity as an ideological support for a regime that was in many ways anti-Christian. For a summary of this debate, see Philip LeMasters, *The Import of Eschatology in John Howard Yoder's Critique of Constantinianism* (San Francisco: Mellen Research University Press, 1992), pp. 102–7.

2. John Howard Yoder, "The Otherness of the Church," *Mennonite Quar-terly Review* 35 (October 1961):212. This seminal essay of Yoder's is now hap-pily more accessibly found in his *The Royal Priesthood*, ed. Michael G. Cartwright (Grand Rapids, Mich.: Eerdmans, 1994), pp. 53–64. Much of the account to follow leans heavily on Yoder. For another, basically congruent account, see David J. Bosch, *Transforming Mission: Paradigm Shifts in Theology of Mission* (Maryknoll, N.Y.: Orbis, 1991). Besides providing historical detail throughout, Bosch observes that "the Roman Catholic (or Western) Church was always compromised to the state. The same was true of the Byzantine Church, only more so" (p. 205). He also notes that the Reformers (excepting Anabaptists) did not break with the medieval understanding of church and state: "Since Con-stantine the idea of a 'Christian' state . . . was simply taken for granted" (p. 240).

3. Cochrane, *Christianity and Classical Culture*, p. 211.

4. *The Book of Common Prayer* (New York: Church Hymnal Corpora-tion and The Seabury Press, 1979), p. 302.

5. John Howard Yoder, *The Original Revolution* (Scottdale, Pa.: Herald Press, 1977), pp. 72–73.

6. Yoder, "Otherness," p. 288.

7. Ibid., p. 289.

8. Ibid.

9. John Howard Yoder, *The Priestly Kingdom* (Notre Dame, Ind.: University of Notre Dame Press, 1984), p. 138.

10. John Milbank begins his magisterial *Theology and Social Theory* (Oxford: Basil Blackwell, 1990) with the words, "Once, there was no 'secular'" (p. 9). He then uses much of his first chapter to provide an account of how the church in fact created the conceptuality and institutions of secularism, with more sympathy for the synthesis of Christendom than Yoder's account allows. But Milbank sees changes that, by the time of the late medieval and then Reformation periods, issue in the sorts of developments Yoder deplores. Thus Milbank laments the "self-understanding of Christianity arrived at in late-medieval nominalism, the protestant reformation and seventeenth-century Augustinianism, which completely privatized, spiritualized and transcendentalized the sacred, and concurrently reimagined nature, human action and society as a sphere of autonomous, sheerly formal power" (p. 9).

11. H. Richard Niebuhr, *Christ and Culture* (New York: Harper Torchbooks, 1951), pp. 2–3.

12. Obviously I borrow this essay's title from John Howard Yoder's influential work, *The Politics of Jesus,* 2d ed. (Grand Rapids, Mich.: Eerdmans, 1994). Yoder was one of the first theologians to crystallize the political aspects of Jesus' life and ministry, and push their implications. In this chapter I will largely rely on more recent New Testament scholarship, particularly that of N. T. Wright and Ben F. Meyer. But it is important to emphasize that what follows is, in broad strokes, hardly an account put forward by a mere handful of theologians and biblical scholars. As Yoder makes clear, his 1972 book (the first edition of *Politics*) was "*then* a summary of the widely known scholarship of the time." Yoder especially made use of the work of Amos Wilder, Oscar Cullmann, Otto Piper, Paul Minear, and Markus Barth. In his revised edition, Yoder correctly notes that, in the intervening decades since his book was first published, scholars now "less than ever . . . make Jesus apolitical." (Yoder, pp. vii, x, 13–14.) The list of active biblical scholars alone, which Yoder might cite as vivid proof but does not, includes, in New Testament studies, John Riches, Gerd Thiessen, Wayne Meeks, William Herzog, Gerhard Lohfink, Ched Myers, Walter Wink, Marcus Borg, Richard Hays, E. P. Sanders, and Richard Horsley; and in Old Testament studies, Walter Brueggemann, Paul Hanson, Christopher J. H. Wright, Patrick Miller, and Norman Gottwald. For a helpful overview of some of the studies especially concerning politics and Jesus, see Ben Witherington III, *The Jesus Quest: The Third Search for the Jew of Nazareth* (Downers Grove, Ill.: InterVarsity Press, 1995), pp. 16–17, 100–102, 116–18, and especially 151–60.

13. N. T. Wright, "The New Testament and the 'State,'" *Themelios* 16, no. 1 (October/November 1990):11.

14. See Ben F. Meyer, *The Early Christians: Their World Mission and Self-Discovery* (Wilmington, Del.: Michael Glazer, 1986), p. 61.

15. Roman occupation was "simply the mode that Israel's continuing exile had taken. . . . As long as Herod and Pilate were in control of Palestine, Israel was still under the curse of Deuteronomy 29." N. T. Wright, *The Climax of the Covenant* (Minneapolis, Minn.: Fortress Press, 1991), p. 141. See also his *The New Testament and the People of God* (Minneapolis, Minn.: Fortress Press, 1992), pp. 268–72.

16. For a helpful survey of these options as theological and political, see Yoder, *The Politics of Jesus*. Meyer comments that much theology (I would note pietistic evangelicalism and existentialist neo-orthodoxy) has misconceived the career of Jesus "as an individualistic call to decision, in almost complete abstraction from its Jewishness and from the intra-Jewish historical context of religious competitor's for Israel's allegiance (Pharisees, Zealots, Sadducees, Essenes, baptists. . . .)" (*Early Christians*, pp. 43–44).

17. Wright, *New Testament and the People of God*, p. 169.

18. Troeltsch, *The Social Teaching of the Christian Churches*, vol. 1, trans. Olive Wyon (New York: Macmillan, 1931), p. 40.

19. All quotations from Wright in this paragraph are from *The New Testament and the People of God*, pp. 169–70.

20. Yoder, *Politics*, p. 28.

21. Allen Verhey, *The Great Reversal* (Grand Rapids, Mich.: Eerdmans, 1984), p. 74.

22. Charles P. Price and Louis Weil, *Liturgy for Living* (New York: Seabury, 1979), p. 21; Yoder, *Politics*, pp. 206–07.

23. Robert Banks, *Paul's Idea of Community* (Grand Rapids, Mich.: Eerdmans, 1988), p. 34.

24. Wayne Meeks, *The Origins of Christian Morality: The First Two Centuries* (New Haven, Conn.: Yale University Press, 1993), p. 45.

25. Wright, *New Testament and the People of God*, p. 120.

26. Ibid., p. 350.

27. See John H. Westerhoff, "Fashioning Christians in Our Day," in *Schooling Christians*, ed. Stanley Hauerwas and John H. Westerhoff (Grand Rapids, Mich.: Eerdmans, 1992), p. 280. Cf. Wright: "The Christians, meanwhile, do not seem to have taken refuge in the defence that they were merely a private club for the advancement of personal piety. They continued to proclaim their allegiance to a Christ who was a 'king' in a sense which precluded allegiance to Caesar, even if his kingdom was not to be conceived on the model of Caesar's" (*New Testament and the People of God*, p. 355).

28. Meeks, *Origins*, p. 110. So far was early Christianity removed from its later liberal, individualistic incarnation that the eminent historian of antiquity Peter Brown comments that its appeal "lay in its radical sense of community" (*The World of Late Antiquity: A.D. 150–750* [New York: Harcourt Brace Jovanovich, 1971], p. 68). In another place he observes that the church was concerned to create a "society in miniature, a 'people of God'; its appeal lay in its

exceptional degree of cohesion" (*Religion and Society in the Age of St. Augustine* [New York: Harper and Row, 1972], p. 136).

29. Robert W. Jenson, *The Triune Identity* (Philadelphia: Fortress Press, 1982), p. 5.

30. Ibid., p. 7.

31. Ibid., p. 47.

32. For a fuller account on this point, see my *Families at the Crossroads* (Downers Grove, Ill.: InterVarsity Press, 1993), pp. 9–26 and 174–79.

33. Matthew Arnold, *Culture and Anarchy: An Essay in Political and Social Criticism* (Ann Arbor: University of Michigan Press, 1965), p. 164.

34. Meyer, *Early Christians*, p. 46.

35. Ibid., p. 47.

36. Wright, *New Testament and the People of God*, pp. 247–48. Elsewhere Wright remarks that Jewish theology was a "fighting doctrine." In the same vein, for the early church, "The major issues at stake . . . were monotheism, idolatry, election, holiness and how these interacted. And if that list sounds abstract, removed from the actual life-setting of actual churches, it is because we have forgotten, or have not yet learned . . . that precisely these 'theological' issues functioned as shorthand ways of articulating the points of pressure, tension and conflict between different actual communities, specifically, Jews and pagans" (*Climax of the Covenant*, pp. 125, 122).

37. Meyer: "Neither the primitive Christian proclaimer nor the point and function of his proclamation is intelligible in historical terms apart from this biblical and ecclesial legacy" (*Early Christians*, p. 47).

38. Ibid., p. 38–39.

39. Ibid., p. 65.

40. See E. J. Tinsley, *The Imitation of God in Christ* (Philadelphia: Westminster Press, 1960), p. 177. As Tinsley eloquently puts it on the same page, Jesus was not simply "a copyist, but a creative artist, in relation to his nation's history."

41. Wright, *New Testament and the People of God*, p. 225, n. 29. I have added Hollywood to Wright's list.

42. See Meyer, *Early Christians*, pp. 60–61.

43. Ibid., p. 64. See also Wright, *New Testament and the People of God*, pp. 306–7.

44. God "sees that the only way of rescuing his world is to call a people, and to enter into a covenant with them, so that through them he will deal with evil. But the means of dealing with evil is to concentrate it in one place and condemn—execute—it there. The full force of this condemnation is not intended to fall on this people in general, but on their representative, the Messiah" (Wright, *Climax of the Covenant*, p. 239).

45. Ibid., p. 151.

46. On the significance of resurrection, see Wright, *New Testament and the People of God*, pp. 328–34.

47. Meyer, *Early Christians*, p. 96. See also Wright, *New Testament and the People of God*, pp. 93, 96; *Climax of the Covenant*, pp. 150–51. The church

as "new Israel" does not nullify God's election of "old Israel" and those within it who do not now believe in Jesus. I take this to be one of the main points of Paul's difficult argument in Rom 9–11. Put in terms applicable today, the existence of the church does not mean present-day Jews are no longer God's chosen people. God has not forgotten, and will never forget, this "Israel."

48. Meyer, *Early Christians*, p. 43.

49. John Milbank, *Theology and Social Theory* (London: Basil Blackwell, 1990), p. 388 (emphasis in original). Compare E. J. Tinsley: "The life of the Christian is the life of itinerant Israel over again, with the same trials and temptations (1 Cor 10:5–13), but the Christian now knows that what was being rehearsed in a preliminary way in the history of Israel was the life of Christ with his faithful followers. Because in Christ the Christians are the New Israel, their life is bound to be a series of variations on the theme of the 'Way' of the Old Israel as it has been summed up for them in Christ" (*Imitation*, p. 157).

50. Gordon Lafer, "Universalism and Particularism in Jewish Law," ed. David Theo Goldberg and Michael Krausz, *Jewish Identity* (Philadelphia: Temple University Press, 1993), p. 196 (emphasis added). Lafer's point is quite explicit in Jer 12:15–16: "And after I [God] have plucked them [the nations] up, I will again have compassion on them, and I will bring them again to their heritage and to their land, every one of them. And then if they will diligently learn the ways of my people [i.e., the culture of Israel], to swear by my name, 'As the Lord lives,' as they taught my people to swear by Baal, then they shall be built up in the midst of my people."

51. See "The Church," in Geoffrey Wainwright, ed., *Keeping the Faith* (Philadelphia: Fortress Press, 1988), pp. 193 and 183. I am indebted to Inagrace Dietterich for calling my attention to Lindbeck's extraordinary essay.

52. Booth, "Individualism and the Mystery of the Social Self," in *Freedom and Interpretation*, ed. Barbara Johnson (New York: Basic Books, 1993), pp. 81, 87–88.

53. Quoted from Slater's *"The Earth Walk without Further Attribution,"* in Lawrence Stone, *The Past and the Present Revisited* (London: Routledge and Kegan Paul, 1987), p. 325.

54. Booth, "Individualism," pp. 78 and 79.

55. For a classic statement, see H. Wheeler Robinson, "Hebrew Psychology," in *The People and the Book*, ed. A. S. Peake (London: Oxford University Press, 1925), pp. 353–82. Robinson remarks that such doctrines as Original Sin are incomprehensible without a notion such as corporate personality. I would add that our thoroughgoing individualism also threatens to render incoherent the doctrines of atonement, of the church, and even, most fundamentally, the Trinity.

56. Bruce J. Malina, *The New Testament World: Insights from Cultural Anthropology* (Atlanta, Ga.: John Knox Press, 1981), pp. 54 and 55 (emphasis in original).

57. Charles Talbert, *Reading Corinthians: A Literary and Theological Commentary on 1 and 2 Corinthians* (New York: Crossroad, 1987), p. 31. Con-

fer J. Paul Sampley: "Paul thinks of believers' relationship with Christ in terms of solidarity with, participation in, or belonging to Christ. . . . Those who have faith are one together in Christ. This solidarity with Christ is Paul's primary identification of believers." And: "Just as surely as one does not snub the workings of the Spirit, one does not disregard the community in one's life of faith." And: "Paul's great interest in the health and growth of the individual's faith is always set within his concern for the well-being of the community, and his commitment to community is always located within his conviction that God's renewal of the entire cosmos is under way." See his *Walking between the Times: Paul's Moral Reasoning* (Minneapolis, Minn.: Fortress Press, 1991), pp. 12, 43, 118.

58. Booth, "Individualism," p. 79.
59. Meeks, *Origins,* p. 6.

2

Always in the Shadow of the Empire

Walter Brueggemann

The community of faith, of course, never lives in a vacuum. It is always in the midst of cultural reality that is thick and dense and powerful. As Richard Niebuhr has made clear in his classic study, the relationship between cultural reality and a community of baptismal faith is endlessly unsettled, problematic, and under negotiation.[1] That this present volume is conceived, written, and (hopefully) read indicates that we are now in a season when we are commonly aware that the community of faith must stand in some tension with dominant culture; thus the theme of this book.

The reasons why our time is now commonly judged to be a season of tension are not difficult to detect. It seems evident that *technological individualism* coupled with *unlimited and unbridled corporate power and corporate wealth* that appears to be beyond the governance of nation-states has created a set of cultural values that are aggressively antihuman.[2] There are times when church and cultural context can live in some kind of mutuality; but this is not one of those times, for gospel rootage requires resistance to such aggressive antihumanism. Such resistance in turn requires great intentionality, embodied in concrete disciplines of body, mind, and heart. For without such disciplines, it is evident that the church community will either be massaged and seduced until it is co-opted, or it will end in the powerlessness of despair.

My own field of study and reflection is the Old Testament. For that reason, in what follows I will explore some of the ways in which the Israelite faith community practiced its intentionality as a community called and mandated by a God with a quite peculiar purpose in the world.

Only the most naive reading of the Old Testament can imagine that ancient Israel was a sweet, serene, religious community of pure motives. Any alert reading makes clear that Israel was endlessly conflicted. Much

39

of the conflict, moreover, concerns ways of relating to the cultural environment in which it was embedded. It is unmistakable that ancient Israel had a rich, ongoing, variegated interaction with its cultural environment, ofttimes being imposed upon by that environment, sometimes being coerced to accommodate, and sometimes willingly appropriating from its environment. In sum, it is plausible to suggest that the *actual practice* of Israel was largely synergistic. That is, Israel was not so different from other peoples and freely adapted and adopted, likely in quite pragmatic ways. Over against that actual practice, however, the Old Testament itself is likely written from *a distinct, self-conscious theological-ideological perspective*. That perspective challenged the actual practice of synergism (syncretism) and championed the practice of distinctiveness that is rooted in distinctive disciplines and expressed in distinctive ethical consequences.[3] It is no easy matter to assess the relationship between common practice and self-conscious perspective, for they no doubt overlap as well as stand in tension. For our purposes, however, we may attend primarily to the theological-ideological perspective of distinctiveness, for it is here that we arrive at the closest parallels to our own resolve to resist aggressive antihumanism by a countercultural approach.

The relationship between Israelite faith and an environment that variously nourishes, empowers, distorts, and opposes is an ongoing one of incredible density. I purpose, however, that one available way to consider this tension and interaction over time is to organize our reflections around the several empires, which in rough sequence dominated Israel's public life. These several empires had proximately different policies and attitudes toward subjugated peoples. Consequently Israel's response, in each case, is commensurately different. But in all of these cases, we can learn of Israel's characteristic resolve to maintain its distinct identity and to protect space for its liberated imagination and, consequently, for its distinctive covenantal ethic. The maintenance of distinctive identity, protection of space for distinctive imagination and ethic takes some intentional doing. Israel's achievement in this regard is at best mixed. It is clear, nonetheless, that it did try.

ISRAEL IS AN INTENTIONAL, DISTINCTIVE COMMUNITY IN THE WORLD DOMINATED BY EGYPT

Life lived under Egyptian hegemony was surely inevitable, given geopolitical reality. Even as Egypt constitutes the most stable reference point for the foreign policy of contemporary Israel, so in the ancient world, Egypt occupied the southern end of the Fertile Crescent and was in every season a force in the life of Israel. Egypt, moreover, had as a constant of its foreign policy the effort to claim the area of Palestine for its own sphere of influence, in order to create a buffer zone against the various formidable powers to the north.

There can be little doubt that Egypt was a constant pressure upon the community of Israel all through the biblical period. That geo-historical reality, however, is transformed in the Old Testament so that Egypt is not simply one of several such impinging powers. Rather Egypt takes on paradigmatic significance in the imagination of Israel. Thus Egypt is portrayed as the quintessential oppressive power, and Pharaoh is rendered as a representative rival to the authority of Yahweh. Thus the socioeconomic reality of Egypt takes on mythic proportions. This preoccupation, always fed by concrete reality, is especially evident in the liturgical account of the Exodus in Exod 1–15, which concerns the thirteenth-century clash in the time of Moses, and the incessant meddling of Egypt in Judean matters in the sixth century.[4] This latter in turn produced the tradition of Jeremiah (43–44), that a return to Egypt gives closure to the story of faith begun with Exodus, and the tradition of Ezekiel that critiques Egypt for its arrogant defiance of Yahweh (Ezek 29–32).

In the memory of Israel, the ancestral narratives of Genesis are framed in the beginning by an acknowledgement in Gn 12:12–20 that Egypt has a monopoly of food in the ancient world, and at the end by an account of the actions of Joseph, progenitor of Israel, who aids and abets Pharaoh's monopoly of food in a way that reduces the agricultural population to debt slavery (Gn 47:13–26). Thus Egypt is presented as a source of life for Israel, but also as an aggressive agent that enslaves those who seek its resources for life. Much of Israelite imagination consists in coming to terms with the Catch-22 of food and bondage, or conversely, no-bondage/no-food.

There can be no doubt, moreover, that Pharaonic notions of exploitation, that fated individual persons to be submerged in and for state purposes, operated in Israel. Thus Pharaoh is reported to be father-in-law to Solomon (1 Kings 3:1), and Solomon's policy of forced labor echoes Egyptian practices. In Egypt's own imperial practice and in the derivative practice of Solomon within Israel, the threat against Israel's distinctiveness has a socioeconomic, political cast. The social practices enacted in the name of Egyptian gods are deeply antihuman, and in Israel's purview anti-Yahwistic, for the peculiar God of Israel intended a human community that does not exploit. The resistance Israel is to practice against this alien ideology that legitimates alien social practice is as paradigmatic as is the role of Pharaoh. That is, the way in which Israel resists Egypt is the characteristic way in which Israel will subsequently resist every aggressor empire.

We may identity *two disciplines of resistance* that mark the life of Israel in its relation to Egypt. The resistance Israel practiced vis-à-vis Egypt is rooted in the most elemental conviction that Yahweh wills otherwise. Yahweh wills otherwise to the state building project that monopolizes labor power. Yahweh wills otherwise to surplus wealth, whereby some live indulgently from the produce of others. Yahweh wills otherwise than exploitative oppression. Yahweh wills otherwise than the Egyptian socio-theological system. Yahweh engages in counteractivity and therefore Israel, as subject of Yahweh, must resist.

Israel developed and practiced *liturgical resistance* by a stylized, regularly enacted drama whereby Egyptian power is given liturgical articulation and Israel is invited—through the course of the drama—to move outside Egyptian hegemony to its own distinctive practice of life.

The substance of Israel's resistance is through the regular reenactment of the Exodus liturgy of Exod 1–15 that is presented to us as a historical narrative. Each time, over the generations, that Israel participated in this drama of counter-reality, Israel imagined and construed a social world outside the hegemonic control of Pharaoh. Indeed, the very doing of the drama itself permitted emancipated imagination that refused the definitions of reality sponsored by Egypt.

The liturgy provides a script for a season of counterbehavior.[5] The first aspect of counterbehavior is *the public voicing of pain*:

> The Israelites groaned under their slavery, and cried out. Out of the slavery their cry for help rose up to God. God heard their groaning, and God remembered his covenant with Abraham, Isaac, and Jacob. God looked upon the Israelites, and God took notice of them. (Exod 2:23–25)

The world of Pharaoh produced great pain, but it was silenced pain in which brick-producing slaves were to accept their suffering and abuse as appropriate to their condition. The public voicing of pain is the refusal to accept suffering in docility, and to resist the status of slave and the abuse that comes with that status. The very first utterance in the liturgy makes available that which Egypt forcibly denied.

Second, this liturgy dares to offer *a critique that ridicules established power*. Obviously such actions are precluded in the empire, for the maintenance of illicit power depends upon the stifling of dissent. The long recital of the plague narrative (Exod 7–11), however, is shot through with mockery whereby Yahweh "makes sport" of Pharaoh and thereby erodes that authority (cf. 10:1–2). The critique includes (a) the assertion that Egypt "could not," that is, that it had reached the end of its technological capacity (Exod 8:18), (b) the futile attempts at deceptive bargaining that seek to deceive Moses (8:25, 10:80–10, 24), and (c) the final, pitiful capitulation of Pharaoh who slowly and progressively must concede everything to Yahweh (12:32). This liturgy is a scenario of reality that contradicts Egyptian reality. This distinctive community is invited to affirm that *the world constructed in liturgy* is more reliable and more credible than the world "out there." The purpose of such liturgy is to nurture imagination and to equip Israel with the nerve to act out of its distinctiveness in the face of formidable, hostile power.

Third, the payoff of such daring imagination is the dance and song of the women, enacted as a gesture of defiance:

> Sing to the Lord, for he has triumphed gloriously;
> horse and rider he has thrown into the sea. (Exod 15:21)

It is clear that this liturgical act—liturgical dance?!—is an act of unadministered, unauthorized freedom whereby the erstwhile slaves give bodily expression to their freedom, the very freedom of bodies Pharaoh could not permit.

The very process of liturgy thus created an environment and a community that understood itself to be special, under a special mandate of emancipation from that Holy Power that Pharaoh could not withstand. There can be little doubt that intentional resistance is rooted in the imagination and maintenance of an alternative world in which ostensive powers of intimidation are narratively discredited and dethroned.

The form of the liturgy is detailed in Exod 12–13 in the provisions for Passover. We do not know about the actual "history" of the Passover festival. What we do know is that Passover emerged, is situated in the text, and is regarded in Israel as the occasion and script for the periodic, disciplined, intentional reenactment and replication of the Exodus narrative. It is the cultic staging whereby in every circumstance, through every generation, this community sustains and makes visible and unavoidable a distinctive identity of emancipation and of resistance to the pressures of Pharaonic culture.

We may identity three facets of this form of reapplication. First, it includes detailed, carefully observed bodily gestures—concerning specific foods prepared in specific ways, markings of blood on doorpost as a visible announcement of protective inscrutability in this community not subject to Pharaonic administration. These sacramental acts deny the legitimacy of the brute power of Pharaoh. Second, along with bodily, sacramental gesture, there is prescribed wording designed to inculcate the young and to socialize them into this perception of reality. It is abundantly clear that the adults who preside over and reiterate the wording understand it to be a political act of emancipation and resistance always again to be undertaken:

> When your children ask you "What do you mean by this observance?" You shall say, "It is the passover sacrifice to the Lord for he passed over the houses of the Israelites in Egypt when he struck down the Egyptians but spared our houses." And the people bowed their heads and worshipped. (Exod 12:27)

This community does not flinch from the violence of these founding narratives, the violence enacted by Yahweh on its behalf. It does not, moreover, blink at the claim of oddness and privilege in the eyes of Yahweh, a privilege never granted to the community by Pharaonic power.

Third, the provisions for Passover make clear that this is a theological-ideological act not contained in ethnic boundaries:

> Any slave who has been purchased may eat of it after he has been circumcised. . . . If an alien who resides with you wants to celebrate the passover to the Lord, all his males shall be circumcised; then he may draw near to celebrate it . . . there shall be one law for the native and for the alien who resides among you (Exod 12:44–49).

The offer is inclusive. But it is not casual. One must be prepared to accept a costly mark to qualify for this community of emancipation and resistance.

Along with liturgical reiteration, this community accepted *rigorous disciplines* for the sake of alternative community. These disciplines we regularly call *commandments* or even *laws*. The emancipating, resisting community, in the imagination of its self-presentation, moved along to Sinai.[6] Mt. Sinai, in this tradition, is *the mountain of address*. There Israel heard the very voice of Yahweh (Exod 20:1–17), and then it heard the mediation of Yahweh in the voice of Moses (vv. 18–21). In this holy voice and in its Mosaic echo, they heard a voice of summons and assurance, a voice of demand and of promise, a voice guaranteeing a peculiar identity. And there they listened. Thus emerges the verb *shema'* as the defining claim of Israel's life. In listening, Israel knows itself not to be self-made, self-invented, or self-imagined. In that listening, moreover, Israel knows it must cease to listen to the voice of Pharaoh that defined realty in terms of brick quotas. In listening, Israel comes to the startling, dangerous conviction that its life consists not in bricks for the empire, but in acts of neighborliness whereby Israel replicates Exodus for its neighbors.

The Sinai address of command is complex and varied, and often contradictory. I will mention only two commands that epitomize the best of Israel's counter practice, while acknowledging there is much else that is not so noble.[7] First, there stands at the center of Torah commands the practice of sabbath, the steady practice of work stoppage that makes visible the claim that life consists in being and not in doing or having. I have no doubt that the recovery of this discipline is decisive for the reenactment of this community of emancipation and resistance.[8] Second, the first specific law in the Sinai utterances after the decalogue, given in Exod 21:1-11, concerns "the year of release," whereby Israel is enjoined to engage in a counter economics that willingly cancels the debts of neighbors, and permits the indebted to rejoin the economy as a full and viable partner. It is this neighborly act of debt cancellation that is the taproot of all Jewish and Christian notions of forgiveness.[9] Forgiveness is cancellation of debts in every zone of existence; this counter community takes as its foremost social characteristic the refusal to exploit the poor, the refusal to get even, the refusal to hold grudges, the refusal to exact vengeance. All of these practices, to be sure, are at the core of the Pharaonic enterprise; but Yahweh authorizes and summons otherwise.

Israel knows that Egypt is endlessly resolved, vigilant, and canny for its way of life. In the narrative of counter reality, however, it becomes clear—over and over in reenactment—that the Egyptian project is doomed. In the end, Pharaoh is desperate and must say to Moses, "Bless me!" (Exod 12:32).[10] In the end the repressive achievements of Pharaoh are empty. This little community that begins in pain and ends in dancing, that stops its life for sabbath, that cancels debts for the sake of neighborliness, in the end this community has in its midst the force for life, and is the wave of the future. It is so because in the end, Yahweh denies Pharaoh any authority, even over Egypt. (Cf. Exod 19:5: "The whole earth is mine.")

ISRAEL IS AN INTENTIONAL, DISTINCTIVE COMMUNITY IN THE WORLD DOMINATED BY ASSYRIA

The rise of Assyrian power with Tiglath Pilezer III in 745 B.C.E. created a new culture of domination that pressured Israel and Judah for a century until the fall of Asshurbanipal in 627 B.C.E. and the destruction of Nineveh in 612 B.C.E. The Assyrians are a most formidable power, at one point extending their hegemony even into Egypt. They are also, in their own annals, portrayed as uncommonly cruel and brutalizing. In response to the formidable and intimidating power of Assyria, Israelite and Judean kings were wont to give in and accept Assyrian definitions of reality.

It is clear, nonetheless, that there was maintained in Judah an insistent alternative to Assyrian hegemony, an alternative endlessly reiterating the claim that Judah's *sure future* could be based only upon loyalty to Yahweh, the emancipating, commanding God, and consequently in resistance to Assyrian hegemony. I will mention three literary evidences of this alternative identity. First, the prophet Isaiah offers in most magisterial form an alternative vision of reality. He does not so much address the ethical detail of Judah's life, but rather focuses on the large issuer of competing political-theological loyalties. Isaiah endlessly reiterates that Judah must *trust* in Yahweh who governs history and who will guarantee Judah in the face of imperial threat.

We know very little about the tactical ways of prophetic utterance in Israel. What is unmistakable, however, is that the prophet endlessly invites Israel to an alternative imaginative scenario of reality, wherein Assyria is denied domination and Yahweh is shown to be an adequate guarantee of life. Thus in the well-known word play of 7:9, in a bid for loyalty to the world construed around Yahweh, the prophet asserts:

> If you do not stand firm in faith,
> you shall not stand at all.

In the Isaiah tradition faith is engagement with all of the distinctive practices of covenant, most particularly the practice of justice and righteousness (cf. 5:7).

The alternative of *unfaith* is to abandon the defining marks of Yahwism, and to embrace the world of anxiety, collusion, and self-indulgence authorized and defined by Assyria. Indeed, the prophet is reductionist in insisting that these are the only two options.

The same poignant contrast is voiced in Is 8:5–8:

> Because this people has refused the waters of Shiloh (*shalom*) that flow gently, and melt in fear . . . therefore the Lord is bringing up against it the mighty flood waters of the River, the King of Assyria and all his glory; it will rise above all its channels and overflow its banks; it will sweep into Judah as a flood, and pouring over it, it will reach up to the neck.

The poet uses the metaphor of *gentle waters* (Yahwism) and *raging waters* (Assyria) as the only alternatives available. Here the poet does not enumerate the disciplines of Yahwism (cf. 1:16–17), but surely alludes to the Sinai requirements of loving God in holiness and loving neighbor in justice.

This contrasting image culminates:

> And its outspread armies will fill the breadth of your land,
> O Immanuel (8:8).

The address to "Immanuel" is ironic. It alludes to the abiding promises made to the house of David, only to announce that the throne of David is precarious and will be overwhelmed:

> No faith . . . no standing,
> no obedience . . . no promise.

Except that the Isaiah tradition cannot ever leave it there. For the Davidic-Immanuel imagery is endlessly resilient for Isaiah. In the very next chapter, the scion of David is celebrated:

> There will be endless peace
> for the throne of David and his kingdom.
> He will establish and uphold it
> with justice and with righteousness
> from this time onward and forever more (9:7).

Judah is warned and threatened about Assyrian definitions of reality. In the end, however, Assyria is no match for Yahweh's promises to David.

Micah is a sometime contemporary of Isaiah and, in a different way, makes the same affirmations. First, of the texts I will mention, the poet castigates the greedy who "covet fields and seize houses" (2:2).[11] The ones who violate Yahwism's covenantalism in such a way will lose out when the land is redivided, perhaps by the Assyrians (v. 4). Thus the expectations of Yahweh that will secure the community concern economic covenantalism in which the claims of the neighbor are not disregarded. Judah as a "contrast society" is premised on the elemental command, "Thou shalt not covet" that is here understood as broad social policy and practice.

The devastating warning that such coveting will bring disaster is matched in the Micah tradition by two assurances. In 5:2–6, it is anticipated that a new governing authority will reestablish Judah and give peace and security (5:4), and if necessary, will defeat Assyria and occupy the land. In the end, however, what is envisioned is not simply the defeat of the empire, but a great scenario of reconciliation, in which "peoples and nations" will submit to Yahweh's Torah in Zion, and will decide for disarmament and peace (4:1–4; cf. Is 2:1–5). What is so remarkable is that the commitment to *Torah* and to *peace* is a peculiar vision of Judah against the military inclination of the empire. In the imaginings of the poet, however, the peaceable Torah vision of Israel prevails, so that the "contrast community" of Yahweh offers the model and option eventually embraced by all nations. The Micah vision bespeaks the deep resolve and resilience of this alternative. Holding to the vision itself is a discipline and a mark of this community, a long-term refusal to give in to a more accommodating but hopeless social practice.

Third, it is plausible that Deuteronomy, the most intentional theological ecclesiology in the Old Testament, is offered as a contrast to Assyrian power. In its fictive articulation, Deuteronomy assaults the "Canaanites." Common scholarly judgment, however, regards Deuteronomy as an eighth–seventh century document, so that "the Canaanites" are stand-ins for the Assyrians, the central power of the time that sought to erode Israelite nerve and insinuate Assyrian claims into Israel's imagination.[12] (See the scornful attempts in Is 36:13–20, 36:4–10, 37:8–13.)

It is widely recognized that covenant receives its definitive voicing in Deuteronomy, the covenant tradition par excellence.[13] "Covenant" is not to be understood as simply a religious slogan, nor as one model among many for Israel's faith. It is rather the quintessential, normative theological-ethical accent of Israel's faith. Deuteronomy offers covenant as a radical and systemic alternative to the politics of autonomy, the economics of exploitation, and the theology of self-indulgence. The model of social reality offered in Deuteronomy is that this community—in all its socioeconomic, political, military aspects—is relational, with each taking responsibility for the neighbor. This notion of social reality touches every phase of social interaction and every exercise of social power. The pervasive discipline to which Deuteronomy summons Israel is precisely to give up autonomy for the sake of committed, neighborly relatedness.

I may cite three facets of this summons:

Economically, the practice of neighborliness is in "the year of release" (Deut 15:1–18). This command, likely the quintessence of neighborliness, seeks to prevent the emergence of a permanent underclass by providing that regularly and frequently, the poor shall have their debts cancelled and be equipped for reentry into the economy in a viable way.[14] It is impossible to overstate the radicality and subversive threat of this provision that undermines any conventional economic practice, and that intends to make Israel a peculiar community in the world.

Liturgically, the teaching of Deuteronomy accents the Passover as an affirmation that Israel's life shall be intentionally situated in the memory of the Exodus. If, as is generally judged, Deuteronomy is set in an Assyrian context, then this liturgical practice transfers the Egyptian miracle into an Assyrian matrix. In 2 Kings 23:21–23, moreover, in a text intimately linked to Deuteronomy, King Josiah is presented as the one who recovers Passover as a disciplined way of sustaining a peculiar identity in the world.

Politically, Deuteronomy acknowledges royal power and severely curbs its drive for autonomous control. The law envisions Torah-based power, for the king is enjoined to study "this Torah" day and night, so that even Davidic kinship is finally located in the covenantal context of Deuteronomy (Deut. 17:14–20). Negatively, moreover, the king is to shun the easy temptations of commoditization by refusing accumulation of silver, gold, wives, horses, or chariots. All of those possible gains are fundamentally irrelevant to a covenantal community and such offers are simply distortions of Israel's true life.

To be sure, the traditions of Isaiah (royal), Micah (peasant), and Deuteronomy (Mosaic-covenantal) give differing nuance to the life of Judah. All are agreed, however, that in every sphere of its life, Judah must be a community of intentional resistance, refusing to let dominant, imperial definitions confiscate the life of Judah. The community is enjoined to great vigilance, lest it lose is *raison d'être*, which is as a Yahwistic, alternative mode of life in a world of acquisitive, exploitative power (cf. Deut 8:1–20).

ISRAEL IS AN INTENTIONAL, DISTINCTIVE COMMUNITY IN A WORLD DOMINATED BY BABYLON

According to common critical judgment, Israel's situation in Babylon as deported, displaced exiles is the clearest, least complicated moment of *intentional community* vis à vis *dominating power*. (Cf. Ps 137 for a voicing of the mood of the exiles.[15]) Because the exiles were now displaced from their homeland and from all its sustaining institutional markers, the power of Babylonian culture to assimilate and the capacity of the Babylonian economy to substitute satiation for a faith-identity are indeed an intense threat. The intensity of the threat in turn evokes the most intentional efforts at community maintenance. Of the many efforts at such maintenance, I will mention two.

First, it is conventional to locate the Priestly material of Genesis-Numbers in the exile, as a strategy for sustaining the *sacramental* sense of community.[16] The Priestly materials, which became the decisive ordering of Israel's Torah, are aimed the maintenance of *order* in a social context of acute disorder and chaos. The Jews in exile had no stable reference points (as with appeal to the temple), and so this tradition offers alternative practices in lieu of such supports. In Gn 1:1–2:4a, the tradition provides a litany that is presumably liturgical, whereby the creation is celebrated, affirmed, and experienced as an ordered, reliable environment for life. That is, the liturgy itself intends to challenge and override the chaos of exilic social circumstance. Among the features that provide liturgical stability are the following:

- The assurance that God's powerful spirit is at work in the world that is therefore an arena of blessing. Generativity for life is assured there.
- The process of ordering is articulated in *separating* elements of creation into their proper zones (Gn 1:4, 6, 7, 14), and by assuring that all fruitfulness is "of every kind" (Gn 1:21, 24–25). This is a world in which nothing is out of place.
- The ordering is repeatedly acknowledged to be "good," and finally "very good." It is probable that "good" here means lovely, aesthetically pleasing. This is a beautiful place in which to reside!
- The liturgy culminates in sabbath rest, whereby the members of this community desist from production, and do so without anxiety. They are sure that the world will hold, because it is authorized by the creator God.

We may imagine that this liturgy provided focus, coherence, and assurance that made the exiles less vulnerable to the threats and to the seductions of Babylon. This tradition, however, championed not only order, but also *presence*.[17] Thus the Priestly materials also provide the exactitude of authorizing (Exod 25–31) and constructing (Exod 35–40) a tabernacle as a place suitable for God's dwelling in the midst of Israel. With great care and attentiveness, according to this imaginative tradition, Israel is able to host the holiness of God, thereby acknowledging that even severe cultural dislocation cannot impede Israel's ready access to the God it loves and serves.

In addition to *order and presence*, this tradition also insists on a *self-conscious ethic* commensurate with God's own holiness:

> You shall be holy, for I the Lord your God am holy. (Lev 19:2)

The commands of Leviticus, that often strike us as excessively punctilious, are an effort to assure the community of a distinctiveness that devotes its entire existence to the will and purpose of Yahweh. This tradition quite clearly accepts a vocation of oddity:

> You shall not do as they do in the land of Egypt, where you have lived, and you shall not do as they do in the land of Canaan, to which I am bringing you. (Lev 18:3)

This text does not mention Babylon, for such a mention here would be anachronistic. If, however, the text is dated to the sixth century, then we may understand "Egypt" and "Canaan" as capable of extrapolation to Babylon. Moreover,

> I have separated you from the peoples. You shall therefore make a distinction between the clean animals and the unclean. (Lev 20:24–25)

The practice of distinctiveness must pervade every aspect and dimension of Israel's life, down to the last small detail.

Second, this sacramental practice of distinctiveness in the Priestly tradition has as its counterpoint a much more dynamic, promissory tradition in the poetry of Is 40–55. Whereas the Priestly material makes the case for distinctiveness in a rather static way, the Isaiah poetry calls Israel to enact a transformed life in the world. Thus the gospel announcement of Yahweh's new governance surges in upon Israel, creating a new social possibility for homecoming and a new ground for communal joy:

O Jerusalem, herald of good tidings,
lift it up, do not fear;
say to the cities of Judah,
"Here is your God." (Is 40:9)

How beautiful upon the mountains
are the feet of the messenger . . .
who says to Zion,
"Your God reigns." (Is 52:7)

In these twin assertions, the power of Babylon is said to be broken. Babylonian gods are defeated. Babylonian power is overcome. Babylonian futures are nullified. Babylonian definitions of reality are overthrown.

Israel is free for life under the aegis of Yahweh who wills well-being, justice, and homecoming. This poet is a voice of hope to a community near despair, ready to give up on Yahweh. Indeed, great oppressive regimes aim at despair. For the killing of a hope-filled future renders displaced people powerless and easy to administer. Thus the poetic, lyrical, liturgical practice of hope is foundational for the sustenance of an odd community. Such practices of course can easily become sloganeering self-deception, unless the community is able to point to signs in the actual course of affairs. Poetic imagination in Isaiah was able to transpose observed public events into gifts Yahweh had performed for Israel. The emancipation of hopefulness engendered liturgical freedom that in turn produced ethical and eventually geographical freedom. This community knows itself, soon or late, headed home in a triumphant procession (cf. Is 35:8–10, 40:3–5).

The text makers in exile were able to defeat the grip of Babylonian hegemony upon the imagination of Israel. The *sacramental* and the *lyrical* both operate in the same tension; it is equally clear that both articulations and practices were crucial for the survival and missional buoyancy of this community so deeply in jeopardy.

ISRAEL IS AN INTENTIONAL, DISTINCTIVE COMMUNITY IN A WORLD DOMINATED BY PERSIA

The rise of Persia under the leadership of Cyrus had been voiced and anticipated in Is 44:28–45:7 as a gift from Yahweh for the sake of the community of exiles. And indeed, it is evident that compared to Babylon's policy of coerced deportation, Persian policy toward conquered peoples (including the Jews) was much more humane, permitting deported peoples to go home, and providing financial assistance for local religion. For that reason the interaction between Persian power and Jewish distinctiveness is not at all antagonistic, for the key agents of Jewish distinctiveness, Ezra and Nehemiah, are authorized and funded by Persia.

It is not for nothing that the peculiar work of Ezra and Nehemiah is commonly termed a "reform." Their work is the imposition of a particularly intense form of Judaism, propelled by a self-assured, self-conscious elite company of Babylonian Jews, upon the populace of Jerusalem. These leaders are indeed fanatical about the reestablishment of a self-conscious, intentional community of discipline that will not accommodate or compromise with cultural pressures.[18] To be sure, these reform measures have often been viewed, especially according to Christian stereotype, as narrow and legalistic. They must, however, be understood in a context in which it seemed clear that the very future and survival of Judaism required stringent and demanding measures.

Concerning the enactment of distinctiveness that characterizes the work of Ezra and Nehemiah, we may mention four elements:

• In what is regarded as the founding event of post-exilic Judaism, Ezra convened "all who could hear with understanding" to the promulgation of the Torah, whereby Judaism is marked as a community that listens to the lore and commands of Yahweh's Torah and shapes its life in glad response to it (Neh 8:1–12). This peculiar community is not self-generated, but understands itself in terms of a special authorization in a script available for steady and regular, attentive reiteration.

• The word-event of Torah is matched by the sacramental gesture of the festival of booths, whereby Israel bodily reenacts the ancient memories of the wilderness sojourn (Neh 8:13–18). In this act, Israel is made freshly aware of the precarious character of its life, and the generosity of God as the ground of its survival and well-being.

• The reformers introduced and required rigorous disciplines commensurate with the jeopardy of evaporation. These included separation from non-Jews (Neh 13:1–3), rejection of mixed marriages (13:27–31), which moves in the direction of "ethnic cleansing," and the observation and payment of regular offerings (10:32–39). While these provisions may strike us as excessive, it is evident that they aim at bringing every aspect of communal life under the intentional governance of Yahweh. Nothing falls outside that commitment.

• Most remarkably, Nehemiah insists on a communitarian economics by rejecting the charging of interest within the community, and binding the haves and have-nots into a practical and effective economic covenant (5:1–13).

It is this series of reforms that sets later Judaism on its way as a community of discipline and obedience. At the end of the Persian period and the rise of Hellenism under Alexander, the maintenance of distinctive Jewishness became urgent. This does not mean that this community remained isolated or insulated. It is clear, and surely inevitable, that Judaism, in a Hellenistic environment, engaged intensely with culture, thus producing what we have come to call "Hellenistic Judaism."[19] What strikes us, however, is not the extent of accommodation, but the capacity to maintain, in an identifiable, self-conscious way a Jewish sense of life in the world.

CONCLUSION

This long review has provided us a long-term menu for Israel's sense of self through the vagaries and challenges of historical experience. We may, from this review, draw three conclusions:

1. In all of these periods, Israel's work of resistance and durability features some common elements:

(a) Israel as a self-conscious community of faith is in every phase of this history profoundly in jeopardy in relation to its context. Its survival depends upon a fluid capacity for resistance and embrace in large part pragmatic. But that pragmatic quality could never eliminate the risk.

(b) There are socioeconomic, political factors and ethnic sensibilities at work in this process in every season. At its core, however, the oddness of this community is theological; it is rooted in the reality of Yahweh, who is seen to be demanding and legitimating.

(c) Such a community requires intentional and rigorous disciplines, so intentional and rigorous that outsiders may view them as excessively demanding. But such discipline is a life-and-death matter. Israel under threat is never an easy "therapeutic" community, and faith in Yahweh is not a massage. It is the embrace and practice of a destiny that makes costly demands in the name of Yahweh.

(*d*)   At the center of these demands are indeed *word and sacrament*—word understood as text production, text reiteration, and text interpretation, sacrament as bodily acts that dramatize full commitment to the rigors.

2. Our question in this volume of essays is not about the past but the present. The visible, intentional community of faith now is not preoccupied with any of these empires. While we may each one give a different name to our comparable matrix of faith identity, I suggest that the task of the beloved community now is *vis-à-vis the "money economy" of Western postindustrial technology that sweeps all before it*, and that seemingly cannot be resisted.[20] The reality of this enterprize—rooted in commodity, aimed at satiation, and unhesitant about brutality—poses acute questions and challenges for a distinctive community of faith. While this imperial context is perhaps not more dangerous than any of the others I have named, it is the one for our time and place.

Perhaps this review may suggest some of the particularities that we may enact as our own, whereby to refuse the complete triumph of military consumerism. Thus the real quarrel is not between believing Christian liberals and believing Christian conservatives, or between publicly inclined and sectarianly inclined Christians; it is rather an issue between baptized Christians and those for whom Yahweh has dropped out of the narrative of the world. Distinctiveness depends upon telling and enacting the story of the world with Yahweh—the governor of Israel and the lord of the church—as the key character.

3. The new situation of Christianity in the West, with the demise of institutional power, poses problems, but also offers great opportunities for a serious church. Because the church has been dominant in the West, often in brutalizing ways, its present circumstance cannot be at all likened to the ongoing social location of Jews. Having said that, it is nonetheless possible that in a new decentered position, *Christians may learn from Jews.* I commend the study of Jacob Neusner concerning *The Enchantments of Judaism*, the daily disciplines and practices of Judaism that keep identity vibrant and available.[21] Neusner observes that such practices abet the daily task of "imaging Jewishness," for without such intentional imagination, says Neusner, Jews cannot be sustained in faith.[22]

Mutatis mutandis, the new cultural dislocation and disestablishment of the church suggest a like mandate of imagination for Christians. Daily imagining of Christian baptismal identity is urgent. Word and sacrament are decisive practices in this task. Finally, however, the urgency is to opt for an actual social reality in which Yahweh is a key player. Powerful forces want to defeat that account of reality. It is the vocation of this peculiar community of faith to keep available and credible the Yahweh account of reality. That requires careful utterance and daring enactment, clear thinking, and bold living.

NOTES

1. H. Richard Niebuhr, *Christ and Culture* (New York: Harper and Brothers, 1951). Niebuhr's classic presentation still provides a way into the subject, although the book is now criticized, especially because the notions of gospel and culture in the book are both monolithic, without taking into account the reality that the gospel takes many forms, and culture is inevitably pluralistic in any context. See Robert E. Webber, *The Church in the World: Opposition, Tension, or Transformation?* (Grand Rapids, Mich.: Academie Books, Zondervan Publishing House, 1986), pp. 261–78.

2. See Charles Reich, *Opposing the System* (New York: Random House, 1995) and Richard J. Barnet, *The Global War against the Poor* (Washington, D.C.: The Servant Leadership School, n.d.).

3. There is, no doubt, according to current scholarly judgment, a deep and pervasive tension between the *practice* of Israelite religion on the ground and the *ideology* which is imposed on the Old Testament that comes to be "normative" for the Old Testament. It is likely that it is the tension itself that is the subject of our study, rather than one or the other of these alternatives. For a comprehensive discussion of the matter, see Rainer Albertz, *A History of Israelite Religion in the Old Testament Period I: From the Beginnings to the End of the Monarchy* (OTL; Louisville, Ky.: Westminster John Knox Press, 1994), *A History of Israelite Religion in the Old Testament Period II: From the Exile to the Maccabees* (OTL; Louisville, Ky.: Westminster John Knox Press, 1994).

4. On the "mythic" component in this "historical narrative, see Frank Moore Cross, "The Cultus of the Israelite League," *Canaanite Myth and Hebrew Epic: Essays in the History of the Religion of Israel* (Cambridge: Harvard University Press, 1973), pp. 79–144.

5. See Walter Brueggemann, "The Exodus Narrative as Israel's Articulation of Faith Development," *Hope within History* (Atlanta, Ga.: John Knox Press, 1987), pp. 7–26.

6. Frank Crüsemann, *Die Torâ; Theologie und Sozialgeschichte des alttestamentlichen Gesetze* (München: Chr. Kaiser Verlag, 1992), p. 75, nicely makes the case that "Sinai is an u-topian place . . . that is the archimedean point of the law that is not bound to the power of the state." That is, Sinai stands behind and outside every historical explanation and is the ultimate source of command.

7. The "downside" of the Torah tradition is made clear, for example, by Carolyn Pressler, *The View of Women Found in the Deuteronomic Family Laws* (BZAW 216; Berlin: De Gruyter, 1993), who demonstrates that the laws are rigidly patriarchal in orientation.

8. See the fine study by Marva J. Dawn, *Keeping the Sabbath Wholly: Ceasing, Resting, Embracing, Feasting* (Grand Rapids, Mich.: Eerdmans, 1989).

9. See Moshe Weinfeld, *Social Justice in Ancient Israel and in the Ancient Near East* (Minneapolis, Minn.: Fortress Press, 1995) who demonstrates that justice in the Old Testament pivots around the "sabbatic principle" expressed in sabbath, the year of release, and the year of jubilee. On the latter, see Maria Harris, *Proclaim Jubilee! A Spirituality for the Twenty-First Century* (Louisville, Ky.: Westminster John Knox Press, 1996).

10. On this remarkable text, see Hans Walter Wolff, "The Kerygma of the Yahwist," *Interpretation* 20 (1966): 152 and passim, and Walter Brueggemann,"Subversive Modes of Blessing," (forthcoming).

11. On this text, see Marvin Chaney, "You Shall not Covet Your Neighbor's House," *Pacific Theological Review* 15, no. 2 (winter 1982): 3–13.

12. On the term "Canaanite" as an ideological marker, see Niels P. Lemche, *The Canaanites and Their Land: The Tradition of the Canaanites* (JSOT Supp. 110; Sheffield: JSOT Press, 1991).

13. See Ernest W. Nicholson, *God and His People: Covenant and Theology in the Old Testament* (New York: Oxford University Press, 1986).

14. On this text, see Jeffries M. Hamilton, *Social Justice and Deuteronomy: The Case of Deuteronomy 15* (Atlanta, Ga.: Scholars Press, 1992).

15. On Israel amidst the Babylonians, see Daniel L. Smith, *The Religion of the Landless: The Social Context of the Babylonian Exile* (Indianapolis, Ind.: Meyer Stone, 1989).

16. On the Priestly material, see the review by Robert B. Coote and David Robert Ord, *In The Beginning: Creation and the Priestly History* (Minneapolis, Minn.: Fortress Press, 1991).

17. Generally on the theological problem of presence in the Old Testament, see Samuel L. Terrien, *The Elusive Presence: Toward a New Biblical Theology* (San Francisco: Harper and Row, 1978). On the Priestly materials, see especially pp. 161–226.

18. One must of course notice the irony that this vigorous form and concern for purity and separatism is *funded* by the Persians. One might expect that a movement for purity and separation would insist upon the avoidance of such external funding, as in the case of the "Three Self" movement in the Chinese church. But alas (cf. Neh 9:37)!

19. See the magisterial study of the subject by Martin Hengel, *Judaism and Hellenism* (Philadelphia: Fortress Press, 1974). The "Maccabean revolt," whatever its intention or historical shape, stands as the definitional marker for resistance to Hellenization and any other such option for accommodation.

20. See Reich, *Opposing the System*, Theodore H. von Laue, *The World Revolution of Westernization: The Twentieth Century in Global Perspective*

(New York: Oxford University Press, 1987), and less directly Jacques Ellul, *The Technological Society* (New York: Knopf, 1965).

21. Jacob Neusner, *The Enchantments of Judaism: Rites of Transformation from Birth through Death* (New York: Basic Books, 1987).

22. Neusner (ibid., 214) concludes, "We are Jews through the power of our imagination."

3

Salt and Leaven: Resistances to Empire in the Street-Smart Paleochurch

Marianne Sawicki

Driving north from the Bluegrass toward Chicago, I never cross the Ohio River without thinking of the Underground Railroad and the courageous people who waded to freedom where the I-275 bridge now leaps from bank to bank. The broad Ohio was their Red Sea, Kentucky their Egypt, and northern cities their Promised Land. Crossing the waters was a decisive event of liberation for the slaves, for the nineteenth-century Americans just as for the ancient Hebrews.

A landscape that is cleanly split into two opposite banks can appropriately symbolize a discrete "before" time of bondage and an "after" time of liberty. At the water, something ended and something else began. Evil and tears lay behind the fugitives, and hope lay ahead. They crossed one way, once, and never went back. It's a simple and powerful image: the image of *exodus*, literally the "way out" toward freedom. A theology of liberation discerns and celebrates the ways in which God still leads people out from oppressive situations toward horizons of possibility for fully human life. In ancient times the people of Israel defined their community as that people who had been liberated from bondage in Egypt and now served only the God who had led them through the perils of water, desert, and mountain to take over the land of Canaan.

A compelling theological vision. But it was *not* the vision of the early Jesus constituencies. They defined themselves quite differently. To be sure, the Exodus pattern was well known to the Jews of Roman Galilee.[1] Motifs lifted from it have been worked into some of the literary compositions that became the New Testament (such as Matthew's parallels between Jesus and Moses as lawgivers, or Mark's paschal interpretation of Jesus' death). But there was a time before the churches dared to improvise on the Torah in such terms. More important, the spatial deployment of the Jesus event simply was quite unlike an exodus. Jesus' first followers knew that there was no escape, no place to go to get away from the civil and personal evils confronting them. They had to figure out how to live in a landscape compromised by colonial oppressions. They would seek and find God's Kingdom precisely in the midst of that. The Kinneret was not designated a Red Sea, nor the Galilee an Egypt. There was no thought of attempting a Moses-style exodus from the bondage of Roman occupation toward a new space of freedom. Instead, paleochurch practices were symbiotic with Roman power.

This was deliberate, by design. Jesus' followers used the metaphors of salt and leaven to describe their stance toward imperial power. They understood the gospel to be both corrosive and preservative like salt; it was to be infectious, expansive, and profane like leaven. These metaphors express a theology of digging in and staying put, an ecclesiology of infiltration rather than escape and conquest. I believe that it is vitally important for today's churches to consider this early ecclesiological option. Why? Because it is older, more primitive, more radical, and yet more adaptable to our own political situations than "liberation theology" is. In this chapter I make my argument in five steps. I begin by clearing up the confusion between real and metaphorical space-talk that has hindered our understanding of the paleochurch's deployment across its indigenous landscape. Second, I debunk the claim that disciplined historical inquiry must be positivistic, oppressive, and therefore useless to any progressive political program. Those two moves set the stage for my presentation of the theology of subversive cohabitation that I find in early parts of the Gospels, where there is no "discipleship of equals," no ecclesial democracy, and no impetus toward liberation from patriarchy. Fourth, I compare the coping tactics of the Jesus movements with resistive adaptations to Roman imperialism that were developing at the same time in mainstream early Judaism. Finally, I conclude with the suggestion that "to salt and to leaven" are canonical ecclesiological directives that we must follow not by slavish imitation, but rather by creative analogy in Christian confrontations with present-day empires, as we look for the kingdom that Jesus was talking about.

SPURIOUS SPATIALIZATIONS

To say that Jesus was a historical person is to say that he lived and worked *somewhere*. Roman Galilee was a real place. Roads crossed it.

From the northeast, the route from Damascus and Babylon funneled merchants and tourists into the Kinneret region. About the year 20 C.E., Herod Antipas built his seaside capital city, Tiberias, on the southwestern shore of the Kinneret to attract those wealthy and well-connected travelers into his territory on their way to and from Jerusalem via the Jordan valley. The lake already had thriving industries ringing it, such as the shipyards and fish packing plants at Magdala. Galilee exported foodstuffs and textiles throughout the region and the world. There were fortunes to be made when Roman administration introduced worldwide market efficiencies, but the cost was the realignment of traditional small-scale village relationships as imperial cities drew labor away from the land.

The physical configuration of villages, cities, trade routes, and nutritional resources comprising the Galilean landscape must be understood before we can understand how Jesus went looking *there* for what he called God's Kingdom. Unfortunately we have a bad intellectual habit that may keep us from taking the *real* space of Galilee with due seriousness. We talk about space *figuratively* in various metaphors borrowed from materialist literary theory. These figures have become so familiar that we forget they are only figures of speech, and that the real spaces do not behave like the literary figures.

Take, for example, the notion of "discursive space." Since Heidegger, it has become customary for theorists to describe the event of reality-recognition as an "opening up" of a space of disclosure.[2] Habermas' theory of communicative action calls for the establishment of a democratic "public space" where all concerned parties may freely communicate and negotiate their interests.[3] Such "spaces" do not open up automatically, but must be deliberately established. The protocols of communication constitute the "space." Fair enough; it's an apt metaphor. Yet we must remember that *physically* open spaces do not automatically result in unimpeded information transfer. Conversely, disclosure and communication can be "opened up" (figuratively speaking) under conditions of very confined and restricted real space, and even under conditions of real physical absence. (The myriad connections of the Internet are only the latest illustration.) The figurative "opening" of a conversation may coincide with, and may even require, closures and exclusions of various kinds.[4]

Another example of a spatial figure is the Greek term *ekklēsia*, which designates the paleochurch in the texts of the New Testament. It connotes a calling out, a gathering together. The image is one of selection, displacement, and physical propinquity. This term was commonly used to designate secular political assemblies in which people met to decide various matters of common concern. The ideal of democracy, forged in ancient Athens, requires citizens to meet in a self-governing assembly. Participation in such an *ekklēsia* was restricted both socially and physically. Socially, only free male property owners were allowed to participate. Physically, the assembly was limited by the size of the physical enclosure, the reach of the human voice, and the distance people could travel to participate. It is conceivable that the intention to belong to an *ekklēsia* might outweigh physical barriers to someone's actual presence there. On the other hand, historically, the church very soon transcended *ekklēsia*. The paleochurch's intention to scatter and diffuse across the empire was literally the antithesis of "ecclesial" gathering. For example, the spatial sundering of *ekklēsia* is mandated in the "Great Commission" of Mt 28: 18–20 and in the diffusion of information and personnel after Pentecost, Acts 1:8.

Exodus, already discussed above, is a third spatial motion metaphor. To escape, you cross over from one place to another. Physical distance separates and insulates you from the evil that is left behind.[5] But liberation from the bondage of sin is not a theme of the teaching of Jesus or of the gospel narratives; it is a Pauline metaphor, in which "distance" stands for time. The "before" state is the religious ideology of Jewish law, as Paul saw it. The state of liberation is freedom from the law; that is, Torah, villainized to suit Paul's rhetoric.[6] Today's so-called liberation theology extends this Pauline metaphor, aspiring to put an end to oppressive conditions, not by physically exiting, but by politically vanquishing certain evil economic and social structures.[7] The incongruity built into this metaphorical use of the "exodus" motif is that one tries to "get away" from evil temporally without being able to move away from it physically. Liberation is proclaimed while evil circumstances are quite plainly *still here*. This liberation is not real. It does not materialize, but is supposed to subsist as the invisible engine propelling historical events toward some always future goal.

Contemporary social theory invokes a fourth spatial metaphor, *colonization,* to describe cultural appropriations or "displacements" engineered by a dominant group. Real, historical colonization occurred in space. That is, people from one land went into another land, where they altered the landscape to siphon off wealth. The colonizers dominated both in the material realm and in cultural affairs. Colonization produced secondary real displacements for the subjugated people: emigration, migration of labor, urbanization, homelessness, and so forth. Real physical goods were caused to circulate in new patterns, and wealth flowed away from the colony to the colonizing country. Roman imperialism, therefore, was a reality that was spatially deployed.

To be sure, cultural distortion accompanied and facilitated these real displacements. Rome achieved cultural hegemony by granting concessions to a class of collaborating indigenous rulers. Thus the Herodian princes were raised and educated offshore with the sons of elite Roman families. Antipas went away from Palestine to learn how to be Roman, and he came back to redesign Israel's landscape as a little Italy. During his administration, Lake Kinneret became the Mediterranean Sea, with shipping routes presided over by Antipas' new tourist attraction Tiberias, a little Ostia. From the Kinneret, the Jordan valley led tourists and merchants to Jericho, gateway to Jerusalem, just as the Tiber led from the port of Ostia inland to Rome. John the Baptist's effective opposition to this Italianization of Israel was spatially deployed as well. John situated himself astride Herod's little Tiber and used its very water to signal repentance—literally, "turning back"—for the tourists and business travelers making their way between Tiberias and Jerusalem. Jesus' own baptism by John signaled his disengagement from the colonial Kinneret industrial complex in which he may well have been participating as a shipwright. Colonization and colonial oppression in the real world are always embodied in material features such as these. Oppression as a subjective or psychologically felt experience is devoid of meaning if it lacks reference to transactions in real space.

A fifth spatial metaphor commonly misused today is that of *social situation*. In real space, an individual human being can occupy only one place at a time and can see only the objects that are relatively nearby around her. Physical vision is both enabled and limited by real location. This "standpoint" determines knowledge and praxis. Metaphorically, empirical knowledge is *somewhat* like vision, and one's distinctive demographic peculiarities are *somewhat* like a location on a grid defined by all possible human variations. Thus it can be said metaphorically that knowledge itself is both enabled and limited by social location. That much is clear. However, equivocation and confusion creep in when we confuse the properties of real space with those of metaphorical, epistemological space. While *real* distance inhibits communication, people can and do understand others who *metaphorically* occupy very distant social spaces. Empathy does not require that one displace the other, or move into the space of the other.[8] Conversely, understanding is not guaranteed by similar or identical social location. All of which indicates that knowledge can transcend perspective. If epistemological space were real space, we would indeed be trapped in relativism with no hope of reaching consensus. Scientific historical claims would then be nothing but attempts to achieve arbitrary hegemony for one's own view, simply because it is one's own. But epistemological space is not real space. Empirical knowledge is grounded in a priori rational structures that are the common heritage of all human beings, wherever they happen to be and no matter how they came to be there. Knowledge is possible apart from "standpoints," and there are some profoundly important truths that are not "situational."

My argument has had to begin with a critique of these metaphorical equivocations about space. Without having distinguished between real and figurative space, we could not proceed to investigate the interplay between the two or appreciate the resistive practices deployed by the early church. In the next section, I pursue and challenge the implications of the relativistic epistemology that stems from perspectivalism and spatial equivocation.

THE POSSIBILITY AND THE
USEFULNESS OF KNOWING HISTORY

Much has been written in the last decade about "the historical Jesus," that is, the profile of Jesus of Nazareth before Calvary as it can be drawn through critical cooperative study of the textual and material evidence available to us. Oversimplifying for the sake of argument, one might say that there are currently four theological options represented in the literature, which might be summed up as follows:

1. The gospel portraits are substantially reliable and can be taken more or less at face value.[9]
2. Profiles of Jesus are mere ideological constructions. We are free to portray him in any manner that furthers the interests of our community, just as the canonical evangelists did. "The name of Jesus" has always been elastic enough to cover innovative interpretations. It's up for grabs.[10]
3. Scholarly consensus can be achieved concerning some important aspects of Jesus' career and message, though not all. This consensus should confront and override the nonscientific memories of Jesus, particularly the cultic and devotional memories.[11]
4. Remembering Jesus occurs authentically in various places and practices, among which are liturgy, charity, teaching, and healing, as

well as disciplined study of the gospels. Scholarly historical investigations of *who Jesus was* and of *how he was remembered by the paleochurch* are a vital component in the contemporary discernment of *who Jesus is*.[12]

If this were a chapter about Jesus, I would now proceed to defend option 4. But the chapter is about the precanonical church, whose discernment first identified Jesus. My argument here is that the paleochurch was not just redesigning Jesus and his message ad lib as it went along, in whatever way best served the needs of the moment (option 2), but rather was already operating on the premise of option 4. That is, from Calvary onward, the wonders wrought and the words spoken "in the name of Jesus" were intended to have some real historical continuity with him and his practices, even as they creatively adapted to changing circumstances. Most important, today *we can understand* this intention and how it operated. We can adopt it and derive guidance from it. And this is precisely what theology should do.

I am optimistic about the possibility of acquiring reliable information concerning the intentions and practices of the paleochurch. My optimism has two sources: the breadth of evidence that is emerging, and the depth of analysis made possible by contemporary critical social theory.[13] We have evidences of several kinds. We have ancient texts: the canonical books of the New Testament as well as other first-century religious and secular writings. We have material remains: the landscape of Israel and the ancient Near East, artifacts, architecture, and floral and faunal traces of ancient dietary and labor patterns. We have comparative anthropological and socio-political data. To collect and analyze all this evidence, we have a repertoire of social theory. The blindly reductive "systems theory" of the 1960s has given way to more subtle postprocessual cultural analysis in archaeology. Moreover, professional practitioners of scientific historical analysis now are drawn from a wider sector of society than ever before.

These are developments of the 1990s. Biblical scholars trained in the 1960s may not be taking them into account when they indict *all* historical investigation as necessarily positivistic, or when they charge that data are produced arbitrarily from social-scientific modeling. As advances in archaeology become more widely known, the claim that historical study is *necessarily* positivistic and patriarchal will be seen to be without merit.[14]

Paradoxically, ideological rejection of any possibility of historical data has gone hand-in-hand with the importation of anachronistic principles and concepts into first-century Galilee.[15] There is a certain logic to this. If nothing from the first century constrains our description of that era (that is, if the evidence can fit equally well into *just any* scenario that we might contrive), then we may as well make up a universal law from which to deduce a portrayal of first-century practices. For example, we may as well assume that women are oppressed always and everywhere, and that they always resist oppression.[16] Then we can syllogistically (but spuriously!) deduce the statement that first-century Galilean women were oppressed and resisted oppression. This deduction can become the hermeneutical engine that pumps out convenient descriptions of paleochurch practices. In the midst of the cities of the early Roman Empire, we would then be free to find the democratic polity described in fourth-century B.C.E. Athenian texts, or the ideology of liberty, equality, and fraternity espoused in eighteenth-century Euro-American texts. Plato's Athens, Paul's Ephesus, James's Jerusalem, Voltaire's Paris, Jefferson's Virginia—their texts would be interchangeable. Mix and match.

No matter how exhilarating such an ideological interpretive project may feel to its practitioners and consumers, it obviously cannot forge a theological consensus within the whole church or a scholarly consensus within the academic community. Only some factions can accept it. But that is not the most telling indictment of this project. More problematically, it silences the voices of women and men in the first century. This hermeneutic of deduction obliterates the words of Jesus' first witnesses. The campaign to find "democracy" and "equality" in the paleochurch drowns out those indigenous expressions in which its members actually named, reflected upon, and propagated their practices. "Salt" and "leaven" are two of those indigenous critical namings, as I will show in the next section. We can indeed understand what the paleochurch was trying to say, but only if we listen without hastily assimilating their imagery to anachronistically imposed categories of liberation, equality, democracy, and so-called open discourse.

WHO DID *THEY* SAY THEY WERE?

In the first section I criticized the spatial equivocation that produces five metaphorical terms commonly used in contemporary ecclesiology: *discursive space, ekklēsia, exodus-liberation, colonization,* and *standpoint.* I am ready now to show how strikingly those metaphors clash with the imagery in which Jesus' first followers named their own practices. The imagery of leaven and salt describes deployment strategies for the kingdom of God that are not at all open, democratic, or liberating. Nor do these strategies constitute a discrete "standpoint." Rather, the paleochurch is a stealth operation. It presumes that imperial structures will remain intact so that they can be infiltrated. This is a resistance that exploits the empire; it does not defeat, neutralize, kill, or escape from its host. The paleochurch looks for the kingdom of God in the midst of occupied Palestine and Syria, not on some far shore where oppression has been left behind.[17]

First, the "discursive space" of paleochurch practice is closed and secretive. This is abundantly clear in texts from the earliest stratum of the Sayings Gospel Q, and is corroborated in rabbinic traditions. The historical recovery of evidence for the practices and the teachings of Jesus' first followers is more easily accomplished than the recovery of the deeds and words of the "historical Jesus" himself. For this task, we don't have to determine whether a given practice that is reflected in early texts comes originally from Jesus or was an innovation by his followers. Either way, the practice is something that they embrace "in Jesus' name." The words of Jesus, as distinctively remembered and performed by some sector of the early church, disclose a great deal about that community's ideology and about its practices of memory and performance.[18]

The parables of the mustard seed and the leaven are juxtaposed in Q and they address the missionary work of the Q community.[19] In Q 10:2–11 the disciples of Jesus are sent out into dangerous circumstances, like lambs among wolves. Although they use the roads like tourists and business travelers, they go incognito, creating the false impression that they are locals by carrying no baggage. In towns they are to indigenize themselves by attaching to the family that employs them, "growing roots in the community in an unobtrusive manner."[20] The stealth tactics are understood to be temporary and provisional, for in Q 12:2–3:

> Nothing has been covered up that will not be revealed, or hidden that will not be known. What you have said in the dark will be heard in the light, and what you have whispered into the ear shall be proclaimed from the housetops.

To these people it seems only natural that God's Kingdom must germinate and foment secretly at first, and that its eventual success is assured. In Q 13:19–20:

> It is like a grain of mustard which someone took and cast it in his own garden, and it grew and became a tree and the birds of

the sky made their nests in its branches. . . . The reign of God is
like leaven which a woman took and hid in three measures of
flour, till it leavened the whole mass.

In fact, mustard is not a tree but a big aggressive weed. Cotter points out
that mighty trees like the oak and the cedar commonly represented political systems organized for domination; the pesky mustard shrub that the
birds prefer is a parody. As for the leaven, it is "hidden" in the flour
before it raises the whole wad of dough. Cotter concludes that the Q
missionaries "had to hide their efforts from formal public scrutiny."[21]

After sheltered beginnings hidden in the dark and in secret, the practices of the Q missionaries were supposed to burst forth into visibility:
like a mustard plant, like a risen loaf, like a lamp on a lampstand
(Q 11:33), like a shout from a housetop. Other early Jesus constituencies apparently chafed at the stealth tactics of the Q people and wanted
to "go public" more rapidly:

Is a lamp brought in to be put under a bushel, or under a bed,
and not on a stand? For there is nothing hid, except to be made
manifest; nor is anything secret, except to come to light. (Mk 4:21)

A city set on a hill cannot be hid. (Mt 5:14)

A city being built on a high mountain and fortified cannot fall,
nor can it be hidden. (GThom 32)

No one after lighting a lamp covers it with a vessel, or puts it
under a bed, but puts it on a stand, that those who enter may
see the light. (Lk 8:16)

No one after lighting a lamp puts it in a cellar or under a bushel
but on a stand, that those who enter may see the light.
(Lk 11:33 = Q 11:33)

Note the hiding places mentioned in these texts: under a bed, in a cellar,
under a bushel, within a city. These would be places where *a person*
could hide if the police ("those who enter," *eisporeuomenoi*) were
searching house to house for troublemakers. In effect, these sayings propose a policy shift from secrecy to confrontative engagement with the
authorities. (But note that there is still no hint of escape, exodus, liberation.)

Matthew's Jesus underscores the point of the metaphor: *That lamp
is you.*

You are the light of the world (*phōs tou kosmou*). . . . Let your
light shine before people so that they may see your good works
and give glory to your Father who is in heaven. (Mt 5:14, 16;
compare Jn 8:12 and 9:5, where the light of the world is Jesus.)

Matthew puts the same point on the salt metaphor: *You* are the salt of
the earth (*halas tēs gēs,* Mt 5:13). The salt sayings that follow are noto-
riously obscure.

If salt be tainted, by what shall it be salted? It no longer has any
potency except to be thrown out and walked on by people.
(Mt 5:13)

Salt is good; but
if salt be tainted, by what shall it be seasoned? It is suitable neither for soil (*gēn* = earth) nor for manure. They throw it out.
(Lk 14:34–35 = Q 14:34–35)

Everyone is going to be salted with fire.
Salt is good; but
if the salt becomes saltless, what are you going to season it with?
Have salt in yourselves and be at peace with one another.
(Mk 9:49–50)

These sayings baffle interpreters. Chemically it is not possible for salt to
become unsalty; some sort of mixture or unrefined raw material must be
intended.[22] The authors of the gospel texts also seem to have amalga-
mated several diverse salt sayings whose meanings may already have
become obscure by the end of the first century.

Fortunately, they can be brought into clearer focus by considering the
Galilean lakeside context in which they first circulated. Salt was used
industrially in fish packing. Kinneret producers exported a briny gourmet
fish sauce that was used as a condiment. A little of it went a long way.
The "tainted" salt may refer to the occasional batch that was spoiled in
production. When a load of fish spoiled, the mess could be composted as
fertilizer to enrich the soil. But if the brine was brewed up wrong, it could
not be dumped in a field because doing so would prevent any crops from
growing there. In fact, to salt a field would be an act of sabotage and
would disrupt agricultural production. Bad brine would have to be
dumped on bad land, that is, on a city pavement where it would do no
more harm to the environment, but would actually improve the walking
surface by sterilizing the urban filth and killing weeds.

"Earth" in Mt 5:13 doesn't mean the planet; it means the soil. Salt disables soil from producing crops. On the other hand, salt preserves food. It prevents fish from rotting so that they can be shipped from the Kinneret to distant markets. The fish-packing plants in Magdala, on the shores of the freshwater "Sea of Galilee," would have to import salt overland in bulk from southern Judea or Idumea, on the other side of the Dead Sea. There may very well have been spillage and agricultural damage along the roads, both from the raw salt and from the finished product. "Traveling salt," then, is a hazardous material. If it leaks it can ruin crops and corrode metal. Perhaps salt was shipped in unmarked containers to avoid arousing hostility from landowners along the way. This would make it something of a stealth commodity. Its potency would have been essential to the economy of the region, yet it would have to be brought in very discretely. My suggestion is that the industrial perspective aligns the metaphor of salt with the metaphors of the mustard seed, the leaven, and the oil lamp. Accordingly, paleochurch practices are such that they "turn on the lights" in a dark world that doesn't appreciate being lit up, and they "ship salt" across agricultural land. "You reveal the cosmos, you salt the soil," says Matthew (Mt 5:13–14). We may read this as self-portraiture by the paleochurch.

If, as I suggest, salt was a controversial commodity, the controversy set one socioeconomic class against another. In the first century it was increasingly common to find large tracts of agricultural lands held by absentee landlords. More and more farmers were working for somebody else. Not so the fishing fleet. Family-owned boats seem to have been the norm, although many people also fished for hire. But you could always cast a net from the shore and sell your morning's catch to the fish-packing plant.[23] Nobody owned the lake. The "pro-salt" faction in the controversy, then, would be made up of small-scale boat owners, freelance fishers, and workers in allied industries like shipbuilding, fuel gathering, and pot manufacture. If the Q missionaries are "salt of the soil," then they are in solidarity with all those workers as the workers resist powerful agribusiness interests. They have to be strategically sneaky in order to bring the harsh light of reality, and the purifying corrosion of salt, to bear upon the invisible interlocked web of imperial collusions by the wealthy estate-owning class. The metaphor seems to indicate as much.

How did these sneaky practices look from the other side? Rabbinic tradition offers further evidence that the paleochurch made its initial approaches one-on-one through stealthy infiltration. According to the Mishnah, indigenous Judean authorities caught *someone*, maybe Peter, sneaking around in Lod and whispering heterodox teachings to one person at a time. Schwartz examines the mishnaic and talmudic traditions about an individual identified as Ben Stada who is placed in Lydda under circumstances similar to those in which Acts 9:32–35 places Peter there.[24] The crime of beguiling people into false religious beliefs and practices was punishable by stoning. But *two* witnesses ordinarily were required to establish guilt in a capital case. The crime of the enticer (Hebrew *mesit*) was so serious and dangerous, however, that some of the legal requirements of due process could be relaxed in order to enable the authorities to entrap the offender. The *mesit* was like salt in the soil. Schwartz writes:

> The *mesit*, according to the Rabbis, threatened the very fabric of Jewish survival. The *mesit* preached action. . . . The *mesit* preached his message only in secret and often disguised it as a social encounter, preaching at a meal. The *mesit* spoke in a "low voice" and preferred to preach to individuals since "an individual does not ask outside advice and will err after him (= the *mesit*) while groups of many will seek advice and not err." . . . A *mesit* was neither a sage, Rabbi or prophet, but rather a "common man" . . . someone who would not automatically be recognized.[25]

Schwartz argues persuasively that Peter operated in just this manner, according to details of his activities recorded in the Acts of the Apostles. When Peter healed, he did it privately, without fanfare. If people heard about the healing and came to him to inquire, Peter chose his words very carefully to avoid charges of blasphemy. He played cat-and-mouse with the Sanhedrin and, unlike Paul or Stephen, preserved "the delicate balance of public and private activity" so as to keep one jump ahead of the law.[26]

It's difficult to see how this sort of opportunistic infiltration could have been carried out under the guidance of a democratically self-governed assembly of Christians, the alleged "discipleship of equals."[27] We have no evidence for any social mechanism to build consensus or to set policy. The paleochurch does not "gather" for social visibility; it scatters for invisibility and maximum disruption of other targeted institutions. Even in the best of times, democracy is hard to manage. It requires coordination of the judgments of individual members whose interests and insights are divergent. Decisions must be made in light of a perceived common good that may not coincide with the individual preference of anyone. The first century was not the best of times. Democracy no longer existed as a form of social organization at the level of the empire or its client states. Nor were there any democratically governed cities, industries, families, religions, or businesses. As the Stoic philosopher Epictetus amply attests, the realm of public affairs had become chaotic and precarious. The best that one could do was to govern one's own unruly desires and achieve an internal serenity. "Have salt in yourselves and be at peace with one another" (Mk 9:50); Epictetus could certainly agree with that.

One searches in vain for traces of democratic polity amid the vignettes of paleochurch decision making that have been recorded in Acts. Consider these examples. The replacement for Judas is not elected, but chosen by lot (Acts 1:26). The material needs of the community are provided by benefactors who are wealthy merchants and householders, not by egalitarian tax or tithe (Acts 2:45; compare Rom 16:1–5). Christians who run afoul of community mores are summarily dispatched without benefit of due process (Acts 5:1–11). On his own initiative Peter makes important policy changes regarding gentiles, and explains it later to his associates (Acts 10:1–11:18). The Jerusalem church holds an assembly that issues orders to the church in Antioch (Acts 15:28–29). None of this is democratic.

But do these details perhaps pertain only to a relatively late period, after the paleochurch had abandoned some primitive form of governance in which property was communally owned and democratically administered, and in which teaching activities were coordinated by consensus? That seems unlikely; the practices listed above match the prevailing customs of that time and place. For example, Essene documents indicate that common ownership of property was an indigenous cultural practice in Palestine. Yet it was not egalitarian; it entailed a two-tier social structure. Members who had permanently given over their property were an elite inner circle within a probationary group whose commitment was temporary.[28] We must conclude that the urban churches generally operated ad hoc, by whatever means seemed expedient. They organized their activities according to available indigenous and colonial cultural patterns. We cannot conclude that they were any more democratic or egalitarian than any other institution taking shape in the Greco-Roman cities of the eastern empire.[29]

In the fifth and final section of this chapter, we are going to consider the question of whether there is any enduring significance to the institutional contours emerging in the early urban churches; that is, whether the character of that institutionalization constitutes an imperative to be followed today. But our next step is to compare the paleochurch's stealth tactics to the tactics defining another resistive constituency in first-century Palestine.

ALTERNATIVE RESPONSES IN EARLY JUDAISM

Judaism as we know it today acquired several of its most pro-foundly self-defining practices through confrontation with the Romanization of Judea and Galilee. The historical term "Judaism" refers to the modification of Israelite religion socially and textually produced by the generations living from the late second-Temple period through the time of the editing of the Mishnah (roughly the middle of the first century B.C.E. to 200 C.E.). After the Romans tore down Jerusalem's Temple in 70, the *sacrificial* practices set forth in the Torah no longer could be followed. However, the *legal* and *instructional* practices of the indigenous population continued and adapted. After 70, these practices were significantly shaped by the intention to preserve technical information about conducting the cult, and to preserve the lineage of cultic personnel (priests and levites), until the Temple could be rebuilt. But that hope gradually faded. The institutions of the rabbinic study house and the synagogue became more salient in their own right, and the scope of their authority expanded. Early on they seem to have competed for leadership in the Land of Israel. By talmudic times (third and fourth centuries), however, they were architecturally joined. A single edifice symbolized the local Jewish community, its teaching and judicatory and charitable and social functions, its ritual observances, and its professional leadership.[30]

This urban centralization suited the Romans. Their style of colonial administration depended on effective liaison with a few good men, the heads of compliant indigenous ruling families. Long before Rome became an empire, Jews had been a multinational presence. Dispersed among the cities of the Mediterranean and the Levant, Jews (*Ioudaioi*, "Judeans") formed cohesive local communities, also called synagogues, whose functions were housed in distinctive structures when possible. It is plausible that the first synagogues to be built in the land of Israel itself, well before the destruction of the Temple, were built for the convenience of Diaspora Jews on holiday or traveling for business. Although formal prayer meetings may have occurred in them, that was not their primary use. After the Temple was razed, however, the religious practices and the architecture of Jews in Israel gradually conformed to those of Diaspora Jews.

With at least two significant exceptions: the Mishnah and the *miqveh* or ritual bathing tank, both of which originated in the land of Israel under Roman colonial pressures and were subsequently exported to the Diaspora. Let's consider them in turn. The Mishnah is the compiled teachings of the early rabbis: rulings in legal cases, stories illustrating correct religious observances, legends, botanical lore, biblical exegesis, and more. Before being reduced to writing and contained within a definitive text around 200 C.E., those teachings earlier had been produced and "contained" within an architectural innovation, the rabbinic study house. They did not circulate at large. The studyhouse was built to restrict access, keeping the teachings pure, enhancing their prestige, and associating them with an authoritative teacher. The *miqveh* is an architectural form designed to house the practice of ritual bathing, which although mandated anciently in Torah was accomplished outdoors or in ordinary bath facilities until precisely this era. A third tanklike architectural innovation may be identified in a distinctive new design for the synagogue hall. Seating was provided on steps rising along all four walls, so that participants sat in shadow looking inward and downward into a central area lit from above by a clerestory. There was no line of sight to the outdoors, and the flow of people in and out was regulated through two doorways.[31]

These "tanks" are resistive architectural gestures. They assert control and direction over their respective symbolic fluids. The study hall regulates teaching and memory, while the *halachah* (religious law) developing within it reconquers and regulates the times and spaces of everyday living in a colonized land: inch by inch, sabbath by sabbath. The clerestory synagogue hall regulates light for public reading and for observing the community assembled face to face; it also admits, encloses, and then releases the members of the community themselves. The *miqveh* regulates water by catching it from the heavens, without the intervention of Roman aqueducts; this special water therefore has the potency to remove various kinds of impediments to cultic purity.[32] The tanklike structure is analogous in form and function to those of two older indigenous architectures that had embodied the national identity of the people, before being severely compromised by Roman occupation: the village house, and the Temple.

The Romans destroyed lots of houses and ultimately tore down the Temple itself, but that is not the point. The house, with its finely carved threshold, selectively admitted and enclosed the people associated with a patriline. It regulated their identity and their daily activities. Colonial pressures distorted those indigenous work patterns, drawing labor away from the village and into the city, bringing massive social and cultural disruption. Thus the indigenous labor and kinship practices were distorted by Roman presence, often unwittingly. Rome violated Israelite thresholds. Moreover, the Land of Israel itself remained "holy" because its

God-given fertility was tithed and sacrificed. Grain and meat had to circulate in prescribed ways across the landscape and up to Jerusalem to the Temple. The colonial power tapped into those circulating commodities and diverted a great portion of them to imperial cities and other world markets. This produced real *economic* hardship; additionally, it produced *cultural* distress because it symbolically interfered with the indigenous material affirmation of Israel's covenant relationship with the deity.

In the same way, the seemingly benign Roman aqueducts wrested control of water away from the divine hand, secularizing and profaning one of the most profound and poetically powerful symbols of divine providence. (When the aqueduct ran, who cared if God sent or withheld the rains?) The *miqveh* tank and its associated practices constitute an alternative water system to that of the aqueducts. "Living" water—that is, water from rain or running streams that had not been lifted by human technology—was made available for purifying vessels and people. Passage through the *miqveh* tank after menstruation signaled the availability of a Jewish wife for lawful procreation.[33] This new architectural form figured into the complex process of certifying Jewish descent, which became equivalent to Jewish identity. Obviously, a patriline cannot be maintained as a closed system. It must open selectively to admit brides in each generation. The certification of brides, and therefore of continuity for the different castes of Israelites, became a matter of greater cultural concern in the Roman period than ever before. This may be owing in part to the desire to preserve the priestly caste for the day when the Temple might be rebuilt. But it also signals a new strategy for ensuring national identity at a time when the integrity of the Land and its people was gravely compromised.

These "tanks" resist Roman power symbolically, in the indigenous idiom of Israelite religion, and in ways that the Romans would neither care about nor understand. The *miqveh*, the study house, the clerestory synagogue hall, and their associated practices symbolically take over the colonially breached functions of the village domestic threshold and the Temple.[34] In the midst of imperial occupation, everyday life is now "housed" and "sanctified" by an emerging halachic code whose practices erect another kingdom right under Roman noses in Palestine. Was the resistance effective? While not directly hampering the colonial power, these practices did indeed provide for the integrity and survival of a people identifying themselves as Jews. They persist as elements of traditional Judaism today.

Jesus and his followers used the same idiom to offer symbolic resistance, but at a slightly earlier period and in contrasting ways. Jesus lived in Galilee during Herodian times, while the Temple economy was still intact, in an era of increasing Judean hegemony, but before the establishment of Judean-influenced teaching centers at Sepphoris and Tiberias.[35] Galilee had come under Hasmonean influence during the century before Jesus' birth. The Hasmonean dynasty was that of the Maccabees, whose rule was remembered as the last period of self-government in the Land of Israel (164 to 63 B.C.E.). The beginning of the end for the Hasmonean house was their betrothal of Mariamme to Herod the Great, the up-and-coming client king of the Romans, in 42 B.C.E.[36] Herod subsequently murdered not only Mariamme, but three young kinsmen of hers as well: Mariamme's brother Aristobulus (about 35 B.C.E.) and her two sons by Herod himself, Aristobulus and Alexander (in 6 B.C.E.). They were the last Hasmoneans and had been very popular with the people of Judea.

Neither Herod nor his son Herod Antipas, who took over in Galilee in 4 B.C.E. when Herod died, had the respect of the people of Judea or Galilee. The people's desire for a return to Hasmonean rule, and to the independence that it represented, was expressed in an astonishing way. Herod had wiped out the Hasmonean patriline, and in killing Mariamme he had also removed the possibility of any direct Hasmonean descendants at all. People responded to the murder of Mariamme by starting to name their daughters after her. The land began to be populated with new Miriams.[37] If "the virgin's name was Mary" (Lk 1:27) shortly after 29 B.C.E., when Herod murdered the last Hasmonean princess, that had to mean that the child's family wanted symbolically to counteract the effect of Herod's crime and to align themselves with the hope of independence.[38] Virgin wombs all across Israel were designated ready to bring forth babies to reestablish what the Hasmoneans had meant to the people. In effect, to name a girl child "Mary" is to assert that Herod's takeover and sellout to the Romans cannot succeed, because the women of the land intend to bring more "Hasmoneans" into the world than Herod can murder—*even without male Hasmoneans to father them into a proper patriline*. The name Mary is unambiguously political, brave, and resistive. Jesus was born into such a family.[39]

Nevertheless the Herodians still held power after Jesus grew to adulthood. Jesus' use of the landscape and material culture of Galilee responds in some ways to Antipas' manipulation of them. Antipas, like his father Herod the Great, was known for architectural achievements. The Italianization of Galilee with the palace and city of Tiberias was mentioned above. Jesus countered with an architectural innovation of sorts: he taught in the open air, on the slopes overlooking Lake Kinneret. The Lake was Herod's little Mediterranean Sea, busy with wharfs and commercial shipping, visible behind Jesus as he stood teaching people seated on the hillside. Jesus fed people with "free fish" from the Lake. But those particular practices could not be institutionalized and replicated on a large scale by his followers after Calvary, whom I have designated the paleochurch.

The generation after Jesus made the crucial decisions that made it possible for all subsequent generations to "see" Jesus as Lord and Savior after it became impossible literally to see and hear him against the backdrop of Herod's disneyworld, the Mediterraneanized Kinneret. Jesus' refusal of *urban* interior space made sense only in terms of what it was refusing: the Roman disruption of traditional Galilean village networks through establishment of urban centers. Jesus' distribution of "free fish and bread" made sense only as a refusal of the imperial economic disruptions of local-market commodities circulation, including imperial co-optation of the leading priests, hereditary recipients of food tithes. Jesus' trope of "fatherhood" and his rejection of family values made sense in the idiom of lineage strategy as waged by the Herodians and their collaborators, the ruling Jerusalem priestly families. Jesus' detour out of the Jordan corridor after accepting John's baptism was a disengagement from Herodian multinational business traffic in particular and from Roman water management in general, which, again, was the spatial and cultural context in which it made sense. These material aspects of empire—urban architecture, commodities acquisition, manipulation of kinship-based traditional leadership institutions, and control of the water—would later evoke the different but comparable symbolic resistive responses of early Judaism that we briefly mentioned above (that is, novel closures of the architectural space of the synagogue and *miqveh*; elaboration of legal rulings to preserve or reestablish the sacral character of foodstuffs, instructions, and lineages; distinctive dining and washing practices).

These spatial forms and practices, "Christian" and "Jewish" alike, are resistive but not resistive enough to destroy the empire outright. If you will, they contradict the inevitability of the logic of empire. They attack its perceived reasonableness, its aura of efficiency and inevitability. They deprive it of its hegemonic ability to appear to offer the superior rationale for organizing human activities. Moreover, they frame and define the alternative to empire *in terms of what the empire is not*. Therefore, ironically, the paleochurch relies upon having a sound and functioning empire, in order to maintain the resistive character of the

Jesus movement and to retain the focus of Jesus' teaching after Calvary and beyond Galilee. The kingdom of God is not free-standing. It has to be sought in the midst of something else. After Calvary, the physical sites of the Kingdom of God are the Greco-Roman urban spaces of Palestine and Syria. The means of propagation of the gospel within city space become constitutive of the message itself. "*You* are non-cooperation with agribusiness; *you* are non-compliance with the cloaking mechanisms of worldly power."[40] *You* are the real politics of free food in the hungry city.

SALT AND LEAVEN TODAY

The foregoing argument has been premised on a rather large "if" that must now be addressed. I have assumed that an accurate account of the message and practice of the earliest churches is required *if churches today are to conform themselves to their earliest ancestors in faith*. On that basis I have argued that resistance from within imperial structures, rather than liberation from them, was the mode of self-understanding embraced by the paleochurch. It remains now to consider briefly whether and to what extent present-day church practices can or should be modeled after those of the mid first century. The issue cannot be settled here, but we can lay out the possibilities.

The simplest answer is to assert that the actions and intentions of Jesus himself were replicated (perfectly, or nearly so) in the precanonical paleochurch and subsequently in the documentary record of the epistles and gospels and in ecclesiastical institutions. Historically this did not happen, of course, but the *intention* to do as Jesus did remains a theologically powerful motive. A more historically nuanced answer invests authority not in the historical Jesus, but in the version of his life and message that was captured at some stage subsequent to Calvary; for example, in the texts of the canonical gospels, or in early ecclesiastical institutions. They become the authoritative reference point and the criterion against which to measure and correct the activities of today's church. A third possible answer sidesteps historical questions altogether by reducing the tradition to whatever was believed and handed on by the generation immediately before our own. The opinions of our parents then simply stand for "the tradition."

My own proposal is that we take with utmost seriousness the findings of historical scholarship—including the finding that the paleochurch accommodated the words and practices of Jesus to the urban spaces of the empire. The paleochurch achieved solidarity and continuity with Jesus while adapting its activities to the evolving challenges of imperial colonization after Calvary. What continued was refusal of the totalitarian claims of the empire that empire was "the best way, the only way." This innovation was the adoption of what I have called stealth tactics. The way of salt and leaven is not *absolutely* authoritative; it is *relatively* authoritative insofar as churches today encounter circumstances like those in occupied Palestine.[41]

As it happens, we do indeed live in such circumstances. The challenge for us therefore is to devise means of material resistance to the hegemony of empire, by which I mean the economic structures of world capitalism supported by consumer ideology and substance abuse. There is no "liberation" from these. But resistance, in solidarity with the paleochurch, can take the form of small-scale refusals to comply with the alleged inevitability of the pomps and glamours of middle-class life. Among these I would name: automobiles and the commuting lifestyle; so-called life insurance and retirement funds; careerism; the "soccer mom" syndrome and the overscheduling of adolescent activities; fast food; fashionable clothing manufactured offshore under oppressive labor conditions; the subtle self-replicating practices of racism and classism; the relegation of the very young and the very old to caregiving institutions. Many other taken-for-granted practices could be identified as the means by which human life is colonized in our everyday concrete experience.[42]

What the paleochurch understood by Jesus' phrase "the Kingdom of God" was an elusive reality that had to be sought in the midst of imperial distortions of human life. That reality cannot be fully defined on paper, either in the gospels or here in this chapter. My argument has been that the Kingdom of God is sought resistively, and therefore is redefined accordingly as historical circumstances change. The people of the paleochurch found it by working stealthily, on a small scale, and in the symbolic idiom of their own world. Now it's our turn.

NOTES

1. Galilee began to be Romanized in the reign of Herod the Great, beginning in 37 B.C.E. Herod died in 4 B.C.E., about the time Jesus was born. His son Herod Antipas then ruled the Galilee while Jesus grew up and worked there. I use the term "paleochurch" to designate the communities cohering in Jesus' name after Calvary around a shared intention, a continuity of vision and mis-

sion with Jesus. The paleochurch is precanonical because it predates the Gospels and the Epistles, and it is the source of the oral and written traditions that their authors used.

2. See Martin Heidegger's 1935 essay "The Origin of the Work of Art," translated in Heidegger 1971.

3. See Habermas 1962, 1981; Benhabib 1992; and Elisabeth Schüssler Fiorenza 1992b, part 2: "The Hermeneutical Space of a Feminist Rhetoric of Liberation." On the related notion of standpoint, see Hartsock 1983 and Hennessy 1993.

4. An alternative image of resistive communication is the "integrated circuit," suggested by Haraway 1991. The circuit works when "closed." It connects distant individual components, whom Haraway designates "cyborgs," and lets them work together effectively. Cyborg spatiality is counterimperial.

5. Thus the exorcisms of Jesus are not "liberations," technically speaking. The demon is evicted from the body of the victim, but the victim does not go anywhere.

6. Not the whole Torah. See Acts 15:1–21, where a compromise is reached concerning "a yoke that neither our ancestors nor we have been able to bear."

7. There is much of value in the literature of "liberation theology" from the last three decades. For recent introductions to the breadth of its accomplishments, see Musto 1991 and Finson 1991. Liberation theology, as a fully domesticated academic methodology, now is mainstreamed in the publications of the American theological establishment. For example, the Workgroup in Constructive Theology prescribes a regime of "envisioning emanicpatory praxis" as the third step in each of the chapters of its theology primer (Chopp and Taylor 1994). Here the rhetoric of liberation conceals the dynamics of privileged inclusion and censored exclusion by which the textbook was actually produced—I speak as a former Workgroup member whose contributions were suppressed. More successful dissents from the imposition of liberation rhetoric have been made by Myers 1988, by Gottwald 1989, and by several of the contributors to Gottwald and Horsley 1993 and the editors themselves.

8. On the contrary, empathy becomes impossible if the other is displaced and replaced by oneself. Empathy is not primarily an emotion, but a competence to follow the conscious processes of other persons. For a technical study of it, see Sawicki 1997.

9. This is the position of conservative mainstream and fundamentalist Christianity.

10. This assumption, either expressed or implied, is the foundation of liberation theology in general and of the widely accepted theology of "critical feminist biblical interpretation for liberation" propounded by Elisabeth Schüssler Fiorenza. Surprisingly, its premises are shared by the American Roman Catholic theological establishment, which regards the historical facts of Jesus' life as largely unknowable and, when knowable, largely irrelevant to faith. Thus Francis Schüssler Fiorenza (1994: 294–95) rightly complains that Christian symbols have undergone "dislocation from the historical concreteness of the life and

praxis of Jesus." He proposes that "the historical particularity of Jesus" should be a "check" and "a critical corrective" for the creative, interpretive proliferation of symbolic theology, as well as its basis. But clearly, Fiorenza's formulation leaves too much unsaid. It is valid only insofar as this "historical particularity of Jesus" includes elements corroborated by the general contours of Jesus' material culture and economic circumstances, *not simply those attested by the gospel portraits.* In other words, some extratextual leverage is required for any effective "check and critical corrective" upon the christifying symbolizations that are already occurring in the texts themselves. It is the gospels' textual "particularization" of Jesus, lifting him away from general historical conditions of first-century Galilee, that initiates the creative symbolization that requires the "checking." So one must go beyond Francis Fiorenza's formulation to ask, "*which* particularizations of Jesus?"; the various competing particularizations of Jesus are precisely what we need a critical corrective *for.*

11. This is the contention in public communications from the Jesus Seminar, but is not shared by all of the individual seminar fellows. It also expresses the stance of many biblical scholars in the academy.

12. I take this to be the historical consensus of Roman Catholicism, and I argue in favor of it in Sawicki 1988 and 1994.

13. Admittedly, the theory helps to shape the data. But theory does not *entirely* determine data, as proponents of "option 2" mistakenly assume. It is altogether possible to know the past. Faith obliges Christians to learn whatever can be known about the beliefs and practices of the paleochurch.

14. Historical studies in general and historical-Jesus scholarship in particular undeniably *have been* positivistic and patriarchal at times. My point is that historical study can be conducted nonpositivisticly and nonpatriarchally, and that the information produced by such study is indispensable for responsible theology.

15. The ironic but wrongheaded substitution of transhistorical laws for historically derived facts is pursued in the recent and much-copied work of Elisabeth Schüssler Fiorenza 1992b: 79–96 (on the "conflictive model of historical reconstruction") and 1995: 88–96 (on "The Jesus Movement as a Jewish Emancipatory Movement of Wo/men" and the "historical model of struggle"). Earlier, Schüssler Fiorenza had followed more conventional critical historical practices, and the enduring contribution of her scholarship is owing to that. Luise Schottroff adopts the same unfounded axioms in her work: that the gospel is "liberating," that women are universally oppressed, and that early Christian women were primarily struggling against that oppression.

16. One difficulty with this assumption, obviously, is that the practices that constitute "oppression," "resistance," and "womanhood" are culture-specific. Without close attention to indigenous descriptions of the situation, facilitated by empathy, we cannot determine whether a given practice is part of "oppression" or part of "resistance." A case in point is the postmenstrual use of the *miqveh* (ritual bath), discussed below.

17. I do not deny that Christian theologians *subsequently* have been able to accomplish a creative synthesis in which exodus themes, leavening, sowing,

and salting mutually enhance one another. But it seems clear that the notion of stealthy growth originated in a distinctive practice that is obscured if we insist on grasping it in terms of an exodus spatiality.

18. Thus our inquiry draws on the accomplishments of contemporary historical-Jesus scholarship. See Kloppenborg 1996a and 1992 for the state of the question and a plea for the judicious use of Q texts in historical reconstructions of Jesus. My discussion of the parables of the mustard seed, the leaven, and salt is indebted to Cotter 1992 and Kea 1990, but the inferences about industrial use of salt are my own. A reconstructed text of the Sayings Gospel Q is available in Kloppenborg et al. 1990; for parallels see Crossan 1986. By convention, verses in Q are numbered as they are in Luke.

19. See Cotter 1992, 45.

20. Ibid., pp. 45, 47.

21. See Cotter 1992:47. Schottroff 1995:79–80 argues unpersuasively that "the 'hiding' involved here is a normal step in preparing leavened bread." *Ekrypsen* (Lk 13:21) and *enekrypsen* (Mt 13:33) say more than what the bread-making process requires. In order to work, yeast needs to be shielded from chilly drafts and from sunlight; it does not need to be "hidden."

22. A Christian rhetorical practice of self-identification in terms of the potencies of salt may have been current during the time of Rabbi Joshua ben Hananiah, an influential proponent of theological and political moderation who flourished around 70 to 130 C.E. The saying about unsavory salt is woven into a clever polemic that pits Joshua against Athenian philosophers in Tractate Berakot 8b of the Babylonian Talmud. One infers that the saying was being cited by Christians against traditional teachers of Torah, criticizing them as "salt without savor." According to that inference, the competitors of the rabbis would be volunteering to be the new salt that resalts the old salt. Rabbi Joshua's response is, in effect, that it is impossible for the salt of Torah ever to become tainted. The talmudic text in which this story appears did not reach its final form before the sixth century, but numerous traditions portray Joshua as an able opponent of heretics or "ex's" (*minim*), as the rabbis called them.

23. Or directly to tourists and local householders, as presumed in Mk 6:36–38 and parallels.

24. See Schwartz 1995 and 1991, 67–79. The name "Lydda" comes into English via Josephus's Greek version of the Hebrew name "Lod" or "Lud" that appears in the rabbinic texts. In ancient times it was very fertile agricultural land. In the Second Temple period, the agricultural estates of Lod were held by the Hasmoneans. Today Lod is the site of Israel's international airport.

25. See Schwartz 1995, 402.

26. See Schwartz 1995, 409. Compare Mk 14:44–49 and parallels, where Jesus protests to the arresting officers that he has taught openly and lawfully at the Temple.

27. Perhaps *today's* church should be organized as a discipleship of equals; but not because that was the form of polity in the earliest churches. Although I concur with Bianchi and Ruether 1992, with Schottroff 1995, and with Elisa-

beth Schüssler Fiorenza in their present-day social agenda, I cannot follow their attempt to project this vision for the future back onto the first century.

28. See Capper 1995.

29. Kloppenborg 1996b carefully examines the practices of voluntary associations in the Greco-Roman world. He highlights the myth-making dimensions of the rhetoric of egalitarianism in the Pauline churches. Comparative study of indigenous practices, and of paleochurch variations on these practices, makes it very difficult to accept that the paleochurch was a "discipleship of equals," as asserted by Schüssler Fiorenza 1989, 1992a, and 1994.

30. Historians debate the sequence and the mechanisms of this development, and the extent to which it was a reaction to conditions precipitated in the fourth century by the Roman recognition and co-optation of the church under Constantine. Those questions need not detain us here; we are merely clarifying terms and sketching the historical horizon of first-century occurrences.

31. For a detailed description and discussion, see my forthcoming essay "Caste and Contact in the Galilee of Jesus." There I argue that these tanklike structures are variations on the theme of selective letting-in and letting-go expressed in the threshold structure of ordinary houses and in the circulation patterns embodied in the architectural plan of the Jerusalem Temple.

32. Obviously, the "potency" under discussion here is a cultural perception. By modern chemical standards, aqueduct water probably was cleaner than rainwater caught in stone storage tanks.

33. Of course there were numerous other uses for the *miqveh* in domestic and industrial contexts, but the purification of menstruants seems to be the most emotionally salient of them.

34. This conclusion is drawn in hindsight and on anthropological grounds; it is not meant to express any first-century religious understanding.

35. On the prevailing political climate and the transition from Hasmonean to Herodian administration in the Galilee, see Horsley 1995 and 1996. On the cities and architecture of the Galilee and Judea, see Rousseau and Arav 1995.

36. She was about sixteen when betrothed. Herod married Mariamme in 37 B.C.E., having repudiated his first wife, Doris. Herod had Mariamme killed in 29 B.C.E. The forms *Mariamme* and *Mariamne* come from the written Greek inflectable forms of the Hebrew name *Miriam*, which was Moses' sister's name in the Torah. The English form is *Mary*. After Mariamme's death, Herod married another woman by the same name; or, one who took the name. Because Herod's second Mariamme was not of any distinguished lineage, Herod created one for her by installing her father as high priest.

37. Margaret Williams, who studied the frequency of names in Roman Palestine, points this out. See Williams 1995.

38. The name becomes suddenly quite common in first-century inscriptions and texts from the land of Israel. Williams reports that it became popular with the Herodian dynasty itself. This may indicate that there was something of a contest over the name. Herodian daughters were labeled "Mary's" to further the Herodian claim to legitimacy.

39. Surely this is the real political background to the stories of Herod's jealous murder of infants, and of Jesus' trial before Antipas. I have suggested elsewhere that Jesus' mother's family were based in Sepphoris and had ties to Jerusalem (Sawicki 1994: 113–15), and I discuss the connection between Jesus and the Herodian party in my forthcoming essay "Magdalenes and Tiberiennes: City Women and the Entourage of Jesus."

40. Paraphrasing Mt 5:13, 14.

41. In Palestine as Jesus knew it, the central religious authorities in Jerusalem operated in an uneasy alliance with the forces of imperial occupation. Jesus and the paleochurch resisted those religious authorities together with the secular ones. Religious authority is never unproblematic for followers of Jesus.

42. This task of identification and discernment is best done in local communities, but I have attempted something of the sort in my forthcoming essay "Going to Church" and in Sawicki 1991 and 1995.

REFERENCES

Benhabib, Seyla. 1992. *Situating the Self: Gender, Community, and Postmodernism in Contemporary Ethics*. New York: Routledge.

Bianchi, Eugene C., and Rosemary Radford Ruether. 1992. *A Democratic Catholic Church: The Reconstruction of Roman Catholicism*. New York: Crossroad.

Capper, Brian. 1995. "The Palestinian Cultural Context of Earliest Christian Community of Goods." *The Book of Acts in Its Palestinian Setting*, 323–356. The Book of Acts in Its First Century Setting, Vol. 4. Edited by Richard Bauckham. Grand Rapids, Mich.: Eerdmans.

Chopp, Rebecca S., and Mark Lewis Taylor, eds. 1994. *Reconstructing Christian Theology*. Minneapolis, Minn.: Fortress.

Cotter, Wendy J. 1992. "The Parables of the Mustard Seed and the Leaven: Their Function in the Earliest Stratum of Q." *Toronto Journal of Theology* 8: 38–51.

Crossan, John Dominic, designer and ed. 1986. *Sayings Parallels: A Workbook for the Jesus Tradition*. Philadelphia: Fortress.

Fiorenza, Francis Schüssler. 1994. "Christian Redemption between Colonialism and Pluralism." *Reconstructing Christian Theology*, 269–302. Edited by Rebecca S. Chopp and Mark Lewis Taylor. Minneapolis, Minn.: Fortress Press.

Finson, Shelley Davis. 1991. *Women and Religion: A Bibliographic Guide to Christian Feminist Liberation Theology*. Toronto: University of Toronto Press.

Gottwald, Norman K. 1989. "The Exodus as Event and Process: A Test Case in the Biblical Grounding of Liberation Theology." *The Future of Liberation Theology: Essays in Honor of Gustavo Gutiérrez*, 250–260. Edited by Marc H. Ellis and Otto Maduro. Maryknoll, N.Y.: Orbis Books.

Gottwald, Norman K, and Richard A. Horsley. 1993. "Introduction: The Bible and Liberation: Deeper Roots and Wider Horizons." *The Bible and Liberation: Political and Social Hermeneutics*, xiii–xxi. Revised edition. Edited by Norman K. Gottwald and Richard A. Horsley. Maryknoll, N.Y.: Orbis Books.

Habermas, Jürgen. 1962. *Strukturwandel der Öffentlichkeit: Untersuchungen zu einer Kategorie der burgerlichen Gesellschaft.* Neuweid: Luchterhand. Translated by Thomas Burger as *The Structural Transformation of the Public Sphere: An Inquiry into a Category of Bourgeois Society.* Cambridge, Mass.: MIT Press, 1989.

———. 1981. *Theorie des kommunikativen Handelns.* Two volumes. Frankfurt am Main: Suhrkamp. Translated by Thoman McCarthy as *The Theory of Communicative Action.* Boston: Beacon Press, 1984–c1987

Haraway, Donna J. 1991. "A Cyborg Manifesto: Science, Technology, and Socialist-Feminism in the Late Twentieth Century," *Simians, Cyborgs, and Women: The Reinvention of Nature*, 148–81 and 243–48. New York: Routledge.

Hartsock, Nancy. 1983. "The Feminist Standpoint: Developing the Ground for a Specifically Feminist Historical Materialism," *Discovering Reality: Feminist Perspectives on Epistemology, Metaphysics, and Philosophy of Science, 238–310.* Edited by Sandra Harding and Merrill B. Hintikka. Dordrecht: Reidel.

Heidegger, Martin. 1971. *Poetry, Language. Thought.* Translated by Albert Hofstadter. New York: Harper Colophon.

Hennessy, Rosemary. 1993. *Materialist Feminism and the Politics of Discourse.* New York: Routledge.

Horsley, Richard A. 1995. *Galilee: History, Politics, People.* Valley Forge, Pa.: Trinity Press International.

———. 1996. *Archaeology, History, and Society in Galilee: The Social Context of Jesus and the Rabbis.* Valley Forge, Pa.: Trinity Press International.

Kea, Perry V. 1990. "Salting the Salt: Q 14:34–35 and Mk 9:49–50." *Foundations & Facets Forum* 6: 239–44.

Kloppenborg, John S. 1992. "Literary Convention, Self-Evidence, and the Social History of the Q People." *Early Christianity, Q and Jesus.* Semeia 55. Edited by John S. Kloppenborg and Leif E. Vaage. Atlanta, Ga.: Scholars Press.

———. 1996a. "The Sayings Gospel Q and the Quest of the Historical Jesus." *Harvard Theological Review* 89: 307–44.

———. 1996b. "Egalitarianism in the Myth and Rhetoric of Pauline Churches." *Reimagining Christian Origins: A Colloquium Honoring Burton L. Mack*, 247–63. Edited by Elizabeth A. Castelli and Hal Taussig. Valley Forge, Pa.: Trinity Press International.

Kloppenborg. John S., Marvin W. Meyer, Stephen J. Patterson, and Michael G. Steinhauser. 1990. *Q Thomas Reader.* Sonoma, Calif.: Polebridge Press.

Musto, Ronald G. 1991. *Liberation Theologies: A Research Guide.* New York: Garland Publishing Company.

Myers, Ched. 1988. *Binding the Strong Man: A Political Reading of Mark's Story of Jesus.* Maryknoll, N.Y.: Orbis Books.

Rousseau, John J., and Rami Arav. 1995. *Jesus and His World: An Archaeological and Cultural Dictionary.* Minneapolis, Minn.: Fortress Press.

Sawicki, Marianne. 1988. *The Gospel in History: Portrait of a Teaching Church.* New York: Paulist Press.

————. 1991. "Teaching as a Gift of Peace." *Theology Today* 47: 377–87.

————. 1994. *Seeing the Lord: Resurrection and Early Christian Practices.* Minneapolis, Minn.: Fortress Press.

————. 1995. "How Can Christian Worship Be Contemporary?" *What Is "Contemporary" Worship?*, 22–30. Edited by Gordon Lathrop. Minneapolis, Minn.: Augsburg Fortress Press.

————. 1997. *Body, Text, and Science: The Literacy of Investigative Practices and the Phenomenology of Edith Stein.* Phaenomenologica 114. Dordrecht: Kluwer Academic Publishers.

————. Forthcoming. "Caste and Contact in the Galilee of Jesus: Research beyond Positivism and Constructionism." *Galilean Archaeology and the Historical Jesus: The Integration of Material and Textual Remains.* Edited by J. Andrew Overman and Richard Horsley. Valley Forge, Pa.: Trinity Press International.

————. "Magdalenes and Tiberiennes: City Women and the Entourage of Jesus." *Transformative Encounters: Jesus and Women Re-Viewed.* Edited by Ingrid Rosa Kitzberger. Leiden: Brill.

————. "Going to Church: A Social Geography of Parish." *The Material Conditions of the Local Church.* Edited by Michael Warren.

Schottroff, Luise. 1995. *Lydia's Impatient Sisters: A Feminist Social History of Early Christianity.* Translated by Barbara and Martin Rumscheidt. Louisville, Ky.: Westminster John Knox Press.

Schüssler Fiorenza, Elisabeth. 1989. "The Politics of Otherness: Biblical Interpretation as a Critical Praxis for Liberation." *The Future of Liberation Theology: Essays in Honor of Gustavo Gutiérrez*, 311–25. Edited by Marc H. Ellis and Otto Maduro. Maryknoll, N.Y.: Orbis Books.

————. 1992a. "A Discipleship of Equals: Ekklesial Democracy and Patriarchy in Biblical Perspective." *A Democratic Catholic Church: The Reconstruction of Roman Catholicism*, 17–33. Edited by Eugene C. Bianchi and Rosemary Radford Ruether. New York: Crossroad.

————. 1992b. *But She Said: Feminist Practices of Biblical Interpretation.* Boston: Beacon Press.

————. 1994. "The Bible, the Global Context, and the Discipleship of Equals." *Reconstructing Christian Theology*, 79–98. Edited by Rebecca S. Chopp and Mark Lewis Taylor. Minneapolis, Minn.: Fortress Press.

————. 1995. *Jesus Miriam's Child, Sophia's Prophet: Critical Issues in Feminist Christology.* New York: Continuum.

Schwartz, Joshua J. 1991. *Lod (Lydda), Israel: From Its Origins through the Byzantine Period 5600 B.C.E.–640 C.E.* BAR International Series 571. Oxford: Tempus Reparatum, British Archaeological Reports.

——. 1995. "Peter and Ben Stada in Lydda." *The Book of Acts in Its Palestinian Setting*, 391–414. The Book of Acts in Its First Century Setting, Vol. 4. Edited by Richard Bauckham. Grand Rapids, Mich.: Eerdmans.

Williams, Margaret H. 1995. "Palestinian Jewish Personal Names in Acts." *The Book of Acts in Its Palestinian Setting*, 79–113. The Book of Acts in Its First Century Setting, Vol. 4. Edited by Richard Bauckham. Grand Rapids, Mich.: Eerdmans.

4

The Nonviolent Terrorist:
In Defense of Christian Fanaticism

Stanley Hauerwas

ON BEING A FANATIC

I begin with an apology. I cannot meet the expectations of those who organized the conference. I cannot because I represent a different politics than the politics that created the "between" found in the title of the conference, that is, "Christian Ethics between Radicalism and Fanaticism." I want Christians to be radicals. I want Christians to be fanatics.[1] Indeed I suspect that is why I was invited. You wanted an example of a fanatical radical. I will try not to disappoint you.

I must apologize, however, if I have misunderstood my role in this colloquium. In the letter inviting me to address the conference the purpose of the colloquium is said to be an attempt "to analyze the necessity and the dangers of the radicalism of (Christian) ethics." I assume I am to represent "the necessity" of Christian radicalism. Yet I was asked in particular "to deal as an ethicist with the question of the tension between the radicality of the gospel in sociopolitical, peace, and ecological matters and the risk of becoming a fanatic. How can you live out the radicality of the Christian message without becoming intolerant?" I do not want to keep you in suspense. Being a fanatic is not a risk but a requirement and there is nothing wrong with intolerance if you are the kind of Christian radical I believe we are called to be.

I realize, however, that such a summary answer will not satisfy most who are worried about Christians acting responsibly in the world as we

---

The present paper was written for a conference at the Catholic University of Louvain.

know it. Fanatics and radicals are seldom thought to be responsible. In other words I realize I bear the burden of proof. In order to try to make an unapologetic case for Christian radicalism I am going to provide a defense of what to many is the clearest case of fanaticism—terrorism. I realize this will seem a bizarre strategy for a pacifist, but I hope to show why nonviolence cannot help but appear as a terrorist tactic by those who want to make the world safe for war.

In the light of what many take to be the moral anarchy of our culture, it is comforting to think that there is a strong moral consensus about some things—for example, child pornography and terrorism. Therefore my attempt to provide a justification of terrorism, at least, a kind of theological terrorism, cannot help but seem unsettling. Yet I want to try to show that insofar as most continue to believe that war is a necessary instrument for the maintenance of the goods of the human community, then terrorism cannot be automatically subject to moral condemnation.

I want to be candid, however, about where my argument is meant to lead. I want you to be, like me, a pacifist. As a pacifist I obviously think that war and terrorism are not compatible with Christian discipleship.[2] Yet many Christians think that, though war is terrible, under certain conditions it may not only be justified but a duty. Those that would so justify war for Christians usually assume that terrorism is beyond justification. I will try to show that the attempt to save war as a moral project by distinguishing war from terrorism will not work. In short, if you think terrorism is prohibited, then so is war. Christian nonviolence, therefore, cannot help but appear as fanatical just to the extent it challenges the assumed "normality" of war and violence.

The discussion of the ethics of terrorism, however, is meant to provide a context for what I take to be the central question that gave rise to the subject of this conference—namely, how can the radical character of the gospel be reclaimed without making Christians irrelevant or, worse, intolerant. Radical Christocentric ethics, such as I represent, at least to some seems to threaten the ability of Christians to act constructively in a world already far too divided. In such a divided world what is needed, it is argued, is a universal ethic capable of resolving conflict. In contrast, I will try to show that if Christians are to help such a world live more peacefully, we can only be what we are—those who worship Jesus Christ, the Son of God. For that is the basis of our "radicalism" as Christians—that is, we are not radicals because we assume a radical stance on this or that issue that the world understands as radical, but because any stance we assume must be witness to the God of Jesus Christ.

THE "ETHICS" OF TERRORISM

"One community's terrorist is another community's martyr" is the kind of generalization that is as true as it is false. Yet it is not a bad place to begin thinking about terrorism just to the extent such a statement reminds us that any description of terrorism implicates a set of moral practices and presumptions. James Burtchaell rightly argues that it is

> misleading to address the ethics of terrorism and response to terrorism by accepting without question the fashionable presumption that terrorism is a development so discontinuous with the traditions of warfare that it deserves unconventional moral scrutiny. On the contrary, terrorism, like the many enlargements of violence before it, is a lineal descendent of traditional warfare. It can best be understood and evaluated by analogy with conventional conflict. And I am increasingly of the opinion that it raises not old questions about new kinds of combat but new questions about old forms of war. It is warfare's newest and most sobering progeny.[3]

It is interesting to reflect on the Israeli/PLO conflict in the light of Burtchaell's claim that it is by no means easy to distinguish war from terrorism. The government of Israel found it useful to call the PLO a "terrorist organization" because they sometimes killed school children on buses. Yet the state of Israel was brought into power by an extended and very well organized terrorist campaign. It is easy to forget that those who later became politicians in Israel at one time in their lives blew up the Prince David Hotel. To this day Israel assumes it has the right to bomb Palestinian refugee camps in retaliation for "terrorist attacks," but such bombing is not considered terrorism even though the camps house women and children. Is the bombing perpetrated by an established government by definition not terror?[4] Now that the PLO is a government with land does that mean former acts of "terrorism" are now war?

It has been assumed that a strong distinction can be made between terrorism and war to the extent the former fails to observe the civilized rules of war, and in particular, engages in attacks on civilians. Yet from the "terrorist" point of view distinctions between combatants and noncombatants are not easily maintained. For example, some years ago there was a general outrage against those who raided a white man's Rhodesian farm and slaughtered his wife and children. Yet from the perspective of those who had conducted the raid, those killed—women and children alike—had been "washed, dressed, schooled, and conveyed abroad and entertained and cultivated by dint of the occupation of *their* land and low-paid labor of *their* backs and the deprivation and humiliation of *their* children. It had been the white children's father's rifle that violated them and their homeland, but it was his family that lived good naturally on his violence. How could he be guilty and they be innocent?"[5]

Such examples are but reminders that often those who are called terrorist use violence because they have been denied any other alternative by the "recognized government." Of course this goes to the heart of the attempt to distinguish between terrorism and war, since any such distinction gains its moral warrant from the assumption based in just war theory that there is a continuity between the police function of the state and its war-making potential. The justification of war is but an extension of the right of the state to punish. The latter is possible because it is the disciplined use of violence for the good in common including the good of the one punished. Which is but a reminder, as Paul Ramsey emphasized, just war is not so much a casuistry to determine if a war meets prior determined criteria, but rather an account of state action required for the protection of the innocent.[6] So war is but a continuation of the justice internal to the state transposed to relations between states.

There are, however, some strong reasons to doubt that war is but a continuation of the police function of the state. The latter includes not only a prior agreement on what a crime may be, but also requires the criminal be caught, a decision be made of degree of guilt, the appropriate punishment, as well as the carrying out of the punishment. It is instructive to note that the police do not carry out any of the last functions whereas in war all the functions are carried out by the same agent. In short, war lacks exactly the prior institutions and practices that limit the violence intrinsic to the police function of the state and, at least to some extent, make such violence less arbitrary. Yet as we noted above, it is just the assumption of such continuity that has underwritten the distinction between war and terrorism.

Of course it may be objected that this way of thinking about terrorism leaves out the most important aspect of just war reflection—that is, the principle of noncombatant immunity. Those called terrorist, however, do not necessarily attack noncombatants, but if they do they are not without some moral response. Such an attack may be an attempt to make clear the kind of war they understand they are forced to wage—namely, a war of the desperate that must use selective targeting in nonselective ways.

In this respect it is particularly important to remember that even attacks on civilians by alleged terrorists are not indiscriminate. Who gets blown up by a bomb on a bus may be indiscriminate, but that the bomb was planted on a bus is not indiscriminate. Rather, such bombing may be tied to policy objectives that may even make such a bombing analogous to the defense of civilian deaths on just war grounds of indirect effect; for alleged terrorist strategies are meant—like war itself—to make people prefer peace, or at least order, rather than continue the conflict. Therefore the "random violence" of the terrorist is anything other than random just to the extent it is used in the interest of making the adversary sue for peace. Indeed, the terror of terrorism is often designed to brutalize those who must fight the terrorist so that the very means to fight the terrorist becomes self-defeating.

Accordingly, James Burtchaell argues that terrorism will increasingly be seen not as an anomaly but as one of the degenerate progeny of conventional war. He calls attention to three distinct reactions to weapons development, such as the machine gun, elicited in this century. Some thought such weapons so horrendous they were inherently immoral. Others thought them so terrible they would make war less likely. Still others thought such weapons only made clear how horrible war has always been. Burtchaell concludes that terrorism justifies all three conclusions as it is indeed savage and inhumane. Yet so is war. So "inquiry into the nature and ethical imperatives of terrorism is sound only if we do not imagine that it is inhumane by contrast with war, which is humane. Conventional warfare is conventionally inhumane."[7]

Yet this is a conclusion from which most of us would recoil. But if the above discussion of terrorism has taught us anything we must ask who is the "us" doing the recoiling. Max Stackhouse represents what I take to be the most persuasive answer to that question—the "us" must be the universal voice of humanity. Stackhouse argues that we are at a loss to respond to terrorism because some no longer believe in a universal ethic. According to Stackhouse,

> Ethically, we are in an age in which there is grave doubt among theologians, philosophers, jurists, and social scientists as to whether any universal principles exist which can be reliably known and used by the international community to define torture or terrorism as wrong. To be sure, many say that terrorism and torture are terrible. But when the question is posed as to whether there are any universal absolutes, or whether there are

intrinsically evil acts, or whether there are cross-cultural values which could be the basis for declaring such practices to be inherently wrong we find only doubt and skepticism.[8]

According to Stackhouse, without such a universal ethic we have no means to challenge the assumed right of nation-states to make decisions on the basis of self-interest.

Stackhouse's concern to counter the "relativism" he thinks to be the cause of our inability to condemn terrorism could be meant as a critique of me.[9] Since I am alleged to hold the view that no universal ethic exists, I represent a form of confessional theology that has no basis for saying why terrorism is wrong.[10] As Stackhouse puts the issue:

> If we believe terrorism and torture are in fact fundamentally contrary to the truth and justice of God and ought to be stopped everywhere, we must recognize that the theological foundations on which many contemporary contextualist and confessionalist theologies rest are inadequate to this task, whatever their contributions to other areas. Sadly, they do not have the cross-cultural, intellectual or moral amplitude to address these issues.[11]

Without such a cross-cultural vision, Stackhouse argues we will be plunged into a Hobbesian world where all contend against all, a world in which only might makes right. Stackhouse thinks, however, that we do not live in a world devoid of universal principles. Such principles are those found in democratically authorized constitutions, which Stackhouse believes to be the harbingers of the "enormous transformation" the world is currently undergoing toward the creation of a "universal civilization."[12] Stackhouse argues that those who do not recognize the universality of such democratically authorized constitutions should be regarded as not yet fully rational or, worse, morally perverse. A surprisingly intolerant conclusion for someone so committed to tolerance.[13] Yet it is a conclusion that helps make intelligible my willingness to describe myself as a terrorist—from a perspective such as that of Stackhouse, people like me threaten the project to free the world of war because of our unwillingness to assume a universal stance.

EPISTEMOLOGICAL CRISES AND WAR

So how are we to go on? If we are to be "responsible" must we be able to provide, as Stackhouse argues, an ethic of universal principles so that we can distinguish between war and terrorism? Or are we condemned, as I am alleged to be, to represent a "local" or "restricted" morality, even one called Christian, which cannot provide a basis for rational agreements so we might avoid war? I certainly do not think such an alternative to be our only choice, but to show why I will need to explore Alasdair MacIntyre's account of what he calls epistemological crises. In doing so I shall have to ask your patience as it may not be immediately clear how issues of war and terrorism (much less why I characterize my own position as one of Christian fanaticism) are clarified by what at first appears to be a way of understanding scientific disputes. Yet by the time I am finished I hope to have shown you why MacIntyre's account is crucial for helping us recognize that nothing could be more rational than the peace it is our privilege and obligation to witness as Christians and why such a peace, from the world's perspective, may be thought to be a form of terrorism.

MacIntyre's account of epistemological crises is a correlative of his traditioned account of rationality. According to MacIntyre, it was the central aspiration of the Enlightenment to provide standards and rational justification that any rational person, that is a person independent of all social and cultural particularities, would or should accept without recourse to appeals to authority.[14] This ideal has been impossible to maintain because it has proved impossible to secure agreement on precisely those principles that were to be undeniable by all rational persons. Yet what is particularly troubling is any attempt to provide an alternative account of rationality to that of the Enlightenment continues to be judged deficient by the failed standards of that same Enlightenment standard.

Yet MacIntyre argues that an alternative account of rational inquiry is possible as that "embodied in a tradition, a conception according to which the standards of rational justification themselves emerge from and are part of a history in which they are vindicated by the way in which they transcend the limitations of and provide remedies for the defects of their predecessors within the history of that same tradition."[15] Such a view of rationality is historical, since any attempt to justify is to narrate how the argument has gone so far; accordingly, any subject needing justification is itself a concept with a history; which means that there can be no denial of the diversity of traditions of enquiry.

For those schooled on Enlightenment presuppositions this last point is particularly troubling. From such a perspective it is assumed that MacIntyre cannot avoid relativism and, in spite of his denials, may even advocate relativism.[16] Moreover this view, it is alleged, has disastrous political results because if there is no alternative to relativism then we are condemned to live in a world of war. Absent any way of securing agreements between people who otherwise share nothing in common other than their rationality, it seems the only recourse for resolving disputes is war.

Yet MacIntyre argues that traditions may be able to resolve conflicts not only within the tradition itself but between traditions. In this respect, it is important to attend to the anti-Cartesian and anti-Hegelian aspects of MacIntyre's account of traditions. For MacIntyre, unlike Cartesians, assumes that traditions begin not from unassailable self-evident truths, but rather are contingent. Moreover, in contrast to Hegelian presumptions that each tradition must share with all other traditions some final rational state, for MacIntyre "traditions are always and ineradically to some degree local, informed by particularities of language and social and natural environment, inhabited by Greeks or by citizens of Roman Africa or medieval Persia or by eighteenth-century Scots, who stubbornly refuse to be or become vehicles of the self-realization of *Geist*. Those educated or indoctrinated into accepting Cartesian or Hegelian standards will take the positivity of tradition to be a sign of arbitrariness. For each tradition will, so it may seem, pursue its own specific historical path, and all that we shall be confronted with in the end is a set of independent rival histories."[17]

Yet this suggestion is belied by "one particular kind of occurrence in the history of traditions," which MacIntyre calls "epistemological crises."[18] Such crises can occur in the history of particular persons, groups, and for a whole tradition. Indeed, such a crisis in a tradition may well find itself manifest in our inability to tell the stories of our lives with narrative coherence. To share a culture means we share schemata that are at once constitutive of and normative for intelligible actions— that is, it means we can "get" a joke. Yet it may happen that an individual may come to recognize the possibility of different possibilities of interpretation which present an alternative rival schemata of what is going on around him or her. MacIntyre suggests that Shakespeare's *Hamlet* exemplifies in the person of Hamlet as well as the question of how to interpret the play, *Hamlet*, the problem of having too many schemata for interpretation.[19] That such a crisis may occur does not mean it can always be resolved since it may, as it was in the case of Hamlet, make it impossible for him or us to understand what is going on around us. Such a lack of understanding may make it impossible for us to make our own lives intelligible and may even lead, as it did for Hamlet, to madness (or to the necessity to feign madness). Yet even that description may be too comforting since it assumes that in such a situation we are able to distinguish normality from madness.

A new narrative is required for the resolution of an epistemological crisis. Such a narrative must enable agents to understand both how they could have intelligibly held their former beliefs and how they may have been misled by them. When historically founded certitudes are rendered problematic, new concepts are required to enrich our schemes to furnish solutions to problems that seem intractable; an explanation must be given why the tradition had, before these new resources were available, seemed sterile or incoherent; and these tasks must be carried on in a fashion in which the new conceptual resources are seen in continuity with the tradition as articulated to that point.[20] MacIntyre suggests the way the Catholic doctrine of the Trinity was resolved in the fourth century is a good illustration for the resolution of an epistemological crisis. Aquinas, providing the means in which Aristotle could be received into an Augustinian framework, is of course MacIntyre's crucial exemplification of a successful resolution of an epistemological crisis.[21]

Relativism now appears as the doctrine that denies the possibility of epistemological crises occurring, but by the very fact that such crises occur we can now see that relativism as a position is a mistake. MacIntyre, however, is willing to concede to the relativist that over long periods of time rival traditions, both internally and in relation to one another, may develop without encountering more than minor epistemological crises. Yet when this happens such traditions will be unable to encounter their rivals in a way to defeat them.[22] Moreover, there is nothing to prevent a tradition from degenerating into a self-contained enclave to avoid recognizing that it is being put into question by rival traditions. "This is," MacIntyre observes, "part of the degeneracy of modern astrology, of some types of psychiatric thought, and of liberal Protestantism."[23]

MacIntyre's concession that for long periods of time traditions of very different kinds can coexist without bringing their conflicts and disagreements to rational resolution makes clear that an epistemological crisis, while possibly quite painful, is even more importantly a great achievement. Our problem is not that Christians come into conflict with the world in which we live, but that we do not. Indeed, from this perspective war can now be seen as a failure to sustain the kind of conflict MacIntyre describes as an epistemological crisis—war is necessary when traditions are unable to recognize the crises they create for one another. This is not to deny that a war might be the form an epistemological cri-

sis might take or that terrorism could be construed as a desperate way
to force a conflict that is otherwise denied. Yet war and terrorism usually are not well known for providing "conceptual schemes" that allow
continuity with the past to be named.

WITNESS AS THEOLOGICAL TERRORISM

MacIntyre's account of epistemological crises is crucial if we are to
avoid the unhappy choice between Stackhouse's appeal to universal
principles and war. Moreover, if MacIntyre is right, then we can better
appreciate why Christian nonviolence cannot help but be seen from
advocates of both those alternatives as a form of terrorism. For Christians have been sent out into a world of war to challenge the necessity
of war armed only with the weapons of love. Put differently, that
Christians are first and foremost called to be witnesses by necessity
creates epistemological crises for those that do not worship the God of
Jesus Christ. (Of course, I also want to create such a crisis for those
who do worship Christ but think they can still participate in war.)
Such crises may for long periods be irresolvable and the tension created tempt all involved to violence. That Christians must resist such
temptations is not because such violence may not, at least for a while,
seem to provide "peace," but because the peace provided is not the
peace of Christ.

Christian witness so understood is particularly threatening to those
who assume, like Stackhouse, that our only alternative to war and terrorism is to represent a universal alternative.[24] That narrative, in spite of
its great desire for peace, cannot help but attempt to silence those who
represent "particularistic" traditions. "Particularists," particularly those
who refuse to accept the marginalization offered by such universalists,
cannot help but appear as fanatics and/or terrorists who threaten what
appears to be our only hope for peace. From the perspective of liberal
Christianity, Christians who insist on the "politics of Jesus"[25] cannot but
appear like Islamic fundamentalists—not a bad place to be from my perspective.

Witness can be understood as a universal imperative, but it is such
as an expression of hope rather than an assured result. As Emmanuel
Katongole observes, "witness involves the affirmation of the hermeneutical significance of the presence of others. Because human beings are
not accidentally culturally mediated, but necessarily so, truth does not
come as a correspondence to an independently existing reality. Rather,

truth is an interpretative performance realized through and within the cultural linguistic practice. This historical nature of truth militates against any epistemological singularity or self-sufficiency. Witness, as the form of contact between historically constituted traditions, affirms the realization that no one tradition is in possession of *the* truth. If that were the case, contact with other traditions would take the often preferred form of enforcement and imposition."[26]

It is important to observe that witness in no way is meant to avoid the importance of argument. Yet to have an argument requires that Christians first listen to what the other has to say. Such listening, moreover, may well cause us to learn better what we have to say. Such listening may even create epistemological crises within Christian self-understanding. Yet that is the risk we must take, since our tradition is unintelligible if we fail to be witnesses for the peace that God has secured for the world in Jesus Christ. In that name and that name alone is at once the legitimation as well as the necessity of our witness.

Which finally must bring us back to questions of war and terrorism. Does the position I have tried to sketch in this paper mean Christians must finally accept the inevitability of war and, perhaps even, our inability to distinguish war from terrorism? I certainly see no reason why such a conclusion must follow from what I have said. Christian witness is an alternative to war just to the extent Christian witness establishes connections between those who have no reason to be connected. Such connections in themselves cannot insure peace because, contrary to liberal sentimentality that assumes if people only come to know one another better violence is less likely, the exact opposite may be the case. Rather, what is crucial are the narrative connections Christian witness makes possible, believing—as we do—that the story of Christ is the end of all stories.

Such connections, which I believe are but another word for church (for we must not forget the Christian word for universal is catholic), give Christians the resources for distinguishing war from terrorism. For as the analysis above suggests, to be able to distinguish war from terrorism does not finally rest on conceptual distinctions, important as they are; but rather, through the sharing of stories we are enabled to see the children of my enemies are not my enemies. Such a "seeing" is an achievement that requires the slow work of those who must learn to wait in a world of war, knowing as they do that God would not have God's Kingdom accomplished through violence. Without such a fanatical people we literally would be without hope.

NOTES

1. See, for example, my *Dispatches from the Front: Theological Engagements with the Secular* (Durham, N.C.: Duke University Press, 1994), p. 5.

2. Violence and nonviolence are descriptions of behavior that requires analogical display. In other words we do not just "know" violence or nonviolence when "we see it." Peace too often is just another name for the absence of overt hostilities. For an exchange about the "meaning" of nonviolence see Paul Ramsey, *Speak Up for Just War or Pacifism* (University Park: Pennsylvania State University Press, 1988) and my response in the "Epilogue." In *Dispatches from the Front* I argue that we cannot know what violence (and war) is absent the practice of nonviolence. This may appear a "small point," but I think its significance is often overlooked. From a Christian perspective nonviolence is not an exception to war, but rather war and violence are conceptually and in practice parasitical on nonviolence.

3. James Tunstead Burtchaell, *The Giving and Taking of Life: Essays Ethical* (Notre Dame, Ind.: University of Notre Dame, 1989), pp. 211–12.

4. For example, the United States Department of Defense assumes that terrorism is defined as use of violence by those outside a duly constituted government. Thus "terrorism is the unlawful use or threatened use of force or violence by a revolutionary organization against individuals or property, with the intention of coercing or intimidating governments or societies, often for political or ideological purposes." Yet as Burtchaell points out (p. 213), such a definition leaves no room for state terrorism directed to its own population or to another state. In 1954 the U.S. Government engineered the overthrow of the duly elected government in Guatemala, for instance, and has since made every effort to have an obviously terrorist control "duly constituted," while having to overlook its massacres of 100,000 Guatemalans, and the "disappearing" of countless others. (It's interesting that in U.S. news reports those Guatemalans who protest or defend themselves are routinely labeled "rebels.") Burtchaell provides other definitions from the FBI, International Law Association, and others that only help one see that no "definition" of terrorism can be made to do the work of analysis.

5. Burtchaell, *Giving and Taking of Life*, p. 221. My use of this example is not meant to suggest it is impossible to distinguish between combatants and noncombatants. Just-war thinkers have rightly emphasized the importance of that distinction. Yet that distinction in itself is not sufficient to distinguish war from terrorism.

6. In *Christian Ethics and the Sit-In* (New York: Association Press, 1961), Ramsey says, "democracy means justifiable and limited resistance (and thus it refines and establishes procedures for making a justifiable revolution, which is in principle to apply to domestic politics the same line of reasoning that drove Christians in the early centuries of this era to justify and limit warfare for the resistance and correction of evil." p. 93. Later in the same book he observes that democracy is nothing more than *justum bellum*, "both in its origin in Western

history and in the principles of Christian ethics requiring participation in it as a form of regularized struggle between man and man in the midst of which alone we have in this fallen world any life with man preserved unto a higher and more open fellowship." p. 104.

7. Burtchaell, *Giving and Taking of Life*, p. 231.

8. Max Stackhouse, "Torture, Terrorism and Theology: The Need for a Universal Ethic," *Christian Century* 103, no. 29 (October 8, 1986): 861.

9. Stackhouse's most sustained criticism of my position can be found in his "Liberalism Dispatched vs. Liberalism Engaged," *Christian Century* 112, no. 29 (October 18, 1995): 962–67. Though this article takes the form of a review of my book *Dispatches from the Front*, it is a wholesale attack on what he takes to be my position. What Stackhouse thinks I must think is only what someone like Stackhouse can think I think because of the way he thinks. For example, in his review he suggests that I think religious claims are immune to rational criticism. I certainly do not think that to be the case, though I should like to know more what he thinks rational criticism to be. I mention this point since it relates to the general argument of this essay. I certainly have a stake in rational criticism though I am quite suspicious of appeals to rational criticism in the abstract.

10. For a response to the charge I am a "confessionalist" see my "Failure of Communication or A Case of Uncomprehending Feminism," *Scottish Journal of Theology* 50, no. 1 (March, 1997). This article is a response to Gloria Albrecht's review of my book, *In Good Company*. I find it interesting that Stackhouse and Albrecht share the view that I must be a "confessionalist" since they are, politically, at other ends of the spectrum. I think, however, this is but an indication of how deeply each of them is embedded not only in political liberalism but more importantly in theological liberalism.

11. Stackhouse, "Liberalism," p. 862. Stackhouse's assumption that we must have a reason for knowing why terrorism is wrong is, of course, part of the problem. Such a view fails to see that the question is not justification but description. Terrorism is one of those descriptions that work within the practices of a community that make the question, "What is wrong with terrorism?" distinctly odd. Torture works much the same way as do words like murder and, perhaps, abortion. That such words exist can give the impression that a universal ethic of principles exists to justify their use. But such descriptions as descriptions need no justification.

12. Stackhouse, "Liberalism," p. 863. Stackhouse develops this position in his *Creeds, Society, and Human Rights: A Study in Three Cultures* (Grand Rapids, Mich.: Eerdmans, 1984).

13. The very day I was writing this paragraph I received my copy of *The New York Review of Books*, 44, no. 1 (January 9, 1997), which carried a review by William McNeill of Samuel Huntington's, *The Clash of Civilizations and the Remaking of World Order*. McNeill quotes Huntington to the effect that "Western belief in the universality of Western culture suffers from three problems: it is false; it is immoral; and it is dangerous." According to McNeill Huntington

thinks it false because other civilizations have other ideals and norms; it is immoral because imperialism is the logical consequence of universalism; it is dangerous because such universalistic assumptions make war more likely. "Decline of the West?", p. 18. Though I have other things to say, certainly Huntington has said some of what needs to be said in response to Stackhouse.

14. Alasdair MacIntyre, *Whose Justice? Which Rationality?* (Notre Dame, Ind.: University of Notre Dame, 1988), p. 6.

15. Ibid., p. 7. Not enough attention has been paid to the form MacIntyre's argument takes in this book. He cannot provide any argument to end all arguments with those who want to assume Enlightenment views since his own account of rationality can only be displayed. The narrative detail concerning the Scottish Enlightenment in the book is not MacIntyre simply showing he understands Stair, Hutchenson, and Hume, but rather is necessary for his defense of how rationality requires narrative.

16. This charge simply will not go away no matter how many times the point is made that the very "problem of relativism" has been created by the epistemological theories that claim to be our only hope against relativism. MacIntyre's account of relativism as an option that depends on the development of cosmopolitan cultures seems exactly right. See MacIntyre, *Whose Justice? Which Rationality?*, pp. 389–403.

17. Ibid., p. 361. That a tradition is contingent, however, does not mean MacIntyre believes it impossible to arrive at first principles. Indeed, he believes Aquinas exemplifies how the articulation of such principles is possible. See MacIntyre's *First Principles, Final Ends, and Contemporary Philosophical Issues* (Milwaukee, Wisc.: Marquette University Press, 1990).

18. MacIntyre first developed his account of epistemological crises in his "Epistemological Crises, Dramatic Narrative, and the Philosophy of Science," *The Monist* 69, no. 4 (October, 1977): 453–72. This essay has been reprinted in *Why Narrative?: Readings in Narrative Theology*, edited by Stanley Hauerwas and L. Gregory Jones (Grand Rapids, Mich.: Eerdmans, 1989), pp. 138–57. References to this article will be to *Why Narrative?*.

19. MacIntyre, "Epistemological Crises, Narrative, and Philosophy of Science," pp. 138–41. It is important to note that MacIntyre's account of epistemological crisis is not an invitation to resume the Enlightenment presumption that before we can know anything we must first have an account of how we know. As Nicholas Lash nicely puts the matter—epistemology is what we do when things go wrong. *The Beginning and End of "Religion"* (Cambridge: Cambridge University Press, 1996), pp. 112–16. It is not quite right to think an epistemological crisis always indicates something has gone wrong, but at the very least a crisis indicates some sense that we have a problem.

20. MacIntyre, *Whose Justice? Which Rationality?*, p. 362.

21. See in particular MacIntyre's account in his *Three Rival Versions of Moral Enquiry: Encyclopaedia, Genealogy, and Tradition* (Notre Dame, Ind.: University of Notre Dame Press, 1990), pp. 105–26. By focusing on these examples I do not mean to distract attention from the compelling examples that Mac-

Intyre uses that come from the history of science. Yet one suspects that MacIntyre's account of epistemological crisis was first illumined for him from theology and, in particular, Newman. I mention this to suggest that inherent in MacIntyre's account of these matters is, I suspect, a very promising way to appreciate at once the difference and the similarity between the kind of knowledge gained through theology and that gained through science. Not the least result could be that the current prejudice against the former in favor of the latter might be challenged without recourse to Kuhn.

22. MacIntyre, *Whose Justice? Which Rationality?*, p. 366.

23. MacIntyre, "Epistemological Crises, Narrative, and Philosophy of Science," p. 147. MacIntyre no doubt takes great pleasure in providing these three candidates as examples of degenerate traditions. I only wish the list might be taken as a wonderful joke. However, I fear it is unfortunately all too true.

24. It is my view that the significance of MacIntyre's argument in his *Three Rival Versions of Moral Enquiry* has yet to be appreciated. For what MacIntyre attempts in that book is to create an epistemological crisis for the encyclopedist and genealogist. The form MacIntyre's argument takes is as important as its content. Put simply, MacIntyre fights fair just to the extent his argument takes the form of a narrative that invites further response. MacIntyre's work, therefore, must have the same essential incompleteness that he so insightfully suggests in *Three Rival Versions* (p. 124) is the heart and soul of Aquinas' *Summa*.

25. I am, of course, referring to the title of John Howard Yoder's, *The Politics of Jesus* (Grand Rapids, Mich.: Eerdmans, 1994). This is the second edition of the book that contains Yoder's update from the 1972 edition. For a wonderful attempt to work out the politics of a perspective like Yoder's within current discussions in political theory, see Thomas Heilke, "On Being Ethical without Moral Sadism: Two Readings of Augustine and the Beginnings of the Anabaptist Revolution," *Political Theory* 24, no. 3 (August, 1996): 493–517. Heilke develops the Anabaptist practice of the ban as an alternative to the politics of violence. He notes that such a "politics" may not seem such to those who assume that the "effort to sustain a hegemonic, territorial, sovereign entity, embodied in a physical collective of human beings and articulated to action for its own self-preservation" constitutes the only entity that deserves the name "political" (p. 513). Such a view of politics helps make clear why the church cannot help but appear as a threat to such "politics"—the church is a polity that represents no such collective but is at once at home and not at home in all such politics. The church, like many terrorist organizations, can be understood as an international conspiracy against all politics based on "self-preservation."

26. Emmanuel Katongole, *Particularity and Moral Rationality: Questioning the Relation between Religion and Ethics with Reference to the Work of Stanley Hauerwas* (Ph.D diss. Katholieke Universiteit, Leuven, 1996), pp. 208–9. Katongole's claim that truth does not come as a correspondence to an independent reality I take to be a rejection of crude correspondent theories of truth, that is, theories that MacIntyre characterizes as conceiving a realm of

facts independent of judgement or of any other form of linguistic expression. MacIntyre rightly suggests that there is much to be said for correspondence theories and one understands that the relation between mind and its objects is given expression in judgements. See his *Which Justice? Which Rationality?*, pp. 354–60.

5

Solomon's Porch:
The Church as Sectarian Ghetto

Robert W. Brimlow

INTRODUCTION

In the sentences immediately following his often (partially) quoted "What has Jerusalem to do with Athens, the Church with the Academy, the Christian with the heretic?" Tertullian states, "Our principles come from the Porch of Solomon, who had himself taught that the Lord is to be sought in simplicity of heart. I have no use for a Stoic or a Platonic or a dialectic Christianity."[1]

In his inimitable way, Tertullian is not only distinguishing Christianity from the dominant philosophical and ethical systems of the day—the Porch of Solomon is as distinct and far from the porch [Stoa] of Zeno as Jerusalem is from Athens—but he is also recalling and invoking 2 Cor 6:14–18 where Paul calls upon the Corinthian church not to "be yoked with those who are different, with unbelievers. . . . What agreement has the Temple of God with idols?"

Stark, clear and powerful passages such as these from both Tertullian and Paul provoke problems for the contemporary church. It is not clear how we are to be Christians in the world or in what way the church ought to function in the midst of unbelievers. How do we transform the secular, pagan culture around us authentically without becoming pagans ourselves? Can we effect a transformation of the world in such a way that *we* are not transformed into some kind of alien residents within our own church community? The danger is that our efforts to be the church in the world will make the church literally mundane, another social club or social service agency. For we are in the world, after all. We do earn our livings and raise our families and drive our cars within this dominant

105

political and cultural milieu. And clearly this world of ours is not all bad; indeed it can't be all bad, for nothing created by the hand of God—neither the professions, families, nor automobiles—can be all bad. We are located here and now, and our lives are fully integrated with the world; our specific secular polity is as integral to us as the air we breathe, Paul's injunction for us to be separate notwithstanding; all we need is a little more exegesis, a little more subtle ecclesiology to understand that.

Notwithstanding. I do not understand why Paul's injunction to us as church is notwithstanding. It is not at all clear to me, if indeed we as church are authentically transformed by the love, sacrifice, and grace of Christ, why we can not be separate. It seems to me that we are called to reject being yoked with those who are different and called, simultaneously, to give witness to the glory of the Lord and the Truth of the gospel. Our witness to the world need not be accommodating in any sense to the definitions, structures, or values of the society around us; nor should the way we witness or the way we are church be separated from the ways we live otherwise. We should not be living otherwise: there is no reason that our lives should be separated this way into two polities—the one religious and spiritual, the other economic and statist.

Through the gospel we have been given a new way to see and think and be, and our call to be church is to witness this seeing, thinking, and being without modification, that is, without accommodation to or compromise with the principalities and powers set against the Lord and, therefore, us. It is important to argue about and ultimately understand the nature of these principalities in order to begin to formulate how the church ought to be in the world. It makes a difference whether states, economic systems, and the civil authority are essentially good though fallen and in need of transformation, or rather are evil and always in opposition to the Body of Christ. Our response to the call depends on this understanding. In what follows, I will be arguing for the latter view and attempting to show that believing secular social systems are essentially good leads to fundamental incompatibility with the gospel.

THEOLOGY AND SECTARIANISM

Many theologians have worked very hard over the centuries to help the church understand our call and what, precisely, discipleship means in the world. Their powerful and oftentimes inspired words offer a translation of the gospel narrative and an application of the wealth of insights that have accrued over two millenia. It is because of their work that we can speak of a "new" way to see and think and be for this time and place. And many of our contemporary theologians have also worked very hard with Scripture, the writings of the Church Fathers, and our tradition to further develop and maintain an ecclesiology that avoids succumbing to the charge of "sectarianism." It appears, frequently, that the most devastating criticism one theologian can level at another is that her work is sectarian. It is not surprising, then, that theologians have written persuasively, trying to convince the church not to behave tribally or engage in practices or ways of thinking that would render us a ghetto in this world. They offer a faint evocation of John Tracy Ellis' famous indictment of the Roman Catholic academy, and formulate the same point with greater theological sophistication.

The theologian's task as thinker and teacher of the church is not easy. I should know; I am not one. I do not earn my living trying to figure out how we are to be church, what it means in concrete (or even in abstract) terms to be "disciples" or how we can witness in a pagan world—if indeed the world is a pagan one. I teach philosophy, and analytic philosophy at that (no handmaiden to theology, she), and I don't know how to witness in my world of material implications and set theoretic constructions. Nor do I know what Peano's postulates have to do with Jerusalem. What I think, research, and write would have relevance, perhaps, to the work of a bare dozen professional philosophers—not that they would agree with any of it—and my actual audience of readers number the five poor souls on my college's Tenure and Promotion Review Committee. Nonetheless, I think I understand, with the clarity and distinctness only an outsider possesses, some of the difficulties theologians confront.

And, of course, whatever understanding I do have is derived from the work of another philosopher.

The problem besetting theology today seems to be similar to the problem facing Tertullian and Paul: how is the church supposed to interact with the world in which it finds itself? Our contemporary situation has perhaps been best expressed by Alasdair MacIntyre. In his essay "God and the Theologians"[2] MacIntyre writes:

> We can see the harsh dilemma of a would-be contemporary theology.
>
> [1] The theologian begins from orthodoxy, but the orthodoxy which has been learnt from Kierkegaard and Barth becomes too easily a closed circle, in which believer speaks only to believer, in which all human content is concealed.

[2] Turning aside from this arid in-group theology, the most perceptive theologians wish to translate what they have to say to an atheistic world. But they are doomed to one of two failures. Either

> [a]   they succeed in their translation: in which case what they find themselves saying has been transformed into the atheism of their hearers. Or
> [b]   they fail in their translation: in which case no one hears what they have to say but themselves.

If [2a] prevails, MacIntyre argues that the result is a theology with a theistic vocabulary but an atheistic substance. Stanley Hauerwas expands MacIntyre's notion of the effects of [2a] to the whole church—in part because the problems of the theologians are, simply, the problems of the church writ small—when he writes:

> Christians, insofar as they endeavor to remain political actors, must attempt to translate their convictions into a non-theological idiom. But once such a translation is acomplished, it becomes very unclear why they need the theological idiom in the first place.[3]

Thus, with [2a] expanded to the full extent of the church's social and political activities in the world, even the vestiges of a theistic vocabulary become superfluous.

I do not find fault with MacIntyre's and Hauerwas' discussion of [2a]. Indeed, it is precisely because theologians in particular have tried to translate the gospel message into secular language that the church has tended to lose its moorings. Because we the church have followed our theologians in this interpretation of our mission to witness to all nations (Lk 24:46f; Mk 16:15; Acts 1:8), the church has become just another social institution indistinguishable from other liberal and consumerist institutions in our culture; and we espouse views as a church that, for the most part, morally good atheists would not find objectionable—and that is precisely the intent. Christ, the gospel, and church fellowship are so personalized that it is proper to relegate them to Sunday mornings and Wednesday evenings. The transformation of Christianity becomes complete when our spirituality devolves into notions of self-fulfillment and our fellowship becomes a vehicle for self-actualization. The problem of the theologians and the problem of the church ceases to be problematic when our faith becomes compartmentalized as one ancillary aspect of our cultural personae, and the gospel itself becomes the outline of yet another twelve-step program for personal wholeness and a solution for our difficulties with intimacy and other human relations.

That preceeding paragraph voices a complaint and critique that has been expressed and argued more cogently and persuasively by others, notably Hauerwas and John Howard Yoder. My primary concern in this chapter focuses on [1], the first horn of the dilemma MacIntyre delimits. I am not convinced that option [1] poses any problem at all for theologians or, by extension, the Christian church. Unless there is some third way lurking in the background that I neither see nor understand as an alternative—and I tend to doubt that there is one because MacIntyre is such a good philosopher—I do not believe that closed circles are all that bad an option. In fact, I believe and shall argue that a closed circle is the better option for the church and the one Tertullian and Paul insist upon, the "sectarian" nature of circles notwithstanding.

In the first place, it occurs to me that MacIntyre's complaint about closed circles could be applied with the same justification to other, analogous social phenomena and situations just as well. However, in those contexts closed circles would seem delightful and enriching rather than arid and problematic. It would seem very odd to maintain the intuitive view that French culture is not fully French and therefore not fully appreciable in its richness and vitality when it is translated into English; and then simultaneously complain that, unless French cultural institutions, literature, and practices were translated, no one but Francophones could appreciate them. It is evident that, in the latter situation, Francophones would constitute a "closed circle" in which Francophone speaks only to Francophone—and in French at that! This is an absurd antithesis and a nonproblem. If one suspects that the French or Quebecois or Haitians possess something of value or know something that one does not but wishes to comprehend, then it behooves one to learn French rather than expect them to speak in English. If those cultures draw us to themselves, it is our responsibility to become educated and immersed in the linguistic and cultural idiom of the French, the Quebecois, and the Haitian and thereby enter the circle. I do not understand why it should be different for the church.

The problem that the church ought to be confronting when faced with the Lord's charge to us to witness to the nations is *not* that of finding a way to translate the gospel so that pagans can understand it in their idiom. To do that is to fall prey to [2a] and transform the gospel into the values of the world when what we should be doing is transforming the world into the Kingdom of God. Rather, our problem as church is to find a way to let the world know that there is another language and another way of viewing and understanding reality that they should want to learn. Our task would then become teaching them that language and admitting them into the circle. Trying to live the gospel and be church is not easy for believers—which is why God's grace is necessary; it ought not be reduced to an easily classified and simply understandable menu item for the nonbeliever, or merely an alternative lifestyle or even a variant expression of acceptable humanistic values.

WHY SECTARIANISM IS REQUIRED: A BRIEF REFLECTION ON THE WORK OF STANLEY HAUERWAS.

I think because the work of Troeltsch and the Niebuhr brothers has been so influential, theologians have tried very hard to avoid sustainable charges of sectarianism, even when their work tends in that direction. This is a problem that appears periodically in the work of Stanley Hauerwas. Hauerwas has frequently been the focus of much criticism, and many of those who disagree with him have accused him of sectarianism. His work is justly influential and persuasive, and it deserves even more credit and admiration than it has received. Nonetheless, there is an aspect of his work that, in the light of the foregoing, is disturbing. My difficulty with Hauerwas is precisely the opposite of most of his critics: he is not quite sectarian enough.

Throughout his books and articles, Hauerwas mounts frequent and persuasive arguments against nation-states in general and, more specifically, against the liberalism and philosophic foundationalism that underlie many of our American social and cultural institutions. Characteristically, he writes

> It is my view that the concern of the religious right and of neo-conservatives to reclaim "traditional moral values" is ironic since the very values they want to recover have been undermined by the very liberalism they support in other spheres of life. What must be recognized is that liberalism is not simply a theory of government but a theory of society that is imperial in its demands.[4]

Hauerwas does not leave it here, offering criticism with no positive vision of the role of the church. In defining "church" as a social ethic, he argues that the church is an alternative polity:

> The gospel is a political gospel. Christians are engaged in politics, but it is a politics of the Kingdom that reveals the insufficiency of all politics based on coercion and falsehood and finds the true source of power in servanthood rather than dominion. . . . The church, therefore, is a polity like any other, but it is also *unlike* any other insofar as it is formed by a people who have no reason to fear the truth. They are able to exist in the world without resorting to coercion to maintain their presence. That they are such depends to a large extent on their willingness to move. . . . For it is certain that much of the world is bound to hate them for calling attention to what the world is. . . . For as Christians we are at home in no nation. Our true home is the church itself, where we find those who, like us, have been formed by a savior who was necessarily always on the move.[5]

In this extended quotation we can see the major elements of Hauerwas' insights. He sees the church as a distinct community existing in the world but practicing a politics of truth and living a life of discipleship. This vision of the alternative polity that is church seems to entail the rejection of the power, dominion, conventions, and values of the prevalent social assumptions, institutions, and practices. I do not think Hauerwas means—or ought to mean—that Christians should engage in a critique of society and social institutions from inside the tent of society itself. I do not think he means—or ought to mean—that the witness and discipleship Christians are called to gives us a blueprint for being better social democrats, better citizens of the state, or more enlightened capitalists. If we are true to the call of the gospel, we should expect to be hated and persecuted and we must be prepared to move. Hauerwas foresees that our being church and telling the truth most likely will result in pogroms against us.

The gospel has freed us from captivity in our political, economic, and cultural milieu. We are at home in no nation because in Christ "there is neither Jew nor Greek, there is neither slave nor free person, there is not male and female." (Gal 3:28) The gospel liberates the church from those presumably fundamental distinctions that defined us and, by our acceptance of those distinctions and definitions, had enslaved us. The "elementary" powers of citizenship and tribalism, of economic status, of political enfranchisement, and of gender differences—the determinants of self—made us slaves of economics, sociology, psychology, nationalism, and violence. By recognizing that we are children of God we are freed from the bondage of those categories and what follows from them; we, therefore, can not be at home or truthful acting as though they are legitimate.

Further, our adoption as children of God and heirs to the promise of Abraham is subversive. It is precisely because our discipleship is so subversive and dangerous to the established order that much of the world will hate and persecute us. Our response to the call of discipleship not only threatens the powers of the world but positively and publicly overthrows them. Jesus' call of Matthew (Mt 9:9f) is not simply an example of an individual sinner's personal metanoia. By calling a tax collector, Jesus demonstrates his priority over Rome. While tax collecting was a franchise purchased by indigenous people, it was a franchise backed by the authority of Caesar: the empire's taxation of subject nations was not only a way to raise revenue but an expression of Rome's dominion over a captive people. If the empire's tax collectors were called to follow Jesus, the power of the empire would be diminished accordingly. Similarly, in following Jesus, Matthew rejects the lure and power of profit. He leaves his potentially lucrative customs post and refuses to engage in the legal economic exploitation of the Jews, however minimal it may have been. Finally, by calling Matthew, the public sinner and traitor, Jesus rejects and overthrows the religious and cultural ostracism of tax collectors as practiced by the Jewish community in Judea. The Pharisees do not understand how Jesus could eat with sinners and outcasts and thereby become ritually impure.

On so many levels this one act of Jesus early in his ministry sets the tone for the formation of the disciples. The social and cultural categories, distinctions, and practices of society are to be rejected and subverted in favor of the gospel. Jesus' call of Matthew was not "Now go and make a fair profit in your operations" nor did it include instructions regarding the legitimate use of the state's coercive power for the common good. Jesus called Matthew to another, alternative way of life that engendered society's hatred and persecution.

I believe that this all too brief reflection is fully consonant with the main thrust of Hauerwas' work. He sees, in a way that few contemporary theologians do, that the call to be disciples of Jesus radically reorders us and our relation to the world. It is a call that requires the peaceful subversion of the empires. Yet I am not sure how far Hauerwas would go with me along this line of thought.

What I find hard to reconcile with this position is Hauerwas' predilection to simultaneously urge the church's accommodation with liberalism and liberal institutions. For example, Hauerwas contends, "We do not want to call Methodists out of Congress; we just want them to be there as Methodists, for Heaven's sake."[6] In another work, he expands the claim from the purely political (Methodist congresspersons) to the entire social realm—those for whom Congress works and thinks—when he writes, "I have no interest in legitimating and/or recommending a withdrawal of Christians or the Church from social or political affairs. I simply want them to be there as Christians and as Church."[7] I am afraid that "simply" is the wrong adverb.

I hope it is clear that I believe the vast majority of Hauerwas' words are correct and contain blessed insights. I believe with him that liberalism—and I would include other social institutions in the same category as purely political liberalism—is imperial in its demands; and I believe that Hauerwas believes we ought to render to the empires what belongs to the empires and to God what is God's. When we consider the example of Jesus in the gospel and our call to follow Him, and consider that the disjunction is that stark, it is obvious that we ought to render to the empires nothing and to God all. And if this is the case, it is not the withdrawal of Christians and church from social and political affairs that needs legitimization but rather our continued involvement with them. There is nothing simple about that kind of justification. It is as if Hauerwas were to say that he does not want to call Christians out of leadership positions in the arms industry or defense department, but simply wants them to be there as "Christian" CEO's and project managers.

That last sentence is ridiculous. Hauerwas and William Willimon recognize the difficulty if not the inherent contradiction of Christians working for arms manufacturers: "If war preparations are wrong, then do we United Methodists want the offerings of our members who work in defense industries? Should United Methodist pastors admit to the Lord's table those who make a living from building weapons?"[8] Raising these troubling questions is indicative of Hauerwas' willingness not only to speak the truth no matter the cost but also to follow the application of the Lord's injunction for us to be peacemakers to all areas of our lives. Of course, it would have been better if Hauerwas had pursued those questions to their obvious answers and had defended those conclusions in a way that would challenge us further. But there is great value in this kind of reflection nonetheless.

In the same spirit, we need to reflect upon Hauerwas' contention that we ought to continue our involvement in social and political affairs

and at least raise troubling questions about the extent of our involvement and how that is consistent with our call to be church. And it is
important to examine Hauerwas in particular because his theology is
otherwise so good that it is crucial for us to understand where he goes
wrong and why sectarianism is required for the church.

There are three related strands of argument underlying Hauerwas'
position that Christians should cooperate with the dominant powers and
they correspond to his notion of the state, his notion of society, and the way
he understands social activism. Because Hauerwas is not very clear about
any of these—how they function or what they represent—he tends to con-
flate these different categories that can lead to a great deal of confusion
about how he sees the role and function of the church in the concrete.

In a paper devoted entirely to defending himself against the charge
of sectarianism, Hauerwas writes:

> I do not see why the position for which I have argued forces the
> church to withdraw from public policy matters . . . unless you
> think that public policy always involves questions of violence
> and/or coercion. I simply do not believe that. Instead I hold out
> the possibility . . . that a good state can exist as a correlative of
> a good society where coercion is at a minimum precisely
> because people are virtuous. Miscamble [Hauerwas' critic] sim-
> ply seems to ignore entirely my constant emphasis on how the
> church serves society through the training of virtuous people.[9]

One of the difficulties with this statement is that it is not clear what
Hauerwas means by "public policy matters." It could refer to those
issues and problems that confront all of us as individuals—such as trying to figure out solutions to the problem of world hunger[10]—or it could
refer to those issues that affect us as citizens of a state—such as trying
to prioritize items in the federal budget. It appears that Hauerwas col-
lapses the distinction between the two within his framework of church
involvement:

> [W]hile I am not opposed to our trying to harness the resources
> of state power to alleviate the needs of people, I think it is
> unfortunate when we think only in those terms.[11]

Yet such a conflation of our mission to feed the hungry and clothe the
naked with the presumed duty of the state to aid the poor leads to major
problems and, ultimately, to incoherence.

Unless he is utilizing a definition he doesn't specify, "public policy" most commonly refers to the legislative agenda and executive practices of the nation-state. So the issue Hauerwas is discussing would more clearly be expressed in terms of either the church's putative obligation to the state or its desire to influence the formal political processes of the state.

My initial reaction to this question is that I see nothing wrong or misguided with the church criticizing state policies or exhorting it to do good with the resources it possesses. But I do consider it to be misguided and wrong for the church to adopt a role in framing such an agenda or becoming involved in, for example, working toward the passage of particular legislative items or bills. Involvement in the formal political process such as campaigning, lobbying, bargaining, reaching consensus, or even voting requires a prior moral committment to the state and its function. Implicit in formal political activity is the committment to the rule of law, acceding to the primacy of the will of the majority, the prerequisite acceptance of the outcome of the political process no matter what that result consists of.

When the church agrees to become involved in the formal processes of political activity, when Christians pull the lever in the voting booth, we agree to abide by and support whatever the majority of citizens choose—at least until the next election. We can protest, within the bounds of the law; we can argue and exhort, within the bounds of the law. And to effect a change in the public policy of the nation, our protests and arguments and exhortations must be made to appeal to the majority of citizens, which requires us to secularize the theological foundations of our language and church. Thus, the incoherence of Hauerwas' position is that in an effort to change the public policy of the state, the church must engage in [2a]—we must translate what we have to say to an atheistic world and adopt the atheism of our audience for the sake of the common good.

Hauerwas' contention that public policy decisions do not always entail violence or coercion is correct, but his conclusion that liberal political activity is therefore acceptable to pacifists and Christians does not follow. Violence and coercion in liberal politics and public policy decisions are only necessary when the state is confronted by resistance to those processes and policies. If we do not resist the will of the majority, if we are committed to abide by the "fair" result even if we lose in the polling place of the legislature, the state need not have recourse to its coercive power or force of arms. We have freely put the chains of obligation to the state on our own wrists; there is no need for us to be jailed when we are good, law-abiding citizens; nor for us to be threatened when we are in complicity with the state's designs.

Involvement in the political processes of the state entails the commitments of citizenship—patriotism; jury duty; taxation; support of the military, the police, the laws and the prisons—all duly passed according to the legal formulae and constitutionally approved. It entails commitment to the gods and ideals of liberalism and those commitments imply approval, support, and loyalty no matter how much we protest against the imperiousness of such a pretentious state power or complain about the exploitation and domination of people, which is an essential feature of states. What Hauerwas' position ultimately amounts to, what current church practice is (without Hauerwas' critique) is an attempt to reconcile the irreconcilable, to flatter the hangman while consoling the victims.[12] By our actions as Christians and church we agree that we are members and citizens of the state, that we belong; because we belong, we are involved and thus we are required to render the tribute of our lives to the empire; and that required tribute we freely grant rends our souls and divides our loyalties.

In addition to Hauerwas' initial indictment of liberalism, I would like to further specify that capitalism and market economics are no less imperial in their demands and must be considered as mutually supporting liberal political practices. I am not sure whether politics precedes economics or if economics precedes politics. What is evident, though, is that the violence and coercion of nation-states—including liberal nation-states—have an analogue in the exploitation and dehumanization of contemporary economics. What is wrong with liberal political theory is precisely what is wrong with market economics: each involves the exercise of a power that deifies those who possess it and reifies those who do not, while in reality the only thing deified is the power itself.[13]

The imperial demands of liberalism and capitalism are abhorrent precisely because they require us to render to them all of the "significant" aspects of our lives. Indeed, they define how our lives are to be considered significant: in the twin terms of political power and economic clout. Conversely, the politically marginalized and the poor are insignificant precisely because they lack the power that characterizes value in our society. Our call to be poor and powerless in the Beatitudes and throughout the gospel is a call to reject this dominating value system; Hauerwas' overall argument that the church is called to be a social ethic must entail this if nothing else.

Of all the arguments Hauerwas has developed over the years, his position that Christianity entails pacifism has affected me most profoundly and has served as the impetus for me to examine the development, formation, and structure of nation-states as well as liberalism more broadly construed. Yet Hauerwas seems to have a tendency to focus too narrowly on the issue of state-sponsored violence and separate it from the overall context of state-sponsored oppression and economic commodification of human beings. The liberal state, with liberal economics, reduces persons to mere dehumanized elements of larger entities; we become data points in market surveys as well as political polls; we are defined by how well our interests coincide with the common interest and as individuals are dispensible for the sake of the common good. Insofar as Hauerwas' understanding of Christian pacifism is a rejection of a means, it is trivial. Insofar as Christian pacifism rejects physical violence but leaves intact the political and economic oppression that strips us of humanity and value, it is merely a critique of a difference in degree: it is wrong to cut off your opponent's legs, but perfectly alright to lop off a finger or two. The psychological precondition for "acceptable" violence is the viewing of our victims as other, as valueless nonhumans. Violence is wrong because it treats others instrumentally and thus ignores the fact that the other is a locus of God's love. And that is precisely what is wrong with the social preconditions of physical and nonphysical violence and oppression—liberal politics and capitalism.

One may argue that Hauerwas' notion of politics is much more expansive than my criticism of public policy suggests. It certainly seems that Hauerwas has recourse to a notion of society and social activism that is broader or more inclusive than what is captured by the idea of nation-states and public-policy decisions. "Politics" in Hauerwas' terminology may be indicative of a related but still distinct phenomenon, for he writes

> I refuse to accept such a characterization [that a pacifist by definition must withdraw from political involvement] not only because there is no intrinsic reason why pacifists must disavow all political involvement simply because they refuse to kill on behalf of the state, but I also refuse to accept such a characterization because it implies that all politics is finally but a cover for violence. . . . Rather than disavowing politics, the pacifist must be the most political of animals exactly because *poltics understood as the process of discovering the goods we have in common is the only alternative to violence.* What the pacifist must deny, however, is the common assumption that genuine politics is determined by state coercion.[14] (Emphasis added)

While it seems that Hauerwas has some idea of society as distinct from the nation-state—and, arguably, sees the role of the church as operating within this sphere—it is very difficult to know what the "goods" are that he has in mind, how the church has those goods in common with society, how this much more broadly construed "political" process is supposed to function or how the answer to any of these questions is reconcilable with the church's call.

It is possible that the common goods he is referring to in this passage regard issues pertaining to the "quality of life" of members of the polity, taking care of the least advantaged of society in Rawlsian terms. On this reading, our point of meeting or intersection with those not in the church would be the material condition of persons whose lives we can affect. Yet, it is not at all evident to me that apparently common concerns about the poverty in our society, for instance, is the same reality for Christians as it is for humanists and nonbelievers. I don't think the Christian injunction to clothe the naked is ultimately the same as the imperative to find new markets for Nike sportswear, even though the result may be the same for each in the end. Nor do I think that compromising Christian principles by associating the church with the exploitative empires—all in the name of achieving good results—is consistent with the gospel. I believe Hauerwas had it right when he wrote

> For God does not rule creation through coercion, but through a cross. As Christians, therefore, we seek not so much to be effective as to be fruitful—we, thus, cannot do that which promises "results" when the means are unjust. Christians have rightly felt much in accord with those, such as Kant, who argue that there are some things we cannot do, no matter what good might accrue. We must be a people who have learned to be patient in the face of injustice.[15]

Yet he unaccountably seems to retreat from this position in a later work when he writes

> We might be tempted to say that *fruitfulness* rather than *effectiveness* is the goal of a confessing church. Yet we believe this is a false alternative. Few of us would admit to holding an ecclesiology that believes in either fruitfulness regardless of cost or results, or effectiveness that is purely pragmatic. . . . For the church to set the principle of being church above other princi-

ples is not to thumb our noses at results. It is trusting God to give us the rules, which are based on what God is doing in the world to bring about God's good results.[16]

In this latter passage Hauerwas seems to believe that the church can have it both ways with regard to genuine political activity: that we can maintain our faithfulness to the Kingdom while simultaneously operating as an interest group, as subjects of another empire, which can form alliances with other political actors to achieve good results. This is a court chaplaincy argument[17] that states that it is permissible to mollify, advise, and bless caesar and his undertakings if only we can modify his evil effects somewhat. Yet the mechanism necessary to participate in social processes in this way leads to the same incoherence as our engagement in public-policy matters. I would argue that God has given us the rules: that we are to be first and foremost a faithful church that works hard and leaves the results to him.

I tend to lose any notion of distinctiveness for the church when I consider such reasoning—and it is reasoning such as this that has characterized the church through much of its history. If we consider that the church's and the secular society's results are equivalent as Hauerwas' latter passage and his reference to "common goods" seems to imply, then it is not clear that there is a significant difference between Christians and good humanists. Further, it becomes evident that public-policy activity in the liberal state—which exists to advance social goods, after all—is not only permissible but mandatory in some circumstances, that is, whenever the church and other liberal interest groups are pursuing the same end such as nuclear disarmament, feeding the poor, or advancing the cause of social justice. We therefore can and ought to cooperate with the powers and empires whenever our genuine political ends are congruent.

Yet it is clearly not the case, following the general trend of Hauerwas' arguments through the body of his work, that results can be determinative in this way. The whole point of utilizing MacIntyre's narrative structure for Hauerwas' ecclesiology is precisely the insight that understanding an act depends entirely upon the narrative context that explains it. Thus, even though the church and humanists agree with the action of feeding the poor, for the Christian it is an act of discipleship and witness whereas for the humanist it may be better described as a mandate following from a consideration of basic liberal rights derived from Kant or Rawls. It is foolish to blur the distinction between the two, even though the result—full bellies—is the same in either case. They are different acts. In the same sense, it is fundamentally incorrect to disregard the difference between Christianity and humanism, even under the guise of that all-encompassing, idiotic notion of sacramentality so much in favor with my fellow Roman Catholics. By placing too much emphasis on the results we are again forced to follow the path of [2a]—to translate the gospel into a secular idiom and thereby turn our backs on the Lord—because that is the only way we can discover the independent and rationally accessible goods we have in common with others.

MOVING TOWARD A CHRISTIAN GHETTO

As I have tried to indicate, one of the major problems within Hauerwas' work, and a major problem for the church, is the failure to distinguish clearly between states and society. Because Hauerwas and the church do not pay sufficient attention to the difference between the two, both tend to fall into state-centered thinking and, therefore, the activity of the church, more often than not, becomes expressive of accommodation with the dominant powers and empires. What's needed is an understanding of the deeper significance of social structures, a clearer understanding that "the body politic is man [sic] in the sight of God."[18] We must not accept the notion that we must treat secular society, the state, liberal politics, or capitalism as givens in the world to which we must adapt our church practices; and clearly we must reject also their hegemony over significant aspects of our lives. The role of the church in saying "yes" to God is saying "no" to the empires.[19] While the common good for the church and for humanity is the same and is described in the gospel, we must not permit the dominant powers and their values to dictate the terms of that good or the language we use to define it publicly.

In order to begin to understand "the body politic" and the church's relation to it, we need to analyze each. What follows is, by necessity, only a sketch, the details of which need to be specified more concretely. Martin Buber has written

> Every degeneration indicates its genus, and in such a way that the degeneration is never related to the genus simply as present to past, but as in a distorted face the distortion is related to the form persisting beneath it. The body politic, which is sometimes also called the "world," that is, the human world, seeks, knowingly or unknowingly, to realize in its genuine formation men's [sic] turning to one another in the context of creation. The false

formations distort but they cannot eliminate the eternal origin. . . . [T]he man who has not ceased to love the human world
in all its abasement sees even today genuine form.[20]

One of the "false formations" of the world is the nation-state. The
nation-state is defined by borders that are nothing but lines drawn in the
dirt that indicate an "us" as distinct from a "them." And the primary
function of the nation-state is to defend us from them by maintaining the
sanctity of the borders and thus of the state itself. Further, the state
serves to protect private property (understood to be "me and what is
mine") from whichever of our fellow citizens who want it without abiding by the fair rules of acquisition.[21] At least from the time of Locke, private property has enjoyed equal status with an individual's life and liberty, and the state, through all the variations of social contract theory
from Hobbes to Rawls, is the primary guarantor of the sanctity of property—both the property of citizens as well as the property of the state
itself as delimited by borders.

Where the church errs is in accepting the divisions that are states
and the idea of property and property rights that underly states. These
are the closed circles we should fear. We have confused the body politic
of humanity with the political institutions of nations. We as church are
called to be supranational rather than intrastatist: the former is the context of our call to discipleship and genuine formation as the people of
God, whereas the latter, at best, divides our loyalties with the false,
degenerate political formations.

If one of the tasks of the church is to serve society, and society is
not statist, we still need to be very careful. If it is clear that we are called
to serve those with a commonality other than national citizenship, we
still must be wary of other commonalities that exclude, which define
"other." Groups with common cultural identites, such as the society
comprising North America and Europe, or Latinos or Asians, may
prove to be even more oppressive, violent, or insular than the nation-
states that they currently constitute. The hegemonic dimension of Western culture that dominates and commodifies people worldwide is
hardly a more comforting notion than violence-prone nation-states;
and cultural entities such as this will prove to be an even more formidable set of empires standing against the Lord and church in this time
of globalization.

The challenge of the church as closed circle is this: we must maintain our distinctiveness and our separateness while we simultaneously
and steadfastly refuse to define "other."

The first part of this apparent paradox—our distinctiveness and sep-arateness as the people of God—is necessary for us to be sustained as disciples. We see the church as the primary vehicle of God's grace in our lives; we need the collaboration, challenges, and support we give to one another. With God's grace we need to sustain each other as members of the Kingdom and maintain our bonds as God's people doing his work. The church must be its own society. It is too much to expect that we can remain faithful in isolation. Ever since the days of the early church, Christians have come together to live and worship; this must occur no longer only for our "religious" services but also for our daily living.

Secondly, and just as important as living in close proximity to one another, the church must develop its own institutions, including eco-nomic ones. The ongoing problem of believing and being disciples lays not in faithfully enduring the severities of persecutions. To our embarassment, most of us are not persecuted in the United States. The challenge for us lies, rather, in being disciples during the daily grind of "normal" activity—of work and making a living. As long as we must leave church and the Christian community and depend on the secular world to earn our living, we must adopt and accept in some measure the anti-Christian values of the pagan. As long as significant aspects of our lives remain divided, our loyalties must also be similarly divided. In the Catholic tradition, our forebears in this country developed our own edu-cational institutions not only to combat the effects of discriminatory admission polices of the major Protestant universities but also to educate and form the youth of our community in the faith. We need to develop these kinds of institutions and expand them into all areas of our church's concerns.

I have in mind a model for this type of church in the Hasidic com-munity within Judaism. As a young man I worked in Crown Heights, Brooklyn, and was astounded at the vibrant, pulsing community life of the Hasidim. They were clearly visible, spoke to one another in their own language, had their own newspapers and social activities. Most important, though, their lives revolved around the schule. Their days seemed regulated by their faith and they gave each other mutual aid and support in living as observant Jews in a gentile world. Their businesses and overall economic life was likewise—as far as I could tell—subordi-nated to their faith. It seemed to be a community of small businesses all of which closed by sundown Friday when the streets became filled with men hurrying to prayer.

I have no doubt that much of what I had seen and absorbed as an outsider has been romanticized. And I have no doubt that there are profound problems and dangers, within Judaism as a whole as well as within the particular Hasidic community of Crown Heights, associated with living in such a closed, tight-knit arrangement.

And, of course, there are dangers for the Christian church in following this kind of path into the ghetto; I can hear the criticism of this position even as I write. The critics will point out the dangers of insularity and tribalism, the danger of mistrusting whomever is "other." They will say that the church needs to be inclusive but what I describe (even briefly) excludes whatever doesn't fit my narrow definition of "church" and demonizes it as evil or at least fallen. Finally, what is wrong with the ghetto is that it is utopian at best.

To these complaints and criticisms, and to some of the others I have not foreseen, I say yes. It is very dangerous. Communities of the kind I have described, communities that are closed circles tend to isolation and inbreeding. They can stifle their members with a crushing regimentation. They can exagerrate the shadows beyond the small circle of light into all sorts of enemies and monsters. They tend never to accept the other, even if she is admitted into the confines of the ghetto.

This is all true. There are significant dangers we must guard against. My point, however, is that the alternative the church has pursued through most of its history is more dangerous than this. No one doubts that the survival of the church depends upon the grace of God working within us and our remaining open to the gospel. This process is more endangered by our assimilation into and complicity with the powers that stand against the gospel. Our distinctiveness as the people of God is endangered by an overbroad inclusiveness that sees as holy even the most profane and corrupt. We are called to the margins; we are called to be weak and separate and to view ourselves as such. We therefore must turn our back to all that is incompatible with the gospel. Jesus could not have proclaimed the Kingdom while he held a tax collection franchise or was employed as the Sanhedrin's comptroller.

What difficulties lie down this pathway we can overcome with the aid of the Spirit. But in order for the Spirit to work within us, we must maintain ourselves in faith. A significant aspect of that faith is the refusal to view persons who are not in the church as other. In rejecting the categories and values of the empires we are not indulging in nihilism; it is precisely because we are trying to live the gospel that the rejection of the empires is entailed. And our affirmation is the same affirmation that Jesus made on the cross: the death of Christ was not for Jews alone but for all creation. In affirming the universality of the gospel that is required by our discipleship, we must be open and welcoming to all. Beneath the corrupt institutions and false formations there are only people like us who search for God; they are not alien but parties to the covenant and the church is called to be for them a sign of the promise and redemption of the Lord. It is by being a visible and accessible community of faith, by recognizing the love of God in all persons that we can guard against the dangers and remain true to our call to be disciples.

NOTES

1. Tertulian, *De Praescriptionibus Haereticorum*, c. 7.

2. Alasdair MacIntyre, "God and the Theologians," in *Against the Self-Images of the Age* (Notre Dame, Ind.: University of Notre Dame Press, 1978), pp. 19–20.

3. "On Keeping Theological Ethics Theological" in *Revisions*, ed. Stanley Hauerwas and Alasdair MacIntyre (Notre Dame, Ind.: University of Notre Dame Press, 1983), p. 30.

4. Stanley Hauerwas, *Against the Nations* (Notre Dame, Ind.: University of Notre Dame Press, 1992), pp. 18–19.

5. Stanley Hauerwas, *The Peaceable Kingdom* (Notre Dame, Ind.: University of Notre Dame Press, 1983), p. 102.

6. Stanley Hauerwas, *In Good Company* (Notre Dame, Ind.: University of Notre Dame Press, 1995), p. 60.

7. Hauerwas, *Against the Nations*, p. 1.

8. Stanley Hauerwas and William Willimon, *Resident Aliens* (Nashville, Tenn.: Abingdon Press, 1989), p. 160.

9. Hauerwas, "Will the Real Sectarian Stand Up?" *Theology Today*, April 1987, p. 90. Hauerwas makes the same assertion in *Against the Nations*, p. 7.

10. Hauerwas uses this example earlier on p. 90 in "Real Sectarian."

11. Ibid.

12. Paraphrasing Richard d'Harcourt, quoted in Guenter Lewy *The Catholic Church and Nazi Germany* (McGraw Hill, 1964), p. 98.

13. I am not sure Hauerwas is prepared to go as far as I do in considering capitalism an idol every bit as bad as liberalism. For some of his critique of capitalism, see "Work as Co-Creation: A Critique of a Remarkably Bad Idea," *In Good Company*, pp. 109–24; "In Praise of Centesimus Annus," ibid., pp. 125–42; *Resident Aliens*, pp 119–20; *A Community of Character*, pp. 81–82. At times Hauerwas seems to consider capitalism good but fallen.

14. Hauerwas, *Against the Nations*, p. 7.

15. Hauerwas, *The Peaceable Kingdom*, p. 104.

16. Hauerwas and Willimon, *Resident Aliens*, p. 46.

17. I am indebted to Michael Budde for this term, which he has leveled at me in other contexts.

18. Martin Buber, *Between Man and Man* (Boston, Mass.: Beacon Press, 1955), p. 79.

19. I am not sure how far Hauerwas is willing to accept this position. It certainly seems that John Howard Yoder, from whom Hauerwas has derived much inspiration, views states and liberal politics with more validity than I would. In a future work I hope to critique Yoder's twin concepts of discernment and discrimination as they apply to states and their varied functions. Ultimately, I believe Yoder's position to be untenable.

20. Buber, *Between Man and Man*, p. 60.

21. While these two functions are not exhaustive, I think they are fundamental. Further, they encapsulate the notion of the "minimal state" praised both by political conservatives and Hauerwas.

6

Decisions That Inscribe Life's Patterns

Michael Warren

This essay is about Christian living in the future. None of us faces the future with a clean slate. Scribbled all over our slate are inscriptions of our recent past that, like the blood dripping from Bluebeard's tiny key that exposed to his bride his carnage, cannot be wiped away.[1] The inscriptions, like the red flow from the key, scream to us to pay attention to our past as we look to the future. This essay is partly about what is on that slate and partly about the possibility that future churches could repeat the worst lapses written there. Those lapses open the claims of Christian discipleship to ridicule, as much as they summon followers of the Jesus Way to pay more attention to what they actually do. Though these matters sound grim, my essay is written from a deep gospel hope that the Spirit of Jesus will perdure. While most of the essay is about practice, its first section grounds everything that follows in the question of social evil in our century. The next sections look at religious groups as engaged in two kinds of production processes. One is the active production of gospel living; the other, the passive ingesting of socially produced attitudes and perceptions hostile to the Spirit of Jesus. In the final sections I consider the production of conscious communal Christic practice and offer some strategies. As the title suggests, there is a lot here about decisions.

CENTENNIAL/MILLENNIAL QUESTIONS

Persons examining the historical record left by those who lived in the twentieth century will have the right to ask what significance local

127

Christian congregations had in that record. Christians, concerned for their tradition, may have a duty to ask this question. Whatever the social and cultural achievements of that century, they are overridden by the social and cultural horrors it produced. The number of those who died violently by calculated human intent in wars, massacres of civilian populations, and attempts to erase entire peoples from the face of the earth has surely been summed up somewhere. My own count hovers near 200 million, a number fattened by end-of-century horrors in the Balkans, where the religious convictions of Roman Catholic Croats, Russian Orthodox Serbs, and Bosnian Muslims did not check the slaughter of hundreds of thousands, and in Rwanda, where the Roman Catholicism of Hutus seems to have had little influence in stemming bestial behavior. This number does not include those killed by institutionalized social systems that starved and maimed human beings in the specially cruel ways that go with structural injustice. The enormity of the evil here seems to make blasphemous any attempt to do such a count, as if quantifying somehow allows our minds to deal with the evil done.

My question above focuses not so much on the significance of these deaths *for* groups of Christians looking back on them, but on the significance *of* those gospel-oriented groups that lived at the time or in the places where the horrors occurred and the significance such Christian groups may have in the future when similar horrors threaten. In our own century, did the group-life of those pledging fidelity to the words and deeds of the Galilean Jew of the first century C.E. make any difference, or attempt to, when victims were being singled out for killing? How many church-going Christians in Poland risked their lives to save Jews from the horrors awaiting them?[2] How much hatred of Jews existed in Roman Catholic Poland or Christian Germany long before the Nazis took over those lands and what forms did that hatred take? If that hatred was widespread, how did it happen that the sacred texts announced in weekly assemblies had such little hold on the hearts of the assembled? Worse, how did those texts, in their way of being interpreted and applied, provide the context for hatred?[3]

These questions are neither novel nor insightful. They are the standard sorts of questions asked in the face of our century. They need to be pressed on Christian assemblies concerned for the challenges ahead. What are the conditions required for "recognizing the Risen Lord?"[4] Asking such questions, local churches can examine whether their current procedures are adequate and consider new ways. The cultural shifts in the past eighty years call for a studied appraisal of the forms of communication and decision making currently in use in local churches. If a starting place for reappraisal is the condition of misery and suffering, I can turn to the questions the German theologian Metz brings to us about that condition.

Johannes Metz asks why the horrors and suffering of our times show up so little in theology? Is theology itself, as written by the learned or practiced by the "faithful," a conspicuous practice of apathy, that is, a way of ignoring the unjust suffering there in plain sight in our midst? How can theology reclaim its political version as action for the salvation of those who suffer unjustly here and now or its prophetic version as speech about the victims and the beaten-down of history? In Auschwitz, specifically, Metz finds "a horror that makes . . . [all] noncontextual talk about God appear empty and blind," in the face of which he asks, "Is there . . . a God whom one can worship with back turned to such a catastrophe?" At issue here is "the question of how one can speak of God at all in the face of the abysmal history of suffering in the world."[5] How indeed? How, now, in various of the more than 300,000 local religious assemblies in the United States today?[6] Can we speak of God (or of the groups pledging fidelity to God) without pretending there is no human collusion in the creation of suffering?

Metz's question of how to connect God and suffering not only deserves to be asked; he claims it is prompted from within the Judeo-Christian tradition itself, a landscape of cries to God, lamenting and objecting to God about unjust suffering. The talent for God, the capacity for God, found in Israel is marked by an incapacity to be consoled by neat ways of explaining away evil. "The language of [Israel's] God-mysticism is not primarily one of providing consoling answers to experiences of suffering; rather, it is much more a language of passionate requestioning that arises out of suffering, a requestioning of God, full of highly charged expectation." (621) Tied to this mysticism is what Metz calls "anamnestic reason," a reason that resists forgetfulness and instead, attends carefully to the silence of those who have disappeared, as a way of being attentive to Godself.

Metz's question sparks further questions—about the conditions under which a refusal to ignore or forget unjust suffering can become part of a local church. Considering the limitations of each person's attentiveness, how will a local assembly be able to maintain attentiveness to unjust suffering in our world as a condition necessary for the ecclesial landscape of cries and lament? By maintaining its communal landscape of cries and lament, the assembly may over time maintain both attentiveness as a mindset and action as a habit.

RELIGIOUS PRODUCTION

If attentiveness to unjust suffering is called for by our tradition, along with an action stance on behalf of victims, how is this "God mysticism" to be achieved? Another way of asking this question—a jarring way—is, How will it be produced? Can such a religious attitude or frame of reference be produced, or is it a gift of God's own self beyond human production? The question is important because it directs us to the specifics of the particulars of being Christians. Religious sociologist Robert Wuthnow invites us to consider the important matter of religious production: the intentional production of religious insights, convictions, commitments, rituals, patterns of response. With his invitation, however, comes a warning that the very idea of religious production may rub most of us the wrong way.[7] We have been taught to think of revelation as a gift of God, an epiphany disclosing God in God's way and at God's moment, not as a human product. Indeed, the New Testament emphasizes God's free intervention in Jesus' double birth: through Mary at Bethlehem and in the resurrection at Jerusalem. And yet, Wuthnow presses on us our teaching that God reveals Godself through human words and deeds—in a fully accessible human way, through very human processes.[8] This teaching is bolstered by current religious sociology.

Most sociologists of religion today make a distinction between religion and the sacred, with religion being a network of humanly devised procedures and the sacred being religion's inner core, which is of God. Sociologists have not always made this distinction. Like some of today's believers, many nineteenth-century sociologists dismissed this distinction but from an opposite direction. They held the sacred to be a confidence trick produced by religion as a way of making capitalism seem willed by God. In their view, religion takes humanly produced procedures and makes them seem to be made by God, that is, sacred. Thus religion produces a false consciousness, a basic misunderstanding of how the world actually works. The human hands behind various social procedures are disguised and the procedures themselves made to appear sacred and unquestionable.

As noted above, current sociology of religion honors the distinction between the human processes of religion and the sacred mediated by these processes. However, I find the oversimplifications of nineteenth-century sociology to have important lessons for religious professionals today. As a religious believer, I find, even in this perspective's most unnuanced version, a useful reminder of the possible distortions of humanly constructed religious forms. One such distortion is a sort of "institutional blindness" of some believers to the arbitrary character of many of religion's own procedures. Though not actually named as sacred, procedures of the group come gradually and quietly to be awarded an unwarranted sacral character. The way a chemical or mineral can bleed from one substance into another, the sacred can bleed unwittingly into this-worldly decisions and arrangements, rendering them unexaminable, unquestionable, and uncontestable. My essay seeks to unlock the door keeping procedures untouched and instead to invite examination, questioning, and if needed, contestation and reform.

Social science's more recent appreciation of religion's relation to the sacred can be helpful for religionists in their task of renewal, as Wuthnow's book shows. Current social science sees culture as a signifying system communicating a social order, that is, a humanly constructed system of meaning communicated by particular processes: gestures, language, rituals, laws, customs, even ways of cooking and eating. What is true of culture in general is also true of the cultural form called a religious tradition. In such a tradition the sacred is carried by "symbolic frameworks . . . set apart from everyday life, giving a sense of transcendent, holistic meaning."[9] The sacred gives us access to realities not so evident to human perception, but does so only by means of individuals, communities and organizations and the particular procedures they use to communicate.[10] While God may be unfathomable, a religious culture's "ways" can be measured and charted—and examined for appropriateness.

A friend told of his first deep sense of the sacred when he was fourteen years old. His memory of what happened may illustrate the concrete decisions and actions that led to his profound insight. In a large church near his all boys' high school, he was at a worship service opening the school year. Hearing hundreds of male voices singing a particular hymn, he found himself caught up in such a tingling sense of the presence of God that he never forgot the power of that moment, that place, that start to a new period of his life. The reality of God for him then was intense and ecstatic, seeming to lift him out of his own body. To recognize that sense of God was made possible by human procedures in a space constructed by human ingenuity to lend a special quality to the human voice, denies none of its reality. I do not claim that such a life-orienting insight defines the sacred, only that it was mediated by a human event. Nor was that sense of God, in all likelihood, exclusive to my friend but was available at various levels of insight to many others present in that group.

On reflection many recognize that in their own lives the sacred has become accessible and real—produced—through human agents or events that were channels of God's gifts. Some can name those agents and vividly describe places, events, and procedures many years after they occurred. However, the matter is not clear to all. Some think the sacred is communicated only by way of startling interventions of God, in acts that disrupt the laws of nature. Those who have taught the Bible have heard from students this complaint: the God who did marvels centuries ago as a means of communicating with mortals seems to have lost interest in them today. Students' evidence for this assertion is that God currently produces no similar marvels as a way of communicating with them. This misunderstanding, a stubborn one, can be corrected, not necessarily easily, through a more adequate theology, through insight into the interpretation of texts, and through more attention to the role of individuals, communities, and organizations in the communication of religious insight.

Even a quick reflection on the conditions under which my friend had his presence-of-God insight shows how ordinary activities of individuals, communities, and organizations helped shape that moment. He himself did not come into that church devoid of previous influences. He, his brother, and sisters came from a devout family, whose life was marked by regular times of worship and prayer, both within their home and in their local church. When he entered that church with his fellow students, his previous religious formation walked in with him, but accompanied by his religious struggles. He was questioning whether he wanted to accept as his own his family's religious commitments.

I have already mentioned the fact that the space of that church where he and so many others were gathered had been constructed to enhance a sense of God's presence by means of space, light, color, and sound. Further, he was with others, hundreds of them, whose presence was organized by teachers and administrators who awarded worship a significant part of the first day of school. The hymns sung had been taught those students, and the words said in unison were either memorized or available to be read off printed sheets. The orderly sequence of the ritual itself was also planned. What happened to him that day was no accident but an achievement of human intentionality backed by the gift of God.

Robert Wuthnow claims that a useful avenue for systematic reflection on these procedures is the "recent 'production of culture' literature in sociology that emphasizes the role of organizations, professionals, power arrangements, and other social resources in generating cultural artifacts, such as music, books, and art."[11] As a method of studying how cultural artifacts are produced in social contexts by communities and organizations, this perspective can also be used to examine how religious communities and organizations function in relation to the sacred.

Wuthnow illustrates this approach in an examination of how a particular person became an artist, specifically a painter. As I did above, he initiates a series of questions about the social conditions under which the crafting of a particular artwork was possible. Was there special training, and if so, what kind of financing made it possible? In the place where any actual painting was done, what was the physical space like: its dimensions, location, and any other conditions helpful to an artist? Who provided the space? What materials and technologies were used? How were they acquired? Was a particular work commissioned, by whom, at what cost? How did the one commissioning come to know the artist or the artist's work? How did any or all these factors influence the content of a particular painting?

But there is also the question of the artist's own self. How does one come to internalize for oneself the social role of the artist? Who were the mentors who influenced that role for a particular person? Did these mentors operate out of a particular model of an artist? Was there operating here a social process by which funding was made available or by which talent was recognized? Such questions can easily be applied to the cultural artifact we call religion.[12] For example how did the administrators of my friend's high school come to see that a large group worship service might beneficially displace the religious instruction given in a classroom that opening day of school?

Applied to a local church or congregation, these sorts of specific questions get at what I call the material conditions of the local church. They do not always produce exactly what the local assembly wishes; sometimes they produce unexpected results. Wuthnow warns us of this two-sided character of what is produced by these material conditions.

The important issue for our purposes is simply that cultural production results in both products and by-products, that is, intended results and unintended results. . . . Some of what they [organizations that produce public religion in our society] produce is deliberate and some is unplanned and unexpected. In both cases resources are expended, and social circumstances influence what happens.[13]

I think this warning has to be expanded, especially to meet the centennial or millennial critique of actual religious functioning. Sometimes religious groups or organizations produce results that disaffirm or deny the very realities they claim to affirm. Such communities can become radical living disconfirmations of their own sacred texts, official positions, and the very religious rituals in which they themselves engage. Our own century offers numberless examples of religious groupings being unable to break through socially and culturally constructed walls of ethnicity, nationalism, class, regionalism, *and* religion, to encounter the human beings of other religions, ethnicities, and so forth, as temples of the living God. The situation of being immured in one's own world of hate can be so counter to one's religious ethos it is denied to be possible, a denial that refuses to attend to the negative consequences of group decisions. Where this denial is in place, a community in a sense hides from its own self. My question: how can religious assemblies become more aware of what they actually live?

PATTERNING PERCEPTION ELECTRONICALLY

To repeat: these questions are not new. However, the situation in which they are asked is relatively new. A shorthand description of this situation would stress the role of culture in shaping people's perceptions and interpretations of their world.[14] Culture is a system of signs that successfully imprints in people the implicit and explicit codes undergirding a social order and its economic system. Every culture represents a way of imagining the shape of the humanum. Many of culture's codes are so deeply absorbed by being in the signifying system that people ordinarily do not think to explain or even mention them. Of central importance to religious persons is that these codes tend to function as norms for behavior and for ordinary judgments. In Ireland, driving a young woman to her home, I honk at a balky, uncertain driver. My passenger slouches down in her seat, so no one will see her presence with one who impolitely honks from impatience. Her behavior puzzles me, and she explains that *my behavior* violates an unspoken code of road courtesy: honk not, except to avoid an accident. New York's code is not acceptable in Cork.

In an unprecedented way, codes today can be quickly constructed, communicated, shifted, and refocused by means of electronically communicated images and narratives. The unprecedented character of electronically communicated meaning lies not in its character of newness. Because of the way this chain of meaning continues to evolve (or metastasize) exponentially, it is best termed as not just new but endlessly or progressively new. The social order's signifying system is "in our faces" so incessantly it takes on some of the taken-for-grantedness of social codes themselves. As George Gerbner says, "Children used to grow up in a home where parents told most of the stories. Today television tells most of the stories to most of the people most of the time."[15] Ironically, the most effective of these stories are not the main narratives that fill an hour of teletime but the fifteen- and thirty-second mini-tales that spike into the main narrative during commercial breaks. In the face of this electronically maintained world of meaning, one might ask what possibilities assemblies gathering weekly around the altar have of maintaining their alternate view of the world?[16]

Codes are norms; norms fuel judgment—like my passenger's judgment about my rude behavior on an Irish road. But there is a further side to this matter. Religions themselves are true cultures, though they exist within a wider culture. They represent special ways of imagining the shape of the human. They are signifying systems by which a social order is communicated, but a social order called for by God's self, a social order that is more than an idea, because of its being implemented via religious action, though not yet fully actual. Like the wider culture's, a religion's codes are also normative, and they are communicated through signs: narratives, patterns of ordinary action, and ritual actions like sharing bread and drinking from a common cup. Some of these religious codes offer cautionary judgments on the codes of the wider culture. Religion's "Your neighbor's misery is God's call to you," or as Emmanuel Levinas puts it, "The material needs of my neighbor are my spiritual needs,"[17] would be one such example of a commentary on the wider culture's codes. Notice that a consumerist culture does not say, Your neighbor is of no concern to you. Its message is more subtle and nuanced than that. It might rather say, When your neighbor's misery and your wants are in conflict, your wants take priority. Religion's imagination of the humanum contests that conclusion. An important feature of the wider culture's coded norms is that they tend to be implicit. Silently, claimlessly, they work their way into our behavior and "ways." However, religion's norms, coming as they do from a tradition and inscribed in texts, tend to be explicit. Coming from God, they add to their normativeness the edge of ultimacy. With ultimacy bestowed by God, these norms are worth living for and dying for. Here we encounter an irony worth the attention of all following religious traditions: the implicit norms can have greater power than the explicit ones. Implicit norms, ordinarily unspoken, are more difficult to contest than explicit ones with their open claims. Once the implicit norms have been internalized, explicit religious norms may be so used as to rarely intersect with, let alone contest, the norms of the wider culture.

In a time of electronic communications, the norms of consumerist culture, incessantly but implicitly communicated, seem to overwhelm the explicit, seemingly ultimate, not often articulated explicit norms of religion. Inert norms, announced but not embraced, known but not applied, are in fact no norms at all. They are the idea of a norm. Norms, when embraced, configure a stance, a positioning of the self or of the community in the face of situations judged by the norms. In this sense a norm is very much like a belief, as described by Charles Sanders Peirce: "The essence of belief is the establishment of a habit, and different beliefs are distinguished by the different modes of action to which they give rise."[18] When some in an audience stand and boo a poor opera performance, the norm they honor in their noisy, impolite protest to bad singing is that of good singing. In their application, however, norms are not rigid, because seeking benchmarks or standards, they plot possibility along a line of more or less. If applying norms is an art, not a science, they are matters for discussion. Norms are sharpened by being applied, by attention to the specifics and nuance [the materiality] of what is being judged, by remembering conditions under which some past stunning achievement came about, and by maintaining a sense of what "the more" could be. Alas, lacking these efforts, the normative "eye," the sense of what is right, and the ability to make a nuanced evaluation, can be lost through disuse.

If norms fuel judgment and judgment fuels action, the question seems to be: Under what conditions can religious groups embrace their norms, consciously use them in judgments, and opt for forms of action consistent with those judgments? Norms are not only accepted and applied individually. Their chief form is found in the communal dimension of judgment, where persons are invited into the circle of norms to grapple with the problem of application to concrete situations. An individual or a group cannot decide for others or apply norms for others, because deciding, norming, and judging require full human agency, and for a group, result from an interactive process. There is no group stance without the struggle to see how norms apply or to discern the difference they make. Today, deciding or "decisioning" is a key religious act, and its absence represents a yawning religious void. Without decisioning, true religious action is replaced with rote repetition.[19] My purpose here is to foster reflection on decisions and action taken after gospel-based judgments are made. At the start of this essay I alluded to the Bluebeard folktale. The cautionary element in that story in not about Bluebeard himself or how he became a monster; it is the question of how and why the naive young sister came to choose him as her life partner, despite warning clues. In the following paragraphs I will reflect briefly on the consequences of decisions.

JUDGMENT, DECISION, BEHAVIOR, EXCLUSIONS

Social philosopher Albert Borgmann seeks to question the modern segregation of doing and making, of decisions about conduct from decisions about technology. As a result of this separation, morality becomes the realm of conduct, presumed to be segregated from the realm of production. This segregation of doing from producing "fails to see that a technological accomplishment, the development and adoption of a technological device always and already constitutes a moral decision."[20] Products, the material results of production, have profound power to shape our conduct, all the greater when that power is not recognized. Borgmann finds badly flawed and unhelpful any moral theory that dismisses as basically neutral the material setting of society. The materiality of our world has important moral implications for the very specific kinds of decisions we make. Here I will recount some of Borgmann's analysis of decision making as being of potential help to the local church.

Understanding the character of decisions sheds light on the significance of particular decisions for behavior and the overall patterning of our lives. All of us "entrust" our aspirations to various kinds of decisions that anchor our spirits in specific deeds, the specific marks of that self in the world. Borgmann makes helpful distinctions. A daily personal decision is different from a fundamental decision, the daily decision being made on a particular day for that day only. A fundamental personal decision, however, is an action marked by a different character of intention, one binding us to a whole pattern of action over many days into the future. A desire to become more familiar with Shakespeare's plays can lead to either a daily or a fundamental decision. If the desire leads to a daily decision to read some play of Shakespeare's or even something about his plays, that decision must be remade day after day. A fundamental decision is different; it looks ahead and binds us to a chain of actions over many days to come, like enrolling in a course on Shakespeare at a local college, and carrying out corollary actions: paying tuition, buying books, setting aside time for class and study, and so forth. For a fundamental personal decision to be suitable, it must have some promise of being carried out. Records will show that not all who sign up for Shakespeare have made a decision suited to being carried out.[21]

Borgmann makes a further distinction about our decisions. A decision that shapes our material environment he at first calls a fundamental *moral* decision, but quickly shifts to naming it a fundamental *material* decision, calling attention thereby to the moral implications of material decisions. When such a decision is made without responsible insight, that shaping of our environment can be harmful to us or at least can have unforeseen consequences. Parents whose home is hooked up to a cable network decide their nine year old daughter may have a TV in her bedroom at the top of the house. They have decided to allow her, once in that room alone, unsupervised access at any hour to a range of televisual "entertainment," some of it unsuitable to one her age. In Borgmann's view the decision to allow the TV in the bedroom is moral not so much because there may be unseemly programming on it but because the decision shifts the relational patterns between child and parents, among others in the home, and ultimately, the pattern of influences. The child of nine may now find herself in the electronic hands of persons who imagine for her the shape of the human, persons her parents might never have allowed into their home had they met them first.

Borgmann himself uses an astute example, also involving electronic communications, that discloses the importance of material decisions.

> Gary Larsen has pictured his father and his family "in the days before television." Dad is sitting on the couch, son and daughter lying on the floor, the dog between them, all four staring at the same blank wall. Once the situation that was tacitly assumed is rendered explicit, it becomes a cartoon and reveals *the absurdity of the assumption that life has empty slots that can be filled without needing to rearrange the order of life* [emphasis added]. Life is always and already full; it is a total fabric. It may contain empty spaces for inconsequential additions. But if anything is added to life that takes time, the web of life is torn and rewoven; a hole is made by the new device. Saving and taking time come down to the same thing here. A time-saving device creates a hole in traditional practices no less than does a device that devours time.
>
> Once a television set is in the house, the daily decision whether to read a book, or write a letter, or play a game, or tell stories, or go for a walk, or sit down to dinner, or watch television no longer really ranges over seven possibilities. The pres-

ence of television had compressed all alternatives to one whose subalternatives are contained in the question: What are we going to watch tonight?[22]

What Borgmann has described here is a "material decision," which in this case was a decision to purchase something that patterned a group's behavior and interaction—the fabric of group life.

Fundamental and material decisions made at a personal or family level can also be made at the collective level, which proves to be the key level in Borgmann's analysis. When made at the collective level, decisions tend to coax along or "preform" the decisions made at the individual and family level. For example, when a collective decision leaves TV signals too weak for good reception in some area, residents may be pushed to rely on a cable system. What Borgmann is sorting out here is a chain of influences in decision making. In his schema then,

1.   fundamental personal and material personal decisions preform the daily decisions by shaping the context of those daily decisions. The fundamental personal decision to study for a degree or the material decision not to own an automobile affects many daily decisions.

2.   Collective material decisions preform the personal fundamental and material decisions. Collective decisions about public transportation and about the nonimportance of sidewalks also shape decisions at the individual level, like the purchase of an automobile. The already constructed patterns of cable TV fare preforms or shapes what results if a decision is made to allow a TV in a child's bedroom.

Borgmann's point is that decisions are particular and affect behavior. His chief concern is to cast more attention to material decisions, both personal and collective. Churches would do well to consider the implications of this point for their own group life. By naming these categories of decisions he helps us attend to them more thoughtfully and intentionally They shift the particularities of our lives. Such attention is important: "The moral fabric of family life is typically patterned not so much by practices as by acquisitions, by material decisions, as I will call them, rather than by practical decisions."[23]

Borgmann's analysis of modernity also provides an interesting way of looking at judgment, of some importance to religious persons. He notices that modern common sense distinguishes between private and public, with the private seen as the sphere of individual discretion and the public the sphere of collective regimentation. Admittedly this polarity has ancient roots in seeing family life as the zone of intimacy and seclusion as opposed to the open, inclusive life of civic engagement. Today, however, the realm of the private has come to be seen as a place where "commodious individualism" can be pursued—but protected by "privacy," a word that designates the essence of the private realm. Borgmann notes that increasingly in our time privacy has been defined as *"freedom from intrusions that can lead to an unwarranted judgment* [emphasis added] on the person whose sphere of intimacy has been invaded."[24] Family members who comprise our private circle and those friends allowed into that circle may make judgments, but no one else is entitled to. What is being protected here from judgment is "the unencumbered enjoyment of consumption goods or commodities . . . , the collective affirmation of consumption as an exercise of freedom."[25] In the end no judgments about consumption are to be made by any person at all, because the ultimate space of privacy is not occupied by a single person but by a single *consumer*.

Borgmann's analysis is cited here in detail for its way of getting at a little noticed but important exclusion of a whole area of life from reflection in religious congregations. Obviously the entire private realm is not excluded, since congregations give attention to kindness toward one's loved ones and to sexual fidelity. Excluded is reflection on how we think about and use money and leisure, the closely guarded commodities of privacy. A kind of silent, even unwitting collusion has agreed that this vital area is out of bounds for religious discourse—and with it the whole question of public resources. Ironically, what religious discourse dares not discuss, commercial orchestrators of human desire use every conceivable stratagem to manipulate. Once such issues are implicitly agreed to be out of bounds for discussion, no gospel norms are allowed and no judgments, even tentative ones, can be made about money and leisure. The use of an assembly's common funds might provoke vigorous discussion, but the discussion dares not spill over to how we deal with our own personal, private finances. Roman Catholic preaching almost never attends to the use of money as a religious question, except in the case of tithing for the local church. In considering this matter, I came to ask myself what of value a church might say even should it attempt to do so.

This matter is not settled by mathematical formulas but by a communal grappling with scriptural texts and with the various ways the tradition has met the question. Norms are not be imposed from outside, any more than religious conviction are. Are there conditions under which a worshiping assembly can begin to ponder personal finances and similar questions and respond to them? Religious texts raise important questions about our responsibilities to others and the use of resources, including money, in meeting those responsibilities.

I am aware that thus far I have intentionally sketched in bold strokes outlines that need to be filled in. Attention to human misery of our time, recognition of the materiality of religious living, facing the problem of the two cultures and of religious judgment, and understanding how decisions shape our private and collective lives—these tasks provide important lines of ecclesial self-reflection. I now proceed to another broad area that may help us reflect on the materiality of the church.

PRACTICE GUIDED BY VISION

In the preparation of this essay I found myself studying various proposals for Christian living. Apparently, the problem of living Jesus' vision of the human never ceases to be a problem, with the most difficult task being "reformulating the assumptions, rules, forms, and practices" of the congregation.[26] That vision tends to go off course, especially from the pulls of culture that are not so responsive to it. Through the ages various strategies have sought to "re-specify" the specifics of the gospel in a way suited for a particular time. Readers will find communities of renegotiated discipleship in their own areas, though not necessarily in their own denomination in these areas. Wherever they are found, communities of radical discipleship deserve to be closely examined for how they have come to embody the gospel in such tangible, believable ways.

One of the characteristics of renegotiated discipleship is the development of "rules" or codes of conduct and practice. Such codes marked the earliest Christian communities and can be found throughout the New Testament. Respecified, such codes also marked monastic groups. The fact they existed at all is instructive, but even more so is that they are still being used by those intent on a community that stands somewhere particular and for something specific. I myself wonder if such specifying codes are not in fact quite normal, even when unwritten and implicit in the sort of "geist" fostered by a local church. Here I will comment on some recent proposals for such rules or codes. However, I warn readers that the matter of these codes is awkward, even dangerous.

Although such codes have been taken up in the interests of reform and renewal, every one I know of has had to be re-reformed and read-justed after a period of time when it became routine. Also, some "rules" became inflexible, not leaving any room for their adherents to adjust to new situations and what they meant for gospel fidelity. Unfortunately, the inflexible love rules. The sorts of rules I will present here are not havens for the inflexible but directives for the creative, carefully engi-neered sextants offering points of orientation in times when careful sail-ing is called for. I first started reflecting on such codes in my attention to the "way" of Transfiguration Parish in Brooklyn. It is an extraordinary local church whose very life is its message and its means of formation. In speaking with those who helped re-found this church in its current renewal that began around 1968, I found they adopted a particular kind of spirituality, as a kind of gospel way within the gospel way. This par-ticular spirituality was embodied in a network of evolving communal practices designed to foster it. These leaders decided they would follow the spirituality of Charles de Foucauld, an agnostic and libertine French military officer who was converted to Jesus and eventually went off to North Africa to live and die among the people he found to be the poor-est of the poor, the Tuareg nomads of the desert.[27] For those who might come to join him, he mapped the way he had set out for himself. This "way" was actually a Christian spirituality that prized solidarity with the poor and a life of poverty. This spirituality now guides a local church in the Williamsburgh section of Brooklyn. Such "ways within the Way" are not unusual.[28]

Though a detailed examination of this particular local church is beyond the scope of this paper, a sketch might help anchor my concerns. From a single base community committed to Foucauld's spirituality in 1969, there are now about twenty-five such communities, of nearly twenty persons each. These groups meet once a week to reflect on the scriptural readings for the coming Sunday in the light of their everyday lives. Representatives of these groups meet on Saturday morning in a kind of assembly to help the pastor prepare his homily. He is enabled to speak both out of the life of the community and into the life of the com-munity. The community has three week-long festivals of learning: in Advent, Lent, and Pentecost, each followed by a street festival of eating, drinking, and dancing. Through discussion and consensus, the homilies for each year all deal with a particular theme, as do the learning festi-vals. Discussion and consensus also mark the process of discerning the gifts of individuals in the community and of calling them to serve the community in particular ways.

In a place teeming with immigrants without documents, the parish has a full-time lawyer advocating for immigration rights and social benefits. In winter, its family shelter cares for about ten families, while up to fifteen undocumented men live in the parish house, originally built for two priests. The parish convent houses more than ten undocumented women. Living in this community of reflection and action is its core way of communicating gospel commitments. Education is endemic, that is, located among the people and flowing from the life of a people. For those seeking it, intensive strategies of Christian formation are available. Those in the base communities make up to two weekend retreats a year at a secluded rural dwelling given to the parish for such purposes.

Such a community sets for itself guidelines that are always flexible, open to reconsideration and revision in changing situations, and attuned to particular needs. Lacking clear and courageous ways of honoring conflicts and dealing with them wisely, such a community would soon move into rigidities and eventually collapse.

Another example of a communal rule of life or set of guidelines is the following sketch of a proposed rule of life written by the New Zealand poet, James K. Baxter for the Jerusalem Community, a Maori settlement on the Wanganui River in New Zealand.[29] Whether it was actually adopted by the community, I do not know, but it seems to have been the rule that guided Baxter's last years of life.

A Cast-Iron Programme for Communal Activity

Feed the hungry;
Give drink to the thirsty;
Give clothes to those who lack them;
Give hospitality to strangers;
Look after the sick;
Bail people out of jail, visit them in jail, and look after them
    when they come out of jail;
Go to neighbors' funerals;
Tell other ignorant people what you in your ignorance think
    you know;
Help the doubtful to clarify their minds and make their own
    decisions;
Console the sad;
Reprove sinners, but gently, brother and sister, gently;
Forgive what seems to be harm done to yourself;
Put up with difficult people;
Pray for whatever has life, including the spirits of the dead.

Where these things are done, Te Wairua Tapu [the Holy Spirit] comes to live in our hearts, and doctrinal differences and difficulties begin to vanish like the summer snow.[30]

While significant for its brevity, this statement is shocking for its difficult particularity. If the gospel itself is an interpretive lens by which to view all reality, the above plan of action is an interpretive lens on the gospel. If followed it would give the gospel an unaccustomed edge in a time of bureaucracy. Rooted in specific words of Jesus, it captures the flavor of the gospel. Baxter calls it a "programme," that is a plan to be followed. I prefer the term "rule" because it suggests a guiding norm against which to measure actual living.

The history of Christianity is threaded with such rules, set forth as a way of making the following of Jesus more specific in particular circumstances. In fact, as hinted above, every Roman Catholic and Protestant religious order I know of lives according to a rule. One of the most famous early ones, the archetype of most that have been written since, is the Rule of Benedict, still followed today. Benedict's rule led to numberless variations found today in the "rules" of religious orders in the various denominations. The Franciscan rule is another famous guide for following Jesus in a particular time. Francis' rule met the rise of a new market economy head on with its own embrace of poverty and the condition of the poor. This latter rule is as instructive in its many revisions as it is in its original insight. Again and again, by becoming gradually accommodated to culture and the comforts proposed by culture, the Franciscan rule lost its radical gospel edge. Endless reforms of Franciscan life—including several breakaway Franciscan orders—were needed to bring the rule back to its original direction.[31]

To repeat, these rules were ways of bringing our sacred texts to bear on very particular social circumstances hostile or at least not open to the words and deeds of Jesus. In effect they proclaimed: having studied our Word of God, this is what we see it means for living in this time and in this place. In our struggle to understand discipleship, we have come to see that these particular ways are how we must strive to live. In such rules, all written after the demise of the catechumenate, the concerns of the ancient catechumenate and the processes of life reform embodied in it were carried on in the church.

Could it be that any gathering of people espousing discipleship would benefit by adopting such a rule for their own local life, if only because such a rule could not be written and accepted except after extended discussion of the character of discipleship today? Here I am thinking of a rule more particular than the ethos of a denomination, which is itself a particularizing and interpreting of the meaning of Jesus' words and deeds. What would happen when a congregation of a denomination began to follow its own adopted rule of what its life stood for and what its priorities would be? Would such a step allow a fidelity focused toward particularities of a congregation's situatedness? A local church is situated in a neighborhood, a city, a state, a nation, and a world.

James K. Baxter's Programme for Communal Activity is clearly focused on very local sorts of needs, though his attention to those needs connected him to a broader vision beyond the local. A year or two before his death he wrote,

> If I say that contemporary society is unfree, I do not mean simply that one can't do what one feels like. Communal freedom itself is never absolute. To be free from the commercial and technological and military obsessions of modern society would mean only to enter a gap, a limbo, an area of unrelated personal isolation, if there were not also the freedom to cooperate and relate to other human beings.
>
> Certainly in contemporary society our personal freedom is absurdly limited. We can be jailed, for example, for swearing in the street or for having no job and no money. But the terrible aspect of our lack of freedom is the fact that we are not free to act communally, when communities are everywhere ceasing to exist, and only a desacralised, depersonalised Goliath remains to demand our collective obedience.
>
> I do not relish the role of David, in confronting that Goliath, who numbs the soul wherever he touches it. But I find myself curiously, perhaps absurdly, cast in that role. And the five water-worn stones I choose from the river, to put in my sling, are five spiritual aspects of Maori communal life—
>
> *arohanui*: the Love of the Many;
> *manuhiritanga*: hospitality to the guest and the stranger;
> *korero*: speech that begets peace and understanding;
> *matewa*: the night life of the soul;
> *mahi*: work undertaken from communal love.
>
> I do not know what the outcome of the battle will be. My aim may be poor. But I think my weapons are well chosen.[32]

A group of priests I know who meet regularly to discuss their ministry, encourage one another, and pray have adopted "Rule for a New

Brother," originally written for use in a Dutch community of brothers. This rule is brief: fifty-eight pages, each no more than twenty-four lines, and the rule is written in verse form, with only a few words to a line. In the genre of a book of advice, this rule sketches the priorities and attitudes needed to be a disciple but also the specific behaviors called for in a community of disciples. A sample:

> The community is the place where you daily share riches and poverty, energy and weakness, joy and sorrow, success and failure, your hope and your doubt. In this kind of community can grow something of Christ's bond with His father: "All that I have is yours, all that you have is mine." Live like a poor person without parading your poverty. Stand by the poor wherever they live and work. Your first love must go out to the least of persons. Don't tie yourself down to the rich or powerful of the world. Get rid of the inclination to court the great and influential. Otherwise you would deform the image of the church.[33]

One of the most imaginative of such rules I have come across is the complete reworking of the text of Benedict's rule so as to apply it to family life, done by Larry Spears, a Quaker husband, father, and lawyer. Spears is well aware of the dangers of writing such a rule for family life, but holds that a rule is actually a living tradition, providing "a means of passing on, adapting and concretizing the previous tradition in a new context," a way "to preserve the guidance of the past in establishing the norms of human life now."[34] Any culture, but especially a religious culture, needs to find a way in a new context to preserve and pass on the wisdom gained in the past. According to Spears, when what is being preserved and passed on is a way of living basically unconformed to a society's lifestyle and values, then special intentionality and conscious effort are needed. Otherwise, the general lifestyle of a society becomes the norm established for and lived by the family.

Spears sees a rule as a guide to right practice, for the ordering of the patterns that determine our attention and our actions. In the Rule of Benedict, he finds a model of practical wisdom capable of being adapted to life today and to families. How credible is his claim? What sorts of problems may underlie Spears' proposal? Can a *monastic* rule devised in the sixth century be adapted for family life in the twenty-first century? Will such an adaptation lead to children unprepared for life in our time? Will it mean the rejection of all aspects of modernity? How will parental authoritarianism or manipulation be avoided, along with the possibility of children rejecting their entire formation as arbitrarily imposed on them? If parents have opted for this rule, under what conditions will their children make this option, especially when they realize it is not followed by the families of their friends? Is Spears' proposal the equivalent of imposing an Amish lifestyle on all Anabaptists or a monastic lifestyle on all Catholics?

Spears answers these questions, not point by point but in general. He points out that all families tend to follow implicit rules set by the patterns of decisions that haphazardly coalesce into patterns of behavior. In some families, such an implicit rule might be, "You can watch any TV program before dinner (or early in the morning) as long as you do not disturb Mom or Dad preparing dinner (or sleeping late Saturday or Sunday morning)." The operative family "rule" is either clear or hidden. An overt rule may prove unwise, but since its presence is not denied it can be challenged. A covert rule, adopted but not acknowledged, is not open to reconsideration or adaptation. "The hidden rule is passed on hidden to new generations, along with habits and ideas of little importance. Undistinguished from the trivia, its impact can generate serious problems in family life" (145–46).

It might be added—though Spears does not advert to the fact—most families have their little library of "how to" guides directing them to specific procedures in children's health care and in shaping children's behavior in matters ranging from eating habits to patterns of preparing children for bed. In many churchgoing families such guides and their specifics, are not supplemented by guides to religious specifics. At the outset of his proposal, Spears challenges families that find his rule unacceptable, to develop an alternative rule. If parts of his proposal seem improper, families should devise more suitable guidelines.

If Spears were to revise his own proposal, I would suggest more attention to influences beyond the household. One of these is the "ways" of other families on any family's life practice, influencing especially through the children. Since such ways can be negative or positive, they call for being decoded in terms of the family's own code of life. If a family were in touch with other families who had also adapted for their circumstances a rule for Christian living—or even with one family who had done so—its own rule would have more coherence. Perhaps a circle of wise parents would be a needed buttress for such a rule. Lacking this attention, Spears' approach might be seen as individualistic. Other influences to be faced but not mentioned in Spears' rule are those of television, film, or radio. Wise rules about these features of current life will probably not come easily.

Spears' insight—and the insight of Transfiguration Parish and the other examples cited here—is that Christian living is forged from the particularities of everyday life, especially from decisions about practices. Circumstances must be discerned in the light of the gospel. Though often ignored, that insight has deep roots in the beginning of the Christian way and at all points in the tradition. It needs to be reclaimed today by the local churches. This insight, further, could ground communal struggle toward a renewed practice. Another way of making the same point:

> [T]he church's practices impede our ability to faithfully proclaim and hear the Scripture. Our failure to understand what Paul "really meant" is not the problem. Our problem is that we live in churches that have no practice of nonviolence, of reconciliation, no sense of the significance of singleness; so we lack the resources to faithfully preach and hear God's Word. If such an approach means that I risk being "unscholarly," it is a risk well worth taking in order to free theology from its academic captivity.[35]

NOTES

1. See Iona and Peter Opie, *The Classic Fairy Tales* (New York: Oxford University Press, 1974), pp. 103–109.

2. For a brief but stirring account of one who did—Maria Bochenek—see Mark Patinkin, "A Narrow Edge of Life, Death," The Seattle *Times*, 21 May 1986, p. A6. Bochenek was honored and memorialized on Jerusalem's Avenue of the Righteous.

3. See Ronald Modras, *The Catholic Church and Anti-Semitism: Poland 1933–1939* (Harwood Academic, 1996).

4. This is the provocative phrase probed by Marianne Sawicki, first in "Recognizing the Risen Lord," *Theology Today* 44, no. 4 (1988): 441–49, and then more comprehensively in *Seeing the Lord:Resurrection and Early Christian Practices* (Minneapolis, Minn.: Fortress, 1994).

5. Johann Baptist Metz, "Suffering unto God," *Critical Inquiry* 20 (Summer, 1994): 611, 612. Dorothee Soelle's eloquence on this matter is well known in such works as *Suffering* (Philadelphia: Fortress, 1975) and *The Strength of the Weak: Toward a Christian Feminist Identity* (Philadelphia: Westminster, 1984).

6. R. Stephen Warner, "The Place of the Congregation in the Contemporary American Religious Configuration," in *American Congregations*, vol. 2, *New Perspectives in the Study of Congregations* ed. James P. Wind and James W. Lewis (London and Chicago: University of Chicago Press, 1994), p. 55.

7. Robert Wuthnow, *Producing the Sacred: An Essay on Public Religion* Chicago: University of Illinois Press, 1994).

8. For an illuminating examination of these human ways, and especially of how language is a key vehicle for encountering God see Nicholas Lash, *Easter in Ordinary*: Reflections on Human Experience and the Knowledge of God (Notre Dame, Ind.: University of Notre Dame Press, 1988), esp. pp. 1–70.

9. Wuthnow, *Producing the Sacred*, p. 3.

10. Paul Berman wrote: "The single greatest shift in the history of mass-communication technology occurred in the fifteenth century. . . . It was a cathedral . . . an awesome engine of communication." The cathedral told the history of Creation and of Christianity itself. Quoted in Vartan Gregorian, "A Place Elsewhere: Reading in the Age of the Computer," *Bulletin of the American Academy of Arts and Sciences* 49, no. 4 (January 1996): 54–64, at 54.

11. Wuthnow, *Producing the Sacred*, p. 6.

12. Ibid., pp. 25–27, passim.

13. Ibid., p. 27.

14. For more detail, see chapters 1 and 2, "The Problem of Popular Culture," and "What Is Culture," of *Communications and Cultural Analysis: A Religious View* (Westport, Conn.: Bergin and Garvey, 1992).

15. George Gerbner, "The Challenge of Television," (unpublished paper, Annenberg School of Communication, University of Pennsylvania), p. 8.

16. This question can be asked about the creation of hate in Rwanda via radio broadcasts by a relatively small group of Hutus bent on genocide. One can ask whether this electronic creation of meaning was countered by a religious proposal of a counter-meaning of love? See, Robert Block, "The Tragedy of Rwanda," New York *Review of Books* 41:17 (20 October 1994): 3–8; and Philip Gourevitch, "Letter from Rwanda: After the Genocide," *New Yorker* (18 December 1995): 77–94.

17. Levinas quotes here the Lithuanian rabbi, Israel Salanter. See Denis Donoghue, "The Philosopher of Selfless Love," New York *Review of Books* (21 March 1996): 37–40, at 38.

18. "How to Make Our Ideas Clear," in *Writings of Charles Sanders Peirce: A Chronological Edition*, vol. 3 [1872–78] (Bloomington: Indiana University Press, 1986), pp. 257–75, at 263–64.

19. A further question, but one I will not deal with here, is: Under what conditions can the best of the norms in each culture enrich the human imagination of the other cultural sector? When each sector is true to the best in its tradition, when each embraces what in its "way" enriches the humanum, then the cross-fertilization of each sector will be fruitful.

20. Albert Borgmann, *Crossing the Postmodern Divide* (Chicago: University of Chicago Press, 1993), p. 110.

21. Of course it is possible to do an action without intending any decision let alone commitment, and still find oneself involved in a network of consequences to which one judges oneself quite unsuited. A casual erotic encounter leading to fatherhood and its cares might be one example. For a stunning nar-

rative of a misdeed unintentionally leading to a lifelong commitment, see Ann Tyler, *Saint Maybe* (New York: Knopf, 1991).

22. Albert Borgmann, *Crossing the Postmodern Divide* (University of Chicago Press, 1993). The quote is from p. 111, but I have summarized here and there from pp. 110–15.

23. Ibid., p. 112.

24. Ibid., p. 42.

25. Ibid., p. 43.

26. Rebecca Chopp, "Situating the Structure: Prophetic Feminism and Theological Education," in *Shifting Boundaries: Contextual Approaches to the Structure of Theological Studies* ed. Farley and Wheeler (Louisville, Ky.: Westminster/John Knox, 1991), pp. 67–89, at 86.

27. A very readable life of de Foucauld is, Marion Mill Preminger, *The Sands of Tamanrasset*: The Story of Charles de Foucauld (New York: Hawthorne Books, 1961); for a more scholarly biography see Philip Hillyer, *Charles de Foucauld*, vol. 9 of The Way of the Christian Mystics, Gen. ed., Noel Dermot O'Donoghue (Collegeville, Minn.: The Liturgical Press, 1990).

28. One passage from this Rule for what he named as "The Little Brothers of the Sacred Heart": "The Little Brothers will not only gladly welcome the guests, the poor, the sick who ask for hospitality; they will invite in those whom they encounter, begging them, kneeling if necessary like Abraham to the angels, not to 'pass your servants by' without accepting their hospitality, their attentions, their marks of brotherly love. Everyone in the neighborhood must know that the Fraternity is the house of God where every poor or sick person is always invited, called, wanted, welcomed with joy and gratitude by brothers who love and cherish them and regard their entry as the discovery of a great treasure. They are in fact the greatest treasure of all, Jesus himself: 'Insofar as you do this to one of the least of these brothers of mine, you do it to me?'"

A Little Brother of Jesus, *Silent Pilgrimage to God: The Spirituality of Charles de Foucauld*, trans. Jeremy Moiser (Maryknoll, New York: Orbis Books, 1977), p. 43.

29. See James K. Baxter, *Collected Poems*, ed. J. E. Weir (Wellington and New York: Oxford University Press, 1980); *Selected Poems*, ed. J. E. Weir (Wellington and New York: Oxford University Press, 1982); and *Autumn Testament* (Wellington: Price Milburn, 1972). Roughly a fourth of Baxter's 2,600 poems appear in the *Collected Poems*.

30. From James K. Baxter, *Jerusalem Daybook* (Wellington: Price Milburn, 1971), pp. 11–12.

31. See Lester Little, "Evangelical Poverty, The New Money Economy and Violence," in David Flood, ed., *Poverty in the Middle Ages* (Werl/Westfl.: Dietrich-Coelde-Verlag, 1975), pp. 11–26. All the essays in this little volume are valuable.

32. James K. Baxter, *Jerusalem Daybook*, pp. 53–54.

33. Brakkenstein Community of Blessed Sacrament Fathers, Holland, "Regel voor een nieuwe broeder." English translation by the Benedictine Nuns

of the Benedictine Priory "Regina Pacis," published as: *Rule for a New Brother* (Springfield, Ill.: Templegate Publishers, 1976), pp. 24–25.

34. Larry Spears, "A Rule for Families of Faith," *American Benedictine Review* 40, no. 2 (June): 142–69, at 143.

35. Stanley Hauerwas, *Unleashing the Scriptures: Freeing the Bible from Captivity to America* (Nashville, Tenn.: Abingdon, 1993), p. 8.

7

Legion and the Believing Community: Discipleship in an Imperial Age

Curt Cadorette

INTRODUCTION

As a graduate student at the University of Chicago several decades ago, one of my New Testament professors often characterized the Gospel of Mark as the least sophisticated of the synoptic texts. His judgement was due to the author's rustic Greek and penchant for healing and miracle scenes that stretched the imagination and presumably offended his theological taste. Surely, Mark is no master of koine, but more recently scholars have come to recognize that the healing and miracle stories in the gospel have deep psychological and theological significance. Mark wants his readers to make a connection between Jesus the Galilean Jew and their own lives as people who have come to understand Jesus as the Christ. Like the woman with a hemorrhage or Jairus' daughter, they count for nothing in the Greco-Roman world, yet they are the recipients of healing grace that has turned them into disciples. Even the Roman centurion who witnesses Jesus' death in the name of the empire proclaims the truth—that an utterly insignificant Jew, crucified by Rome like so many of his compatriots, is the incarnation of God's very self.

Mark wants his readers to recognize that their existence as disciples calls into question the imperial scheme of things that crucified Jesus and now persecutes them as well. The reign of God is a subversive proposition that Rome will not tolerate because it generates hope among the hopeless. It calls everything into question—from daily injustices to the idols of empire—not through political confrontation but rather by making community and equality among the poor and oppressed real, life-giving possibilities. God's reign even overcomes the slow and horrible death of crucifixion. Because Jesus has been raised the empire's victims find hope and life in his person and each other. Mark's lack of literary sophistication is more than compensated for by his powerful description of discipleship as an act of faith and courage in the reality of God alive in Jesus and the believing community that forms the body of Christ.

One of the most intense and unusual healing stories in Mark's Gospel is located at the beginning of the fifth chapter where Jesus exorcises and welcomes into God's reign the most unlikely of candidates, a tormented demoniac. Trained in Western educational institutions, most of us are bound to find this passage a bit jarring, perhaps even embarrassing. We quickly equate the demoniac's behavior with some variety of psychosis. This is not a totally invalid reaction, but it misses the point. By relying on psychological categories we fail to see the deeper symbolism behind the story that is far more important than an empirical explanation. Mark wants us to appreciate the destructive power of Rome manifest in a polymorphous demon called Legion. Rome's power is more than political. The empire is actually a destructive psychosocial reality, a distorted way of being, predicated on the brutal oppression of innocent people. This is the malevolence that has taken over the demoniac's self-consciousness, just as a virus takes over and destroys its host.

Mark wants us to marvel at the way Jesus and his God give new life to the demoniac by forcing him to tell the truth about the malevolent powers within him, despite his initial aversion to the truth. Even more amazing is the fact that he becomes a disciple. In the next few paragraphs I will analyze the deeper significance of the Gerasene demoniac in light of our own tortured world with imperial forces more deadly than those of Rome. Next, I will explore the challenges Christian communities face in the developing world and intentional Christian communities in the developed world where imperial power continues to wreak havoc with people's lives, albeit in different ways.[1] Different socioeconomic and cultural forces are at play at the periphery and center of the empire, which explain the differences between base and intentional communities. Understanding these differences will help us better recognize their more significant similarities as believing communities committed to healing discipleship in a divided, increasingly unjust world. First, however, we need to look at the Gerasene demoniac at closer range.

FRAGMENTATION AND FUSION BY THE SEA OF GALILEE

Mark's description of the nameless demoniac who wanders among the tombs of Gerasene is not nearly as unusual or hyperbolic as we might think. In fact, the demoniac is plausible and his behavior consonant with that of a victim of extreme violence, the political device Rome used with ruthless efficiency to conquer its neighbors in the Mediterranean world. We tend to forget that Augustus' *pax romana*, like the *pax americana*, was made possible by strategic violence and the countless crucifixions of people in the name of imperial "peace" and power. Like many of the victims of incest, rape, and torture, the demoniac's self-identity has been shattered. He is simultaneously one and many people, himself and his tormentor Legion. Literally, he does not know who he is. He cannot distinguish between himself and the forces that attack him. The demoniac's self-mutilation is a classic symptom of trauma-induced disorientation. Enigmatically, it soothes him, not because he is a masochist but because he is used to pain. He equates agony with normalcy. His self-mutilation is also a symbol of the battle that rages within him about who he really is. It is simultaneously a type of self-annihilation and an expression of his desire to be free, to rid himself of the Roman occupation of his psyche. He is trying to answer a fundamental question. Is he a grotesque manifestation of evil or is he a real human being? Jesus' presence helps him to realize that his tormented state, his personal "status quo," is not the final word. It is neither inevitable nor God's will, and he can be free if he wills it. His initial reluctance to tell the truth and be healed, of course, is understandable. He is used to being pathological. It is what he knows and does quite well. There is, however, a spark inside him that helps him realize that his current turmoil and multiplicity is not who he has to be. This grace-filled inspiration is a manifestation of God's reign. Combined with Jesus' compassion, it leads to exorcism and new life. The haughty omnipotence of Legion is transmuted into a herd of swine and a demoniac becomes a disciple who can leave the tombs of Gerasene as someone truly free.

GRAPPLING WITH OUR LIES: EXORCISM IN THE MODERN AGE

Since the 1980s the proponents of free-market, neoliberal capitalism have enjoyed one socioeconomic triumph after another, with little criti-

cal reflection on or effective opposition to their success. Wayward segments of humanity in eastern Europe have been won over to capitalism.
Recalcitrant countries in the developing world have been chastened by
I.M.F. and World Bank "conditionalities" to overturn progressive social
legislation in the name of efficiency and privatization and open their
markets to outside exploitation. Under the tutelage of the Friedmans
and Fukuyamas of the late twentieth century, a technocratic elite has
managed to amass unprecedented amounts of wealth as the masters of a
global, capitalist empire infinitely greater than Rome's. At the same
time, there is grinding poverty and unprecedented violence throughout
the world. In most countries today education and health care are now
"pay as you go" propositions while under- and unemployment have
reached staggering proportions. Political violence in the developing
world and a multitude of addictions in the developed world are telling
symptoms of both possession and a desire to be free. Empires, past and
present, find psychological balance and social justice hard to achieve.
Magic phrases like efficiency, trickle-down, stabilization, and so forth,
make grotesque affluence and immoral poverty seem unavoidable and
even rational despite the fact that they are far from inevitable, irrational,
and deadly. As Ched Myers points out in *Who Will Roll Away the
Stone?*, we all live in the *locus imperii* of global capitalism. Like Legion,
it is a totalizing proposition that sucks energy out of us and numbs our
awareness of each other as we assimilate its lies. On a deeper level we
know that something is terribly wrong, but we find ourselves paralyzed
with fear. Like the demoniac, we are not sure who we are. We find it
agonizingly difficult to separate ourselves from the empire that causes us
so much pain.

There is, however, still a spark of resistance in many people that
helps them counteract possession and despair. They refuse to accept the
global capitalist system as the apex of human development, recognizing
that it is ultimately an idol not terribly different from Rome's. What
exactly is the difference between Caesar's genius and Adam Smith's
Invisible Hand? Are not both, when hypostatized and absolutized, pre-
texts for empire and sources of oppression? The men and women who
raise these questions and objections are often people of faith, members
of base and intentional communities who, otherwise nameless, are enor-
mously important for the creation of a more humane and just world.
These are people who refuse to buy into the imperial system because
they know it is the antithesis of God's reign. They recognize the pathology around them as the by-product of greed and narcissism. They are
responsible people who have an alternative vision and believe in the pos-

sibility of social change. They are not driven by a spirit of political messianism but rather a commitment to honesty and compassion to redress the unnecessary suffering that scars our world. This is the source of hope we will now begin to analyze, focusing on the characteristics and challenges of base and intentional communities, mostly Roman Catholic, in South and North America.

BASE CHRISTIAN COMMUNITIES: THE VOICE OF THE VOICELESS, THE VOICE OF GOD

The emergence of base Christian communities in Latin America in the 1960s is arguably the most important ecclesiological event of this century. As Phillip Berryman points out, there is reason to doubt some of the statistics about the number of communities, which some claim to be in the hundreds of thousands.[2] Nevertheless, there are many of them and they play a significant role in many people's lives, especially those Gustavo Gutiérrez has called the "non-persons" of our age. Base communities are matrices in which oppressed people discover themselves and each other, the inspiration of scripture, and a healthy believing community. Through faith and social action, they escape the numbing effects of the empire's most lethal weapons, fatalism and its inevitable corollary, self-destructive despair. Pooling their energy and insights, members achieve knowledge about themselves and their environment. The poor educate the poor. At the same time, as women and men who form communities of faith, they help each other understand what they believe, unlocking the deeper meaning of scripture and faith. The end result is a community of disciples whose commitment makes the gospel and believing community credible and understandable to others in the larger world. The base community functions as an alternative model of what it means to be human, proving that the excessive individuality and unrelenting acquisitiveness so characteristic of modern capitalism are lies. The poor do not endure their poverty; they celebrate the richness they find in each other. Grateful at having experienced grace in themselves and their neighbors, they believe, think, and act in unprecedented ways. As their lives change so do their neighborhoods and society. On a local, micro level, they help shape God's reign.

Base communities are often explained in light of Vatican II, Medellín, Puebla, and liberation theology. Undoubtedly, ecclesial events and theological movements have given impetus to many communities, but their origin really lies in the collective genius and deep faith of the poor themselves. Despite the ravages of oppression, the poor possess cultural resources and a deep vision of life that sustain them in the most difficult of circumstances. They have their own variety of Spanish and Portuguese, their own indigenous languages, along with song, dance, and a sense of humor specific to victims of oppression. The poor have always been masters at letting the air out of imperial ontology.[3] In the midst of poverty and social pathology, there are intelligent, courageous women and men whose sense of class and cultural specificity helps them to resist and survive. Without this feisty spirit, they would simply die. Many of these men and women are people of intense faith whose convictions are articulated in the complex field of popular religiosity. At its best, popular religiosity gives voice to an alternative vision of the human condition predicated on a strong sense of community and a desire for justice and life. Once considered static and regressive, scholars like Christian Parker in Chile and Diego Irarrázaval in Peru have uncovered the fluid and even liberating qualities of popular religion and culture. At the heart of each base community is a vibrant, alternative vision of what it means to be human voiced in a special language, culture, and religiosity that counteract despair. This is not an easy phenomenon to isolate, even for open-minded outsiders, since it is a multilayered, symbolic reality that cannot be put into words. Nonetheless, base communities bubble with the religious consciousness of the rural and urban poor, allowing them to give voice to their humanity through their own rituals. In this way, popular religion becomes a critical and transforming factor in people's lives, rather than something magical or numbing. Ritual becomes heuristic drama bristling with critical insight and social consequences.

Obscene economic disparity predicated on systematic violence cannot survive without ideological justification. Thus, the supposed intellectual and moral superiority of the social elite is central to their undisturbed sleep. Ultimately, it is not the theory behind base communities that causes hostile reactions but rather what the communities do. To put things more bluntly, effective praxis gets them into trouble. Base communities help previously inarticulate and politically impotent people see, analyze, and act in unwelcome ways. People in base communities put together soup kitchens and neighborhood clinics, thus demonstrating to each other their organizational skills and political savvy. Without engaging in party politics, they learn that they can understand and shape their world in a concrete and more humane way. The men and women who make up base communities are committed to living their lives and reshaping the world in light of God's reign. Consequently, they are not easily co-opted or bribed, thus raising the ire of those who wish they would go away. Base communities are frequently lumped together with the political left by right-wing politicians and some conservatives in the church. This specious assertion helps them dismiss the communities as a political plot. Admittedly, in the '70s and '80s segments of the political left in some countries tried to co-opt members of communities and sometimes communities as a whole. The left had little success, however, because members of base communities know the difference between party politics and the reign of God. The men and women who make up base communities know that both Marxism and neoliberalism, predicated on materialism and contempt for the vulnerable and weak, are incompatible with what they believe. Since the reign of God is the ultimate criterion they use to gauge their lives and social environment, social and political propositions are put in proper place. The sociopolitical absolutes that have claimed so many lives in the twentieth century are correctly perceived for what they are—idols that reflect the egos and class interests of their human creators.

Latin Americans who belong to base communities are a small percentage of the overall population, yet they have a positive effect in an otherwise bleak political terrain. Their communities are examples of grass-roots democracy, collective honesty, and real social change. They make faith palpable in soup kitchens, schools, and neighborhood organizations that help others to be free. Opposition to base communities and the popular movement on the part of those who wield power, be they from the left or right, is easy to explain. Be they old-school Leninists in Cuba or members of the neoliberal technocratic elite in Peru, all share contempt for grass-roots democracy and popular organizations. The ability of the poor to organize and articulate an alternative vision threatens their vaunted intellectual superiority and role as social managers. Rather than being hierarchical, base communities are lateral. Instead of being conservative and focused on the past, they are open-ended and work in the present. They are the antithesis to the status quo, which explains the hostility of the ruling class. What is far more difficult to explain, however, is the opposition of many members of the Catholic hierarchy and certain religious movements to their brothers and sisters in the faith.

Since the late '60s the church in Latin America has been at the forefront of social justice advocacy, often paying a very high price. It has likewise committed itself to a new ecclesiology—a church of the poor that reflects the culture, daily life, and deep-seated longing for justice of the

Latin American people. Liberation theologians have played a part in shaping the social ethic and ecclesiology that emerged after Vatican II and Medellín, but it was endorsed by almost all the members of the Latin American hierarchy as a self-evident moral necessity, vital to the integrity of the church and the credibility of the gospel itself. Nonetheless, for at least the last twenty years, conservative members of the hierarchy and whole religious organizations such as Opus Dei have done everything possible to counteract progressive trends in the Latin American church. They have attacked and slandered individual theologians through their neo-conservative media. Simultaneously, they have pressured church-related funding agencies in the developed world to cut off support for programs and personnel crucial to the growth and well being of base communities. They have caused painful divisions in the church, making it weaker rather than stronger. Precious energy best directed to the defense of the poor and the strengthening of the church as a whole has been wasted on internal struggles with no productive gains. Frankly, certain segments of the institutional church have become reactionary and antipopular, coming dangerously close to rationalizing imperial repression.[4]

Base communities have been an exceptionally effective means for evangelization. In countries where Christian identity is more cultural than conscious, they help others understand what the gospel means. Why, then, the opposition and even hostility in conservative Catholic circles to what seems to be an expression of genuine discipleship and saving grace? The explanation frequently offered by analysts points to irreconcilable theological visions and a resultant dialogue of the deaf. Although not incorrect, this single interpretation is inadequate. Unfortunately, the real explanations are far more embarrassing. They are more social, economic, and political in nature than theological. With few exceptions, Catholic conservatives in Latin American are white. Almost all live in a world of privilege, far removed from that of indigenous, mestizo, and black peoples who make up base communities and whom they rarely if ever meet. Afflicted by stereotypes about those the imperial system needs to dehumanize and defeat, and with which the church has had a long and tawdry symbiotic relationship, the existence of vibrant new communities contradicts racial and class-based prejudices that colonial Catholicism helped to create. The poor should not be able to form autonomous faith communities, but they do. They should not be able to understand and live the gospel, but they do. Even more vexing is the way members of base communities express their religious beliefs. Drawing on their experience of oppression and using popular Catholicism to give it voice, their religious lives bristle with energy and opposition to injustice. Catholic conservatives often accuse the members of base communities of politicizing the gospel and proclaiming a heterodox faith. Certainly, members of base communities are convinced that gospel values are central to transforming and humanizing an unjust world. Their concern, however, is not with party politics but in transforming political and social life in light of the God's reign. Such ideas have been part of the Christian ethic and tradition since its inception. What is truly heretical is using Christianity to justify injustice and foster passivity in the face of injustices that mock God's reign.

In the past two decades, strategic alliances have been forged between groups like Opus Dei and neoliberals who control the economic and political system. In Peru members of Opus Dei have openly attacked the cautious, centrist archbishop of Lima for having the audacity to question a neoliberal president who routinely violates basic human rights. Proclaiming their ultraorthodoxy, they turn a blind eye to economic misery, the use of torture, and the forced sterilization of poor women in public hospitals. These aberrations have their explanation in a thirst for power coupled with a pathological religious pride. Conservative Catholics are intent on reestablishing Christendom, somehow convinced that they can make it Christian, historical evidence aside, and ultimately win over or at least minimize the damage caused by their neoliberal allies. They are true believers in religious and social hierarchy and so prefer to align themselves with dictators rather than grass-roots, Christian democrats. It is not the eighth-century prophets and the Sermon on the Mount that fire their religious imaginations as much as Aristotle's *Politics* and Augustine's *City of God*. Like affluence, grace must trickle down channeled through God's moral elite. Base communities, however, are predicated on the assumption that grace flows where it wills, a tenet of Christian faith that calls into question the neo-Augustinian pessimism of certain ecclesiastical leaders. Members of base communities respect the church's hierarchy because they are patient, tolerant people. They also revere courageous church leaders like Oscar Romero. Nonetheless, they assess the depth of religious leaders' commitment in light of what they say and do, not who they claim to be. In short, "the masters of the truth" are those who do the truth. To priests and bishops accustomed to automatic deference, being questioned by the poor and oppressed is something new. It enrages them, but it is long overdue. Too many Catholic conservatives are addicted to hierarchical power that contradicts the message of the gospel while it kills the poor.

Finally, there is the fact that women are the majority in most base communities and are often powerful actors in the popular movement as well. Less prone to compete and more open to work as members of a group, they are natural organizers who can pray and strategize with equal intensity and intent. Believing women from the popular sector of Latin American countries are generating a new vitality in the church while they lend energy and integrity to the political process. They put the lie to elitist categorizations of poor women as human beings whose bodies, minds, and political vision do not count. More and more, women are exercising bottom-up leadership in the church and society in liberating ways. They are not interested in ordination; they only insist on their right to serve. Organic feminists and praxis-oriented disciples, what they believe is what they do. In an ecclesiastical institution steeped in sexism and schooled in compromise, the presence of uncompromising women from the popular sector is long overdue. Once considered "the slaves of slaves," they affirm the validity of Mark's assertion: when we respond to that spark of grace within us we become free.

To characterize base communities as heterodox aberrations, as some conservative Catholics do, is to mock true orthodoxy and the commitment of men and women who make up such communities. Their sole purpose in life is to be disciples to each other and the societies they want to transform. They are not sectarian or unorthodox in any way. They respect the institutional church, aware that it is their ally, not their enemy. Furthermore, they see themselves as part of the larger Catholic community. They are not even vaguely interested in theological novelties, but rather in knowing scripture, tradition, and church teaching in order to better their lives and world. The attacks of Catholic conservatives are the result of bias about people whose race, class, and gender they fear and whose discipleship threatens their self-understanding as "owners" of the church and the only individuals capable of knowing the truth. In their opposition to base communities they thwart the liberating power of the gospel and make the church complicit in injustice. Some seem to revere Constantine and Christendom more than Jesus and the believing community to which they claim to belong.

INTENTIONAL CHRISTIAN COMMUNITIES: THE SUBVERSIVE POWER OF CATHOLICITY

Base communities in the developing world have been the subject of considerable study, both sociopolitical and theological. The members of base communities have helped reverse the legacy of Christendom by giving shape to a dialectical ecclesiology more in tune with the experience of Mark's community and its struggle to overcome Rome's Legion. Their commitment and action have given a new meaning and legitimacy to catholicity as a community of Jesus' disciples that lives his incarnation in the present. This emergence of new types of Christian community, obviously, is not confined to the developing world. It is also happening in North America, Europe, and other parts of the developed world where a wide array of people are committing themselves to discipleship as members of intentional Christian communities. These new expressions of Christian faith are also producing ecclesial and social change, albeit at a different pace and in different ways. Despite Weber's and Durkheim's now dated assertion about the inevitable privatization and diminution of institutional Christianity, believing people and communities have not disappeared. In fact, there is something of a religious resurgence in many developed countries as women and men, sated with materialistic culture, search for sustaining spiritualities that can help them address life's deeper challenges. The search for transcendent values and a life-directing spirituality does not mean that a kinder gentler Christendom looms on the horizon as some neoconservative Catholics assert. In fact, church membership continues to decline in many developed countries, something the institutional church refuses to look at honestly, since it is indicative of a failure of nerve and substance. What we seem to be dealing with is an attempt on the part of middle-class people to achieve a balance between secularity, a sociocultural proposition most continue to accept, and a healthy spirituality that transcends the capitalist fixation with the bottom line and the here and now. Fewer and fewer people are attracted to either neoliberal materialism, especially in its most Darwinian form, and reactionary, pre–Vatican II Catholicism. Both are throwbacks to the nineteenth century and hold no appeal for balanced human beings contemplating the twenty-first.[5]

Most members of intentional communities generally come from the middle class and are well educated. They enjoy social and political rights and a fair degree of economic comfort. Their relationship to the prevailing system is therefore more complex than that of men and women in base communities who, because of their marginalization, have a clear and critical sense of the system that oppresses them. Middle-class Christians in the developing world are not victims as much as unwilling participants in a multifaceted, imperial system they are challenged to understand and change in light of the gospel. This is hard work fraught with difficulties and dangers. Because they are immersed in a culture of acquisitiveness and conformity, raising questions about what the empire is doing seems provocative and potentially destructive. Like everyone else who lives in and off the system, middle-class Christians have been conditioned by education and religious training to raise few if any questions. They are constantly told by myriad ideological apparatuses not to be aware, to induce naïveté if necessary. It is tempting for middle-class Christians never to go beyond their immediate culture and class-based, suburban world, but inevitably some do. Beginning with their own lives, they become conscious of many contradictions that do not square with imperial propaganda. This uneasy sensation can lead to systemic awareness, at least under the right circumstances. When conscienticized members of the middle class encounter a healthy believing community, one whose faith leads to action, they discover a wealth of allies and analytical tools embodied in the community.

It is amazing that there are as many intentional communities as there are in the developed world with its enormous stress on discrete individuality and materialistic superficiality. In fact, they are growing rapidly in the developed world despite the claims of neoliberal and postmodern theorists that religion has been relegated to the private sphere where it may offer solace to weak-kneed individuals, but no longer has any significance in the social sphere. Certainly, the institutional church no longer plays a major role in shaping social policy in most developed countries. Surely this is for the best since it breaks the bonds of an old and insidious relationship between the ecclesiastical and imperial institutions. Those who understand themselves as Christians in the modern world do not need to exercise power and control. What they strive for is the right to live and explain an alternative way of being human found in the gospel. Living this vision is their obligation as disciples and the most responsibly subversive thing anyone can presently do. In terms of the imperial system, such a vision is weakness and folly. For the disciple, however, the gospel is an idol-shattering antipower. As spokespersons for God's reign, they contribute to the liberation of other human beings. Their beliefs and actions transform lives, challenge the church, and transform society. In the very center of the empire, they disprove the assertions of neoliberal materialists and postmodern cynics who would have us believe that impotence and meaninglessness are our inevitable lot. By forming communities and doing everything in their power to transform the world, the women and men who make up intentional communities are giving a new credibility to the believing community in countries where the institutional church is nearly dead.

In France members of L'Arche community work with severely handicapped children and adults whom many would prefer to drug and warehouse as embarrassments in an urbane world. Highly educated young women and men, who could be making money in lucrative professions, prefer to spend their time holding and helping those broken in body and spirit. They live day in and day out with severely handicapped people and when they celebrate the Eucharist they do so as a united, believing community, healthy and sick, strong and weak together. They do so because they believe in the incarnation as the ultimate truth rather than in wealth and power. They are modern disciples who explain the incarnation, the most important of Christian symbols, in an uncaring, disincarnate world. It is their central symbol and the power behind the lives they heal. L'Arche, once a small intentional community found in one French town, has spread throughout Europe and North America. New communities have been founded in Asia and Latin America. In the face of a seemingly all-powerful, dehumanizing system, uncanny grace abounds and people rediscover the joy of having a common identity as God's children.

Intentional Christian communities are faith-based families of people who recognize and respond to the existence of God in themselves, others, and the world. The men and women in them also belong to communities of resistance that refuse to accept injustice and dehumanization in the name of empire. They do not voice their criticism as irrational sectarians mouthing Jeremiads, or revolutionaries addicted to a self-indulgent, imaginary utopia. They are, rather, responsible people who understand what is wrong and want to transform the world in light of what it can be. In short, they are optimists rather than pessimists. They are aware of the reality of sin, but are even more conscious of the power of God's reign. The members of intentional communities live modestly and often pool their resources. Convinced that race, culture, and gender are not barriers to human understanding as much as intriguing facets of our humanity, they do everything in their power to understand each other and people outside the community despite inevitable difficulties. They practice a real-world hermeneutics based on the assumption that we are capable of understanding and appreciating each other. Finally, they insist that society is something that we are called to shape in new and imaginative ways. Grace does not predetermine anything; it merely opens up new possibilities. Other examples of intentional communities come to mind that may add something concrete to what has been said.

The members of the San Egidio community in Rome, made up of young professionals trained in medicine, the social sciences, and law, reach out and help illegal immigrants, prostitutes, and people with AIDS. They teach them Italian, help them acquire legal status as immigrants, help them find jobs, heal their bodies, and sometimes help them die in a loving way. Paid professionals, they pool their resources to carry out their work. They meet every night in a baroque church in Trastevere. They read scripture, reflect on its meaning, celebrate the Eucharist when a priest is available, and then go to the streets. In Rochester, New York, members of Corpus Christi Parish, which contains many intentional communities within the larger whole, brings white, black, yellow, and brown Americans together as a believing community. The members of the community reach out to each other, street people, ex-cons, and any one who comes through the door. A once-dying ethnic parish in inner-city Rochester is now a vibrant example of discipleship. It has broken down barriers between the suburbs and inner city. It has facilitated deep conversation among ostensibly different people and diluted the toxic effects of race and class in one of the world's most stratified societies. Catholic in the best sense of the word, it has made Christians in Rochester conscious of their sisters and brothers in Haiti. Members of the Corpus Christi community go back and forth to a small Haitian town call Bourne. They help there, but they also help in Rochester where they question and challenge the imperial system that is responsible for so much suffering in Haiti and in American inner cities.

Whereas base communities in the Catholic tradition usually are part of a larger parochial and diocesan network, intentional communities tend to be more diverse in their organization and relationship to the institutional church. Some are subunits of parishes, but most are autonomous. Conflicts between intentional communities and the institutional church are relatively rare, but they do occur. In part, this is due to the fact that many members of intentional communities are educated, self-confident people who resent clerical imposition and reject the assumption of ecclesiastical conservatives that the institution they represent is somehow theirs. Few members of intentional communities are anticlerical, even fewer of them are tolerant of clericalism. Conflict can be particularly acute when leaders in the institutional church, driven by a restorationist agenda, try to exert control over communities accustomed to autonomy and equality. When pre–Vatican II clericalism collides with a lay-based, post–Vatican II ecclesiology, the results are disastrous. The community's and church's energy is dissipated on internal struggles better spent on evangelizing the surrounding world. To avoid such conflicts, some intentional communities refuse any sort of connection with local parishes of a diocese. Although this minimizes the dangers of conflict vis-à-vis a conservative priest or bishop, it can minimize the catholicity of the community. Cut off from other parts of the body, isolated communities sometimes implode.

Members of intentional communities tend to be less concerned with Catholicism as a religious institution than with Catholicism as an incarnational way of being human. In this way they distinguish the medium from the message, the institutional church from the gospel. Although intrinsically linked, they are never synonymous. Likewise, they put tradition is proper perspective. The past is not revered as a static reality but a present and future legacy that provides wise experience and principles to present-day disciples. Intentional communities, like base communities, perform an indispensable hermeneutical task. They explain the gospel and the catholic way of being in a dehumanized and oppressive world. Given the paralysis that besets the institutional church at this moment in history, base and intentional communities are the best and most credible means of evangelization. What they do is profoundly simple. They allow people to see. They open up their eyes so they can see who they really are without the distorting effect of the imperial lens that invariably makes us too large or too small, grandiose or self-loathing in unreal ways. Is this not what Jesus did with the demoniac by helping him see that he was neither a demon nor a madman, simply a human being invited to enter God's reign? Without these communities fewer and fewer people will have the opportunity to say yes to their God-given freedom, remaining enthralled to Legion with all the unnecessary suffering such possession demands.

CONCLUSION

More than thirty years after the final session of Vatican II, many facets of Catholicism have yet to change. Many members of the hierarchy still insist on preconciliar, top-down control. The church's relationship with the secular world is reminiscent of a pre–Vatican II state of affairs. There is a growing spirit of sectarian antagonism vis-à-vis modernity that generates more heat than light. Hostility, unfortunately, only makes responsible debate and possible change harder to bring about. People in the secular world who need to hear the church's message dismiss it as an antimodern anachronism. The modern world's legitimate insistence on pluralism and people's right to multiple truths, is negated by the medieval, intolerant mindset of many leaders in the church. Such closed-minded defeatism, however, is irresponsible. The great challenge, as it was for Mark's readers twenty centuries ago, is to understand what is happening and remain firm, even if doing so entails persecution. We cannot run away from Legion. We have to renounce him in an unequivocal way, as the demoniac is asked to do. The result of his honest struggle is freedom from lies and the right to be a healthy human being. Despite the ups and downs of institutional Catholicism with its ongoing obsession with the past, there are countless disciples intent on moving forward. These are the people who make up base and intentional communities. Willy-nilly, they are moving the institutional church forward, despite predictable foot-dragging. We need to recognize that is usually how things happen in institutions. Leaders manage while people lead. This is rarely admitted in Catholicism, but the evidence is irrefutable. As Anselm of Canterbury put it almost a millennium ago, *vox populi vox Dei*.

On an ecclesiological level, base and intentional communities are crucial to keeping Catholicism catholic. They allow people to constantly amplify its incarnation vision with their diverse cultures, humanity, and historical experience. This process cannot be stopped because it is the work of the Spirit. As Walbert Bühlmann has pointed out in several of his works, the demographic center of Catholicism, and Christianity for that matter, now lies in the Southern Hemisphere. The majority of Catholics, and all Christians, are non-Western people. When it comes to Catholics, the adjective Roman will have a new meaning in the twenty-first century. Surely, it will not disappear, but it will not mean what it has in the twentieth century. The majority of Catholics are now "nonpersons" whose humanity is either unrecognized or perceived as a disposable commodity for the well-being of those who control the global economic system. These disciples possess a subversive desire to survive. They refuse to be nonpersons and simply die. The minority of the Catholic population will reside in the developed world where believers will have to grapple with a socioeconomic system that victimizes their sisters and brothers in faith. As outsiders in the heart of the empire, they possess special strategic knowledge about how the system works. Awareness of a shared religious value system focused on the ongoing reality of incarnation, and in real communication with each other, these two parts of the Catholic whole can provide a new dynamics to Catholicism by helping put together desperately needed alternatives to the present world order. In this way they will make the institutional church more prophetic and credible. If such possibilities are truly tapped, Catholicism may be one of the most dynamic and humanizing religious movements in the next century. Few other religious traditions have quite as much potential. None has such a rich history and present-day diversity with nearly one billion members in every part of the world. Of course, so much depends on whether or not we are willing to be free.

NOTES

1. Admittedly, the terms developing and developed are problematic because they are laden with so many presuppositions. Development is far more than a socioeconomic phenomenon. Many developing countries have highly evolved cultures and social systems. What makes them "underdeveloped" is their inability to relate freely to the global capitalist system that exploits their vulnerability.

2. Berryman, Phillip. "Questions about Base Communities" in *Religion in the Megacity: Catholic and Protestant Portraits from Latin America* (Maryknoll, N.Y.: Orbis Books, 1996), pp. 63–70.

3. These insights are drawn from the work of James C. Scott, a scholar at Yale who has studied peasant societies and their multiple ways of resisting oppressors. Since revolutions rarely work, and almost always backfire, Scott insists that the best way to refute the claims of oppressors is through oblique, encoded means such as song, dance, humor, and sometimes religion.

4. The manifestations of a muted "ecclesiastical fascism" of more recent vintage appeared during the so-called Dirty War in Argentina in the 1970s. A growing number of right-wing clerics, some quite young, can be found in every Latin American country today. Some have recently been appointed bishops, a fact that makes one question Rome's wisdom and Latin American agenda. Given their oligarchic self-understanding and resistance to every sort of change, such bishops are usually pastoral disasters.

5. Surely the resurgence of responsible socialism in recent French and British elections (1997), points to growing resistance to unbridled neoliberal capitalism. Likewise, the failure of Catholic restorationists, as well as American Protestant fundamentalists, to win over large numbers of people, points to a rejection of sectarian religiosity.

REFERENCES

Berryman, Phillip. *Religion in the Megacity: Catholic and Protestant Portraits from Latin America*. Maryknoll, N.Y.: Orbis Books, 1996.

Boff, Leonardo. *Ecclesiogenesis: The Base Communities Reinvent the Church*. Maryknoll, N.Y.: Orbis Books, 1986.

Bühlmann, Walbert. *With Eyes to See: Church and World in the Third Millennium*. Maryknoll, N.Y.: Orbis Books, 1990.

Castañeda, Jorge G. *Utopia Unarmed: The Latin American Left after the Cold War*. New York: Vintage Books, 1993.

Lernoux, Penny. *People of God: The Struggle for World Catholicism*. New York: Viking Press, 1989.

Levine, Daniel, H. *Popular Voices in Latin American Popular Catholicism*. Princeton, N.J.: Princeton University Press, 1992.

Myers, Ched. *Who Will Roll Away The Stone?: Discipleship Queries for First World Christians*. Maryknoll, N.Y.: Orbis Books, 1994.

Parker, Christian. *Popular Religion and Modernization in Latin America: A Different Logic*. Maryknoll, N.Y.: Orbis Books, 1996.

Scott, James C. *Domination and the Arts of Resistance: Hidden Transcripts*. New Haven, Conn.: Yale University Press, 1990.

Veling, Terry A. *Living in the Margins: Intentional Communities and the Art of Interpretation*. New York: Cross Herder, 1996.

8

"There You Will See Him":
Christianity beyond the Frontier Myth

Roberto S. Goizueta

Legend has it that once, when asked what he thought about Western civilization, Mahatma Gandhi responded: It would be a good idea." What we call "Western civilization" has, no doubt, enriched human life beyond measure. Western ideals have inspired men and women to spiritual, intellectual, literary, and aesthetic accomplishments that give expression to our human nature at its most noble. The twentieth century, particularly, has been a century of unprecedented progress. Individual freedom, civil rights, and human equality are no longer unthinkable anathemas but fundamental axioms that shape our everyday lives and social institutions.

Despite the many undisputed advances of Western civilization, however, we are all painfully aware of the disquiet and anxiety that pervade contemporary Western civilization. Scratch the placid, well-heeled surface of our culture and one soon uncovers disturbing signs of another reality. Scratch the sanitized, efficient surface of the modern machine and one discovers six million scarred, emaciated Jewish corpses. Scratch the manicured surface of modern suburbia and one discovers the wan, baleful stare of the doped-up, pierced-through, suicidal teenager—or the bloodshot, empty stare of the abandoned, abused, stressed-out housewife. Scratch the egalitarian surface of modern democracies and one discovers the depressive boredom that comes from powerlessness. Scratch the ebullient surface of Wall Street and one discovers the desperate faces of the permanent underclass. Scratch the digitized surface of the computer age and one discovers the passive glare of the virtually real child.

To be living in the late modern, or postmodern period is to have discovered that, in the words of the German Jewish philosopher Walter

171

Benjamin, "every great work of civilization is at the same time a work of barbarism."[1] The legacy of Western civilization is, at the same time, a legacy of barbarism. How do we know? Because the victims of that barbarism are in our midst—and their faces and voices are finally breaking through the placid surface. The corpses are themselves speaking out from the grave. Their long-repressed cries are breaking through the complacent silence. And the victims are asking us how we, as a society, will respond to their cries. At the dawn of a new millennium, this is the question on which the future of Western civilization will depend. Every other question will eventually become irrelevant unless and until we can effectively address this single question: How will we, as a society, respond to the victims of our own progress, the victims of our successes, the victims of our achievements?

Above all, we must first acknowledge the historical fact that the many achievements of Western civilization have, indeed, come only at great cost. In the face of the millions upon millions of victims, dare we continue to beat our breasts and speak self-righteously of the "victory of capitalism" or the "victory of Western ideals"? Or can this society, without denying the obvious achievements of Western economic, cultural, and political ideals, summon the courage to look into the eyes of those victims and see itself reflected therein?

In this paper, I will suggest that U.S. Hispanics in general, and U.S. Hispanic theologians in particular, can be important contributors to our nation's struggle to confront the ambiguities of its own history in order to move toward a more faithful realization of its noble ideals, in order to strengthen Western civilization. What I will argue is that, in the United States, the noble ideals of Western civilization have taken a particular historical, ideological form that undermines their realization in the long term insofar as this ideological form precludes the very acknowledgment of historical ambiguity, itself a precondition for the realization of those ideals. More specifically, the modern "frontier myth," or ideology still underlying U.S. culture impedes our society's ability to promote "life, liberty, and the pursuit of happiness" at a time when the frontier has been replaced by the "border" as the central symbol of U.S. identity *ad extra*. In other words, late modernity is a world of borders, but, given our history, the profound fear of immigrants reflected in recent legislation suggests that U.S. society continues to view these borders through the lenses of a frontier myth, open to economic expansion but closed to human immigration. The consequent distortion has devastating consequences, among them the inability to acknowledge historical ambiguity.

Conversely, I will suggest, the Latino experience is one that, as defined by the experience of living "on the border," allows for ambiguity and reflects an understanding of the border as a true meeting place, where different cultures interact. This historical context allows for an understanding of Jesus Christ and a reading of the gospel texts that yield a prophetic, liberating notion of the border. Finally, I will adumbrate some of the ecclesiological implications of a theology that takes the border rather than the frontier as its *locus theologicus*.

THE FRONTIER

> . . . I am become a name
> For always roaming with an hungry heart,
> Much have I seen and known . . .
> I am a part of all that I have met;
> Yet all experience is an arch, where thro'
> Gleams that untravelled world, whose margin fades
> Forever and forever when I move.
> How dull it is to pause, to make an end.
> To rust unburnished, not to shine in use!
> And this gray spirit yearning in desire
> To follow knowledge like a shining star
> Beyond the utmost bound of human thought.
> . . . Come my friends,
> 'Tis not to late to seek a newer world.
> Push off, and sitting well in order smite
> The sounding furrows; for my purpose holds
> To sail beyond the sunset, and the baths
> Of all the Western stars until I die
> To strive, to seek, to find and not to yield.[2]

With those words from Tennyson's "Ulysses" the American historian Frederick Jackson Turner ended his commencement address at the University of Washington in June, 1914. Tennyson's words evoked for Turner those frontier ideals that had served the United States so well until the end of the nineteenth century: "to seek a newer world . . . to sail beyond the sunset . . . to strive, to seek, to find and not to yield."

Indeed, it does not take much imagination to see reflected in these words not only the spirit of Daniel Boone and Andrew Jackson but also the spirit of Christopher Columbus and Hernán Cortés. The frontier is the foundational myth of modernity; it is our creation myth. The modern world is constructed by forging and conquering new frontiers: "The first ideal of the pioneer was that of conquest."[3]

In what has been called "the most influential piece of writing in the history of American history," his 1893 essay on "The Significance of the Frontier in American History," Frederick Jackson Turner set forth what came to be known as the frontier thesis:

> American social development has been continually beginning over again on the frontier. This perennial rebirth, this fluidity of American life, this expansion westward with its new opportunities, its continuous touch with the simplicity of primitive society, furnish the forces dominating American character. In this advance, the frontier is the outer edge of the wave—the meeting point between savagery and civilization. . . . And now, four centuries from the discovery of America, at the end of a hundred years of life under the Constitution, the frontier has gone.[4]

By the end of the nineteenth century, the western frontier "finally closed forever, with uncertain consequences for the American future."[5]

Yet myths do not easily die when historical conditions change; they may simply be adapted to the new context. Indeed, argued Turner, the values and worldview implicit in the frontier myth have become a part of U.S. culture: "Long after the frontier period of a particular region of the United States has passed away, the conception of society, the ideals and aspirations that it produced, persist in the minds of the people. . . . This experience has been wrought into the very warp and woof of American thought."[6] And Turner's very definition of the frontier myth (as quoted above) already suggests the particular conception of society underlying the myth. Herein lies the fundamental characteristic of the frontier myth, which gives it its power and rationale; the frontier is "the meeting point between savagery and civilization."

In the history and culture of the United States, the very drive to *extend* the frontier came to be seen as a constitutive feature of "civilization" itself: to be civilized *is* to extend the frontier, to expand, to seek new opportunities, to dominate, to conquer (in Tennyson's words, "How dull it is to pause, to make an end"). Conversely, then, to accept limits to this expansion is to undermine the very foundations of civilized society: "once free lands were exhausted . . . the whole moral fabric would collapse and the land descend into the state of depravity and tyranny that overcrowded Europe already knew."[7] Thus, implicit in the frontier myth is the assumption that the only alternative to expansion is decline, or degeneration. This begs the question that Turner and other scholars were asking at the turn of the twentieth century: How will the United States react to the closing of the western frontier? Turner did not live to see the emergence of an answer during the remaining decades of the twentieth century.

As we approach the end of the twentieth century, however, I do think we can suggest an answer, an answer that lies not to the West but to the South. In retrospect, the turn of the century represented not so much the demise of the frontier as the replacement of the western frontier with a southern frontier. The westward territorial expansion, including the conquest of one-third of Mexico in the first half of the nineteenth century, was replaced by a southern expansion. Initially, this latter followed the pattern of military, geographical, and political expansion. Thus, in the first half of the twentieth century, the U.S. frontier became the Caribbean and Central America. Just as the western frontier had expanded into "virgin territory," so too would the southern frontier. After all, there is only one "America," only one "America the Beautiful." "America" *is* the United States.[8]

Thus, a new breed of pioneers rose up in the first decades of the new century, not only individual adventurers but also economic enterprises seeking to expand their markets, often in conjunction with U.S. political interests. The rapid growth of multinational corporations during this period provided possibilities for *economic* expansion unknown to earlier pioneers. When territorial expansion proved impracticable, more benign forms of economic expansion would take its place, even if sometimes with the aid of political and even military intervention. By the 1930s, contends historian Walter LaFeber, overt military intervention "had become too costly. Moreover, such blatantly imperialist gestures were no longer needed. The blunt instruments were replaced with the Good Neighbor's economic leverage."[9] Nevertheless, when the economic leverage weakened, for example, during the period between the Eisenhower and Reagan presidencies, they might require renewed political and military fortification.

Already in 1890, U.S. Secretary of State James G. Blaine had foreseen the form that the new frontier would take: "he pointedly observed, 'Our great demand is expansion,' but only in trade, for 'we are not seeking annexation of territory.'"[10] Between 1898 and 1901, the United States began to export capital to a degree previously unequaled and, by World War I, had erased its trade deficits.[11] As LaFeber has argued, "the dynamic new United States necessarily prepared itself to find fresh frontiers abroad to replace the closed frontier at home."[12] Moreover, U.S.

activity on these fresh frontiers to the south would bear the marks of the earlier westward expansion, drawing on the same historical myth. U.S. attempts to extend its southern frontier "rested on views of history, the character of foreign peoples [i.e., 'savagery'], and politics that anticipated attitudes held by North Americans throughout much of the twentieth century. . . . North Americans seldom doubted that they could teach people to the south to act more civilized."[13]

If, as Frederick Jackson Turner averred, the frontier myth has been "wrought into the very warp and woof of American thought," the end of the nineteenth century did not signal the end of the frontier myth, only its relocation and reconceptualization. The persistence of that myth raises important questions for our society a century later. Standing at the threshhold of the twenty-first century, the United States is once again confronted with questions concerning the relationship between national identity and geographical boundaries. If the United States of the 1890s perceived national identity as linked to the western frontier, and thus feared a future with closed frontiers, contemporary political, military, and legislative attacks against immigrants suggest that the United States of the 1990s perceives national identity as linked, not to the frontier, but to the "border," and fears a future with open borders.

If Turner's suggestion concerning the foundational character of the frontier myth is accurate, we should not assume that, simply because we now prefer the language of borders to the language of frontiers, the difference in terminology reflects a truly different understanding of history and identity. It may be that, in the 1990s, the frontier myth still functions as the lens through which we as a society read the reality of our borders, especially the southern border which, in the first decades of this century, became our new, "fresh frontier."

THE BORDER

In profound ways, the border defines the social existence and identity of U.S. Hispanics. Not surprisingly, then, it is a major theme in U.S. Latino literature, art, social theory, and theology.[14] In many of these writings, "the border" is revealed as much more than a geographical place. For Latinos and Latinas, the border is not only *where* we are located, or *where* we come from; the border is *who* we are, people whose very identity and reality is "in between."[15]

As *theologians* seeking to discover the presence of God in the ongoing life of our Latino communities, U.S. Hispanic theologians are today asking how the God of Jesus Christ may be encountered on the border. If the border is not merely a geographical category but is, more profoundly, an epistemological and anthropological category defining a *human* reality, a human community, is it possible to encounter God in the midst of that reality, that community? If so, how and where? If so, moreover, what is the role of the Church in that reality?

At the same time, however, we must ask how the dominant culture's understanding of that border and the Latino/a understanding of the border may influence our reading of the border as a *locus theologicus.* Thus, before proceeding to the properly theological and ecclesiological arguments, we should ask how those arguments might be influenced by the frontier myth—and how they might be influenced by a Latino/a understanding of the border.[16]

The Latino/a perception of the border is rooted in the distinctive history of Latin America itself. While the modern drive for territorial expansion and domination is at the heart of both the Iberian and British colonization of the Americas, the processes of expansion developed differently in the North and South:

> The difference was that in the north it was possible and convenient to push back the native inhabitants rather than to conquer and subdue them. What northern colonialists wanted was land [rather than slave labor]. The original inhabitants were a hindrance. So, instead of subjugating the Indians, they set about to push them off their lands, and eventually to exterminate them. If the myth in the Spanish colonies was that the Indians were like children who needed someone to govern them, the myth in the English colonies was that the Indians were nonpeople; they didn't exist, their lands were a vacuum. In north Georgia, in the middle of Cherokee County, there is a monument to a white man who was, so the monument says, "the first man to settle in these parts." And this, in a county that is still called "Cherokee"! This contrast in the colonizing process led to a "border" mentality in Mexico and much of Latin America, and a "frontier" mentality in the United States. Because the Spanish colonizers were forced to live with the original inhabitants of the land, a *mestizo* population and culture developed. . . . In contrast, in the lands to the north, the process and the myth were of a constantly moving frontier, pushing back the native inhabitants of the land, interacting with them as little as possible. There was civilization this side of the frontier; and a void at the

other side. The West was to be "won." The western line, the frontier, was seen as the growing edge; but it was expected to produce growth by mere expansion rather than by interaction.[17]

Justo González suggests that this historical difference has given rise to different conceptions of the border. In the North, the border is perceived as moving in only one direction, outward; in the South, the border is perceived as allowing for movement in both directions. In the North, any movement back across the border is thus perceived as "an incursion of the forces of evil and backwardness into the realm of light and progress."[18] If, as Frederick Jackson Turner so explicitly declared, what lies on the other side of the border is mere "savagery," then any movement back toward the north must be prohibited as a threat to "civilization," a threat to national identity, a threat to national security. Above all, however, any movement north forces civilized society to confront its barbaric *alter ego*.

In other words, Turner was right: on the frontier Western civilization *does* encounter savagery. What he failed to see was that the savagery Western civilization encounters is *its own*. And that is why the United States fears any movement back across the border toward the north: not, ultimately, because this country wants to deny the existence of "those" savages south of the border, but because, for its own sense of national identity, the United States—like all Western societies—*must* deny the existence of *its own* savagery. The faces of those "savages" are the mirrors of this nation's soul; they are the "dangerous memory" that is never quite fully repressed. The faces of the "savages" are what the German theologian Johann Baptist Metz has called "dangerous memories, memories which make demands on us."[19] But an acknowledgment of this fact would necessarily call into question the United States' very identity as the "New Jerusalem" (in the words of Ronald Reagan) or a bridge to the twenty-first century (in the words of Bill Clinton). Collective denial is a much more palatable alternative.

"It is precisely in that willful innocence," warns Justo González, "that guilt lies."[20] "The reason why this country has refused to hear the truth in its own history," he continues, "is that as long as it is innocent of such truth, it does not have to deal with the injustices that lie at the heart of its power and its social order."[21] The reason why the myth of innocence, the frontier myth, must be exposed is not to ascribe blame to some while exonerating others. The reason is that only when we are honest about our present and past reality will we be able to more effectively bring our future reality into harmony with our national ideals.

(After all, repressed memories live on under the surface and will continue to re-surface in barbaric ways, such as attacks against immigrants and anyone whose existence recalls those dangerous memories.) To serve as just such a reminder is, according to González,

> one of our functions as a Hispanic minority in this country. It is not a pleasant function, for few love those who destroy the myths by which they live. But it is a necessary function that we must courageously fulfill. . . . In our country, such guilty innocence is the handmaiden of injustice. Injustice thrives on the myth that the present order is somehow the result of pure intentions and a guiltless history. . . . Perhaps once we are agreed that we are all *ladrones* [thieves], it will be easier for all of us to see more clearly into issues of justice.[22]

Perhaps our country will treat its Latinos and Latinas differently when it acknowledges that the Hispanic presence here, in U.S. cities and towns, is a direct result of this country's progress. Can this society admit that that progress, however extraordinary, has nevertheless come at great cost, a cost that our entire nation is currently paying, whether in the physical poverty of our blighted inner cities or the spiritual poverty of our gated suburbs?[23]

The possibility that "every great work of civilization" may indeed also be "a work of barbarism" is inconceivable in the light of the frontier myth that gave birth to our nation; an impenetrable border (i.e., the southern frontier) remains the last hope for maintaining our identity as the greatest country in the world, an example of unimpeded progress in an otherwise barbaric world. "The quest for human purity," contends Virgilio Elizondo, "defines boundaries and very quickly excludes those who have been the product of territorial transgression. There seems to be an inner fear that the children of territorial transgression pose the deepest threat to the existence of the group and to the survival of its purity."[24]

Yet a border need not function as a frontier that only expands and excludes; it need not function as a safeguard for the illusory purity of one side. Even if too often denied in practice, an alternative understanding of the border is implicit in the mestizo history of Latin America:

> A border is the place at which two realities, two worldviews, two cultures, meet and interact. . . . [A]t the border growth takes place by encounter, by mutual enrichment. A true border,

a true place of encounter, is by nature permeable. It is not like medieval armor, but rather like skin. Our skin does set a limit to where our body begins and where it ends. Our skin also sets certain limits to our give-and-take with our environment, keeping out certain germs, helping us to select that in our environment which we are ready to absorb. But if we ever close up our skin, we die.[25]

A border may function to affirm differences while, at the same time, allowing for an interaction that will be mutually enriching. Such a border, however, would presuppose a mutual recognition that "we are all *ladrones* [thieves]," with the humility entailed in such an admission. None of us are innocent, Euro-American or Latino-American:

> Hispanics . . . always knew that our ancestors were not guiltless. Our Spanish ancestors took the lands of our Indian ancestors. Some of our Indian ancestors practiced human sacrifice and cannibalism. Some of our Spanish forefathers raped our Indian foremothers. Some of our Indian foremothers betrayed their people in favor of the invaders. It is not a pretty story. But it is more real than the story that white settlers came to this land with pure motivations, and that any abuse of its inhabitants was the exception rather than the rule. It is also a story resulting in a painful identity.[26]

To be Hispanic is not merely to live "on" the border; it is to *be* a "border," to live "in between" the rapist and the violated woman, to experience the pain of that ambiguity. But, to be Hispanic is also to know that that ambiguity can be the seedbed of new life, the border can be the birthplace of a new human community unafraid of "impurities" because it knows that none of us are "pure." Such a recognition of the ambiguity of *all* human histories is a necessary precondition for an understanding of the difference between a frontier and a border.[27] It is a precondition for understanding the difference between "America" and the United States, between an "American" and an "*estadounidense.*"[28]

THE GOSPEL ON THE BORDER

The border experience is central to the Christian *kerygma*; in the Gospels, geographical location takes on symbolic, theological significance. Place is not just the accidental context of human activity; the place where an event occurs often conveys the theological meaning and significance of that event. Consequently, it is no mere coincidence that, in the synoptic accounts, Jesus comes from Nazareth, in Galilee, meets his end in Jerusalem, and, finally, returns to Galilee, where he appears to the apostles after his resurrection (Mk 14:28; Mt 26:32, 28:7, 10, 16).

In the light of the Latino/a experience of "mestizaje" (racial-cultural mixture), the final sections of this paper will explore the theological, Christological, and ecclesiological significance of Jesus' Galilean identity and the implications of that significance for a Christian understanding of the border. In so doing, we will suggest how these sacred texts of the Christian tradition can contribute to our understanding of the nature and role of territorial borders in a way that is neither expansionist nor exclusivist, whether tacitly or overtly. (It is important to note that, as *both* a geographical *and* a theological category, Galilee has significance not only for our understanding of the historical Jesus of Nazareth but, especially, for our understanding of the Gospels as *theological* texts.)

The theological significance of Galilee in the Gospels is not arbitrary, but is rooted in the history, geography, and culture of the region. Galilee was located in the far northern reaches of Palestine, bordering on the non-Jewish populations of Syria, Philippi, and the Decapolis. It was thus often viewed by first-century Jews as "a Jewish enclave in the midst of 'unfriendly' gentile seas."[29] "The area as a whole, " writes Richard Horsley, "was a frontier between the great empires in their historical struggles."[30] The Roman administrative cities of Sepphoris and Tiberias were centers of Hellenistic-Roman culture. Consequently, Jewish worship in these cities was "dramatically affected by the influences of Hellenistic-Roman culture and political domination."[31] "It is possible, perhaps even likely, . . ." argues Horsley, "that some Jews considered themselves faithful even while they utilized what would be classified as pagan or Greco-Roman symbols as a matter of course in their everyday lives."[32] Their religio-cultural diversity, together with their economic wealth, made the Galilean urban centers objects of resentment and opposition throughout the Galilean countryside, where village life among the peasantry was "guided by Israelite customs and traditions."[33]

Yet even the Jewish traditions of the peasants were different from those practiced in Jerusalem:

> Galilee was heir in some form to the traditions of the Northern
> Kingdom. . . . Torah was important, as was circumcision in

> Galilean society, but not the written and oral Torah as inter-
> preted by the Judean and Jerusalem retainer class and enforced
> where they could by the Temple aristocracy. Rather Galilee was
> home to popular legal and wisdom traditions. . . . Galilee was
> also ambivalent about Jerusalem, the Temple, the priestly aris-
> tocracy, temple dues and tithes.[34]

In short, as Richard Horsley argues, Galilean Jewish practices could be
described as a kind of popular religion:

> The distinction anthropologists often make between the "great
> tradition" and the "little traditions" may be of some help in for-
> mulating the issues. A "society" may develop cultural traditions
> at two levels: the traditions of origin and customary practice
> continue as a popular tradition cultivated orally in the villages,
> while specialists codify those same traditions in a standardized
> and centralized form as an official tradition, which is cultivated
> orally but perhaps also reduced to written form. Something like
> this distinction between official tradition and popular tradition
> may help explain the situation in Galilee as seen both in sources
> from the first century C.E. and in early rabbinic literature.[35]

A major reason for these religious differences was the history of
Galilee as a political and cultural crossroads. Because of its distance
from Jerusalem, its history as a borderland, and, consequently, its culturally diverse population, Galilee gave birth to popular religious practices that reflected those realities:

> The bulk of the Galilean population, . . . while not Judean,
> would likely have been other descendants of former Israelites.
> While sharing certain common Israelite traditions with the
> Judeans, they would have had traditions of their own and dis-
> tinctive versions of the shared Israelite traditions. Yet it is also
> inherently unlikely that all Galileans in late second-temple times
> were descendants of former Israelites. . . . Thus at least some of
> those living in Galilee must have been non-Israelites, ethnically
> or in cultural heritage. . . . Within the same village, Israelites
> and Gentiles lived in adjacent houses or shared the same court-
> yard . . . , or perhaps even shared a house or oven. . . . A great
> variety of cooperation between Israelite and gentile peasants
> took place on a regular basis.[36]

Not surprisingly, then, regional cults existed, especially along the borders, which reflected the influence of Hellenistic religions; one such cult, for instance, was the worship of the god of Carmel.[37] Horsely calls attention to the "survival of local-regional religious customs and symbols that are not suppressed or replaced over generations of pressure from Jerusalem regimes or rabbinic circles for conformity to 'dominant' religious canons."[38]

This was the cultural milieu in which Jesus grew up and exercised his ministry. This was the historical reality that would then take on theological significance in the Gospels: "While each of the four Gospels treats the region differently within the overall purposes of its narrative . . . many of their underlying social and religious assumptions are realistic on the basis of what can be reconstructed historically from other sources."[39] As Virgilio Elizondo contends, "the overwhelming originality of Christianity is the basic belief of our faith that not only did the Son of God become a *human being*, but he became *Jesus of Nazareth*. . . . Jesus was not simply a Jew, he was a Galilean Jew; throughout his life he and his disciples were identified as Galileans."[40] Consequently, argues Elizondo, Galilee should be the starting point for any Christology that claims to be rooted in the Gospels: given the history and theological significance of Galilee, and given Jesus' identification with this region, what are the ramifications of these facts for the Christian community's understanding of Jesus Christ?

In order to answer this question, we must first examine what particular valence these facts would have had for the evangelists and their communities: In the light of its history, what values, or disvalues, did Galilee represent, or symbolize? We have already hinted at what some of these would have been. Galilee, especially its villages (such as Nazareth), symbolized backwardness, ignorance, poverty, discontent, rebellion, and, above all, religious and racial-cultural impurity:

> Scripturally speaking, Galilee does not appear important in the unfolding drama of salvation and, culturally speaking, at the time of Jesus, it was rejected and despised by the Judean Jews because of the racial mixture of the area and its distance from the temple in Jerusalem. For the Jews of Jerusalem, Galilean was almost synonymous with fool! . . . The Galilean Jews appear to have been despised by all and, because of the mixture of cultures of the area, they were especially despised by the superiority-complexed Jerusalem Jews. Could anything good come out of such an impure, mixed-up, and rebellious area?[41]

The answer to this question is what Elizondo calls the "Galilee Principle," God chooses "what is low and despised in the world" (1 Cor 1:28):

> The apparent nonimportance and rejection of Galilee are the very bases for its all-important role in the historic eruption of God's saving plan for humanity. The human scandal of God's way does not begin with the cross, but with the historico-cultural incarnation of his Son in Galilee. . . . That God has chosen to become a Galilean underscores the great paradox of the incarnation, in which God becomes the despised and lowly of the world. In becoming a Galilean, God becomes the fool of the world for the sake of the world's salvation. What the world rejects, God chooses as his very own.[42]

In Galilee, moreover, the border itself becomes identified with rejection insofar as those persons who live in borderlands assimilate a multiplicity of racial, cultural, and religious influences from "across the border." Like Galilee, all borders are seedbeds of impurity. If they are not sealed, they remain vulnerable to foreign influence and penetration. Consequently, the Jewish establishment in Jerusalem could not conceive that God's word could be revealed in such a region: "Search and you will see that no prophet is to rise from Galilee" (Jn 7:52).

Yet it is precisely in the midst of impurity that, in the person of Jesus Christ, God's love and power are made manifest: "he has risen from the dead, and behold, he is going before you to Galilee; there you will see him" (Mt 28:7). Jesus' ministry will end where it began; it is in Galilee that his disciples will see the resurrected Jesus. The chosen place of God's self-revelation is there where Israelites and Gentiles live side by side, where Jewish religious practices incorporate Hellenistic influences, where popular Judaism remains outside the control of Jerusalem's "official" Judaism. The mestizo culture of the borderland is the privileged locus of God's self-revelation. Ironically, then, Ronald Reagan—and, long before him, the Puritans—may indeed have been right: the United States may well be "the New Jerusalem." And the U.S.-Mexico border is the new Galilee. Today, a new humanity is being born, not in the centers of religious and political power, but at the margins; not among the civilized but among the barbarians; not on the frontier but on the border.

Christianity on the Border

Also emerging on the border (both geographical and metaphorical) is a new ecclesial vitality. For five centuries, the Catholic Church has viewed the peoples of Latin America as objects of evangelization: "At best, the Spaniards considered the Indians coarse, childlike, immature . . . , needy of patient evangelization."[43] Thus, through its role in the conquest of the "New World," the Church participated in the drive to extend the western frontier of Western (Christian) civilization: "Cortés carried a banner of black taffeta with a colored cross, and blue and white flames scattered throughout. He inscribed on the border of the banner: *We follow the cross and in this sign we shall conquer.*"[44] The military conquest was thus accompanied by a "spiritual conquest."[45]

Christianity also accompanied and legitimated the establishment of the English colonies in the North: "The Puritans who came to New England frequently drew analogies between their experience and that of ancient Israel . . . for they were in the process of creating a new nation in a new wilderness."[46] By definition, such a wilderness was not inhabited by full-fledged human beings: "Indians were conveniently perceived not so much as ordinary human beings but as part of the fauna, along with buffaloes and coyotes, to be driven off or killed."[47] Thus, in 1645, Roger Williams was able to write: "These *Heathen* Dogges, better kill a thousand of them than that we *Christians* should be endangered or troubled with them; Better they were all cut off, and then we shall have no more trouble with them . . . cut them all off, and so make way for Christians."[48] Forrest Wood notes, moreover, the intrinsic connection between political and religious language: "Barbarian, savage, heathen, pagan. Whatever term was used, it designated an incarnation of the source of all evil—Satan. . . . And early American Protestants saw him connected to Africans and Indians."[49] Hence, there was a similar connection between political ("colonization," "civilization") and religious ("evangelization") imperialism: "It does not require a particularly careful examination to discover that, underneath all of the political shibboleths and economic realizations, Manifest Destiny was, in the final analysis, a *religious* concept that was exalted by Americans of all social levels and had been an essential element in the adventures of every European colonial power. . . . By the sixteenth century, the Reformation itself had become 'the grand means employed by God in preparing a people who should lay the foundation of a Christian empire in the New World.'"[50] And the nature of that Christian empire was specified precisely: "In claiming a divine mandate, Americans did not consign responsibility to some vague universal *élan vital* like 'Providence' or 'Nature,' or, for that matter, even something so general as a biblical God. The Christian imperialist was nothing if not specific. From the first colonial settlement to the late twentieth century, Christian America meant *Protestant* America."[51]

Thus, if Catholic Christianity had been instrumental in the conquest of the South, Protestant Christianity was a dominant (though by no means the only) force in the conquest of the North. They both shared a belief, legitimated by their theologies, that they had been divinely mandated to extend the frontier of "Christian civilization" into the "New World." On the other side of that frontier lay the ever-present threat of contamination and impurity.

Yet, from the beginning, the Christian support for imperialism was not monolithic. Among the Spaniards, Bartolomé de Las Casas was only the most famous of a small but significant number of prophetic voices decrying the conquest.[52] Among British colonists, a few Protestant ministers such as Jeremiah Evarts challenged British expansionism.[53] At great personal cost, prophets arose to challenge the churches' all-too-easy appropriation of the frontier myth as the lens through which they would view their evangelizing mission; authentic evangelization, as Las Casas observed, is utterly incompatible with conquest and destruction—indeed, it is its very opposite.

The contemporary U.S. context is one that, once again, demands that Christians take a prophetic stand against the enduring power of the frontier myth in U.S. society, including the U.S. Church. This will require, in turn, that Christians draw on those resources of our tradition that reflect a very different understanding of the borders that separate peoples from each other. And the central resource available to us is the figure of Jesus Christ himself, the Galilean Jesus of the Gospels. As someone identified with the borderlands, Jesus of Nazareth challenged all those in his society who would turn borders into impenetrable barriers. The "savages" of his society became his friends and companions, the "uncivilized" and "children" became his confidants. And he was crucified for daring to walk with them, for daring to breach the borders that separated them from the "civilized" people of his society.[54] Today, the Jesus Christ of the Gospels challenges all those who would make of the border a new frontier.

U.S. Hispanic theologians, like Elizondo and González, are retrieving the Galilean Jesus as the central symbol of our faith and the foundation of a Christianity beyond the frontier myth. Living "in between" Galilee and Jerusalem, "in between" San Juan and New York, "in between" Tijuana and San Diego, U.S. Hispanic Christians are today in a position of effecting an authentic reconciliation, one that acknowledges the value of the border as necessary for affirming human differences while, nevertheless, rejecting the frontier myth as the controlling paradigm for understanding the border.

A principal manifestation of this practical reconciliation is U.S. Hispanic popular religion, which, incorporating elements of indigenous and African religions, reflects the religious mestizaje of the borderlands.[55] As Galilean Judaism emerged from the multicultural borderlands of Palestine, so too does the Christianity of the Latino community emerge from the mestizo borderland of the United States. And, as Galilean Jewish practices were often derided by the representatives of official Judaism in Jerusalem, so too are the practices of the Latino community often dismissed as syncretistic, infantile, or superstitious. Just as the practices of Galilean Jews "with regard to heave-offerings and 'things devoted to the priests' . . . marriage customs . . . and observance of the sabbath and festivals" raised eyebrows among the official liturgists of Jerusalem, so too have the "unofficial" religious practices of U.S. Hispanics, performed outside the control of clerical, theological, and liturgical watchdogs, raised suspicions among Catholic clerics and liturgical experts.[56] Just as the very architecture of Galilean synagogues reflected "the survival of local-regional religious customs and symbols that are not suppressed or replaced over generations of pressure from Jerusalem regimes or rabbinic circles for conformity to 'dominant' religious canons," so too do the many local symbols adorning the sanctuaries of Latino churches and the "*altarcitos*" in Latino homes reflect the survival of the people's faith in the face of many generations of opposition.[57]

The rituals of Latino popular religion know no frontiers, or unbreachable borders; therein lies their radical, countercultural character. This "mestizo" popular religion reflects the inability of European Christianity to completely subdue or eradicate indigenous cultures and values. In a society and, too often, a Church structured around national, cultural, religious, and theological barriers intended to preserve national, cultural, religious, and theological "purity," the religious life of those Christian communities living "on the border" threatens the artificial peace of a frontier Christianity. Yet, in so doing, that religious life merely carries on the long Christian tradition of crossing religious and theological borders in order to witness to the universality of God's loving presence.

On the frontier of political, military, and economic expansionism a new reality is being born, a new kind of border. This border is also a frontier; not a frontier where "civilization meets savagery," but a frontier where God's reconciling, salvific loves enters into and transforms human history. The border, contends Elizondo, is God's own frontier: "It is consistently in the frontier regions of human belonging that God begins the new creation."[58] On the border, human empires are replaced by God's own reign. And that reign, as Elizondo suggests, is symbolized by the "impure" and "mixed-up" features and skin color of the mestizo and mestiza, by those human communities whose very survival on the borders of our societies witnesses to the permeability of all borders and, therefore, to the folly of the frontier myth. Latino Christian communities are living witnesses to the truth of the Gospel claim that Galilee, or "the other side of the border," is not merely a heathen wilderness in need of evangelization but a privileged locus of God's self-revelation.[59]

The popular religious practices passed down through generations testify to the barbaric consequences of that myth as well as a people's stubborn faith in a God who does not exclude but reconciles. And, unfortunately, that is why even today Christians pay obeisance to the frontier myth, fearing what the border represents and, therefore, what a mestizo, popular Christianity represents, namely, a God who is encountered in the impure ambiguity of Galilee rather than in the pure clarity of Jerusalem.

Notes

1. Walter Benjamin, quoted in David Tracy, *Plurality and Ambiguity: Hermeneutics, Religion, Hope* (San Francisco: Harper and Row, 1987), p. 69.

2. Alfred Lord Tennyson, quoted in Frederick Jackson Turner, *Rereading Frederick Jackson Turner*, with commentary by John Mack Faragher (New York: Henry Holt and Co., 1994), p. 158.

3. Turner, *Rereading Frederick Jackson Turner*, p. 101. The Latin American historian Enrique Dussel argues that, as the first European to extend European civilization westward, Christopher Columbus was the first "modern" person. Modernity is defined by the need to conquer and subdue: "Columbus thus initiated modernity. . . . Because of his departure from Latin anti-Muslim Europe, the idea that the Occident was the center of history was inaugurated and came to pervade the European life world. Europe even projected its presumed centrality upon its own origins. Hence, Europeans thought either that Adam and Eve were Europeans or that their story portrayed the original myth of Europe to the exclusion of other cultures." *The Invention of the Americas: Eclipse of "the Other" and the Myth of Modernity* (New York: Continuum, 1995), p. 32.

4. Turner, *Rereading Frederick Jackson Turner*, pp. 32, 60.

5. John Mack Faragher, introduction, ibid., p. 1.

6. Turner, *Rereading Frederick Jackson Turner*, p. 96.

7. Ray Allen Billington, *The Genesis of the Frontier Thesis: A Study in Historical Creativity* (San Marino, Calif.: The Huntington Library, 1971), p. 72.

8. As Justo González observes: "Even the name 'America' raises the question: What preposterous conceit allows the inhabitants of a single country to take for themselves the name of an entire hemisphere? What does this say about

that country's view of those other nations who share the hemisphere with it?" *Mañana: Christian Theology from a Hispanic Perspective* (Nashville, Tenn.: Abingdon Press, 1990), 37.

9. Walter LaFeber, *Inevitable Revolutions: The United States in Central America* (New York: W. W. Norton and Company, 1983), p. 300.

10. Quoted in ibid., p. 33.

11. Ibid., p. 35.

12. Ibid., p. 36.

13. Ibid., p. 39. The racist worldview underlying these statements is only too clear, especially when one compares U.S. attitudes toward immigration from Mexico with the very different attitudes toward immigration from Europe—at least white, Anglo Saxon, Protestant Europe.

14. See, for example: Raúl Fernández, *The Mexican-American Border Region: Issues and Trends* (Notre Dame, Ind.: University of Notre Dame Press, 1989); Robert Lee Maril, *Living on the Edge of America: At Home on the Texas-Mexico Border* (College Station: Texas A&M University Press, 1992); Milo Kearney, *Border Cuates: A History of the U.S.-Mexican Twin Cities* (Austin, Tex.: Eakin Press, 1995); Federico Campbell, *Tijuana: Stories on the Border* (Berkeley: University of California Press, 1995); Oscar J. Martínez, *Border People: Life and Society in the U.S.-Mexico Borderlands* (Tucson: University of Arizona Press, 1994); Oscar J. Martínez, ed., *U.S.-Mexico Borderlands: Historical and Contemporary Perspectives* (Wilmington, Del.: Scholarly Resources, 1996); Américo Paredes, *Folklore and Culture on the Texas-Mexican Border* (Austin, Tex.: Center for Mexican American Studies, University of Texas at Austin, 1993); Gloria Anzaldúa, *Borderlands* (San Francisco: Spinsters/Aunt Lute, 1987); Ruth Behar, *Translated Woman: Crossing the Border with Esperanza's Story* (Boston: Beacon Press, 1993); Cruz Arcelia Tanori Villa, *La mujer migrante y el empleo* (México, DF: Instituto Nacional de Antropología e Historia, 1989); José Manuel Valenzuela Arce, ed., *Entre la magia y la historia: tradiciones, mitos y leyendas de la frontera* (Tijuana: Programa Cultural de las Fronteras, El Colegio de la Frontera Norte, 1992); Timothy Matovina, *Tejano Religion and Ethnicity* (Austin, Tex.: University of Texas Press, 1995); idem, *The Alamo Remembered: Tejano Accounts and Perspectives* (Austin, Tex.: University of Texas Press, 1995). In theology, see the works cited below.

15. For a personal account of what it means to live "in between," see my *Caminemos con Jesús: Toward a Hispanic/Latino Theology of Accompaniment* (Maryknoll, N.Y.: Orbis Books, 1995), chapter 1. See also the powerful account of Gloria Anzaldúa, *Borderlands*.

16. Different notions of the "border" are already embedded in the English and Spanish languages themselves: "Significantly, in English we say 'border,' and in Spanish, *frontera*. But when we translate the Spanish *frontera* back into English we can come up with either 'border' or 'frontier.' In fact, commonly used Spanish has no equivalent to the English 'frontier' as distinguished from 'border'." Justo González, *Santa Biblia: The Bible Through Hispanic Eyes* (Nashville, Tenn.: Abingdon Press, 1996)., p. 84.

17. Ibid., pp. 85–86.

18. Ibid., p. 86. If one compares, for instance, the view of national borders represented by the North American Free Trade Agreement with that represented by California's Propositions 187 and 209, as well as the 1996 Welfare Reform Act denying welfare benefits to documented immigrants and their children, one receives a clear message: the United States will accord a freedom of movement to financial capital that it will not accord to mere human beings. The natural right of capital ("market forces," the "law" of supply and demand, "free" trade) to expand into new global markets must be affirmed as absolute and inviolable, while the right of labor (i.e., human beings) to do so must be artificially restricted.

19. Johann Baptist Metz, *Faith in History and Society: Toward a Practical Fundamental Theology* (New York: Seabury Press, 1980), p. 109.

20. Justo González, *Mañana*, p. 39.

21. Ibid.

22. Ibid., p. 40.

23. On the theological significance of the increasing physical isolation of the city from the suburb, see my *Caminemos con Jesús*, pp. 173–211.

24. Virgilio Elizondo, *The Future is Mestizo: Life Where Cultures Meet* (Bloomington, Ind.: Meyer-Stone Books, 1988), p. 80. The connection between the concern for purity and the erection of borders is also observed by Charles Lippy, Robert Choquette, and Stafford Poole, who, citing the work of anthropologist Mary Douglas, note that "any group captured by a passion for purity must draw boundaries. It must seek diligently to distinguish between that which will promote the pursuit of holiness and that which endangers such a pursuit. It must avoid contamination at all costs, lest pollution infect and ultimately destroy true purity." *Christianity Comes to the Americas: 1492–1776* (New York: Paragon House, 1992), p. 268.

25. González, *Santa Biblia*, pp. 86–87.

26. González, *Mañana*, p. 40.

27. Such a recognition is not, moreover, a mere utopian ideal. As anyone who has lived in or traveled to Tijuana, El Paso, or Laredo knows, the actual reality of life on the border is very different from that portrayed in the frontier myth. In towns and cities all along the Rio Grande, a truly border culture is emerging in the shadows of the southern frontier's barbed-wire fences and stone walls: "Today, the borderlands between the U.S. and Mexico form the cradle of a new humanity. It is the meeting ground of ancient civilizations that have never met before. Old cultural borders are giving way and a new people is emerging. . . . The borders no longer mark the end limits of a country, a civilization, or even a hemisphere, but the starting points of a new space populated by a new human group." Elizondo, *The Future is Mestizo*, pp. x–xi.

28. This common Spanish word denoting persons who come from the United States would literally be translated as "United Statesans." In English, of course, no such word exists; "*estadounidenses*" are, simply, "Americans."

29. Douglas Edwards, "The Socio-Economic and Cultural Ethos of the Lower Galilee in the First Century: Implications for the Nascent Jesus Movement," in *The Galilee in Late Antiquity*, edited by L. Levine (1992), p. 54.

30. Richard A. Horsley, *Galilee: History, Politics, People* (Valley Forge, Pa.: Trinity Press International, 1995), p. 241.

31. Richard A. Horsley, *Archaeology, History, and Society in Galilee: The Social Context of Jesus and the Rabbis* (Valley Forge, Pa.: Trinity Press International, 1996), p. 55.

32. Ibid., p. 63.

33. Ibid., p. 122.

34. Jonathan Draper, "Jesus and the Renewal of Local Community in Galilee: Challenge to a Communitarian Christology," *Journal of Theology for Southern Africa* 87 (June, 1994): 35–36.

35. Horsley, *Archaeology, History, and Society in Galilee*, p. 173.

36. Richard A. Horsley, *Galilee*, pp. 243–44.

37. Ibid., pp. 252–53.

38. Ibid., p. 254.

39. Sean Freyne, "Galilee," in *The Oxford Companion to the Bible*, edited by Bruce Metzger and Michael Coogan (New York: Oxford University Press, 1993), p. 241–42.

40. Virgilio Elizondo, *Galilean Journey: The Mexican-American Promise* (Maryknoll, N.Y.: Orbis Books, 1983), p. 49.

41. Ibid., p. 53.

42. Ibid.

43. Dussel, *The Invention of the Americas*, p. 54. José de Acosta was more precise in his depiction of the indigenous peoples: "The third-class savages resemble wild animals. . . . There are infinite numbers of these in the New World. . . . For all those who are scarcely human or only half-human, it is fitting to teach them to be human and to instruct them as children. . . . One must also contain them by force . . . and even force them against their will (Luke 14:23) so that they might enter the kingdom of heaven." Quoted in ibid., p. 54. On the intimate connection between military and spiritual conquest, see also Luis N. Rivera, *A Violent Evangelism: The Political and Religious Conquest of the Americas* (Louisville, Ky.: Westminster/John Knox Press, 1992). That Latin America is still "mission territory" is reflected in the fact that, five centuries after Columbus, the majority of Catholic priests in Latin America are still foreign-born. And, of course, only a small minority of the priests ministering to the Latino community in the United States are native to that community.

44. Fray Juan de Torquemada, quoted in Dussel, *The Invention of the Americas*, p. 39.

45. See Dussel, *The Invention of the Americas*, pp. 50–57.

46. Lippy, Choquette, and Poole, *Christianity Comes to the Americas:1492–1776*, p. 268.

47. Forrest G. Wood, *The Arrogance of Faith: Christianity and Race in America from the Colonial Era to the Twentieth Century* (New York: Alfred A. Knopf, 1990), p. 221.

48. Quoted in ibid., p. 35.

49. Ibid., pp. 35, 220.

50. Ibid., pp. 216–17. Martin Marty likewise notes the intimate connection between religious evangelization and military conquest for the English colonists: "The conquering Protestants regularly employed imperial language. As early as 1610 Virginia colonists were connecting missionary work with conquest and barter." *Righteous Empire: The Protestant Experience in America* (New York: The Dial Press, 1970), p. 5.

51. Ibid., p. 223.

52. See, especially, Bartolomé de Las Casas, *The Devastation of the Indies: A Brief Account* (Baltimore, Md.: Johns Hopkins University Press, 1992) and *Bartolomé de Las Casas: The Only Way*, edited by Helen Parish (New York: Paulist Press, 1992). For a magisterial study of Las Casas' life and work, see Gustavo Gutiérrez, *Las Casas: In Search of the Poor of Jesus Christ* (Maryknoll, N.Y.: Orbis Books, 1993). Other critics of the conquest included Dominican friars Juan de Ramírez, Pedro de Córdoba, and Antonio de Montesinos, as well as Bishops Juan Fernández Angulo, Juan del Valle, and, especially, Antonio de Valdivieso. Luis N. Rivera, *A Violent Evangelism*, pp. 235–57; Enrique Dussel, *A History of the Church in Latin America: Colonialism to Liberation* (Grand Rapids, Mich.: Eerdmans, 1981), pp. 49–55.

53. Marty, *Righteous Empire*, (New York: Dial Press, 1970), p. 8.

54. On Jesus' subversion of social and geographical barriers, see, for instance, John Dominic Crossan, *The Historical Jesus: The Life of a Mediterranean Peasant* (San Francisco: Harper, 1991), pp. 278–79.

55. On the mestizo, or "syncretic" character of Latino popular religion, see especially Anthony Steven-Arroyo, ed., *Enigmatic Powers: Syncretism with African and Indigenous Peoples' Religions among Latinos* (New York: City University of New York, Bildner Center, 1995), and Orlando O. Espín, *The Faith of the People: Theological Reflections on Popular Catholicism* (Maryknoll, N.Y.: Orbis Books, 1997).

56. Horsley, *Galilee*, p. 244. Insofar as post–Vatican II liturgical reforms focused on the revision of "official" liturgical *texts* used by the *clergy*, the Council itself reinforced the marginalization of the primarily *oral* and *lay* religion of U.S. Hispanics: "Thus it is easy to see why liturgical reform, with its concern to 'put devotionalism in its proper place' simply succeeded in driving a larger wedge between the official prayer of the Church and the religious life of the people—a religious life and worldview that is fundamentally promoted by popular religion." Mark Francis, "Popular Piety and Liturgical Reform in a Hispanic Context," in Ana María Pineda and Robert Schreiter, eds., *Dialogue Rejoined: Theology and Ministry in the United States Hispanic Reality* (Collegeville, Minn.: The Liturgical Press, 1995), p. 174.

57. Ibid., p. 254. Examples of such symbols are: El Cristo Negro de Esquipulas, El Santo Niño de Atocha, El Divino Rostro de Jesús, and many local or regional Marian symbols, especially Our Lady of Guadalupe.

58. Elizondo, *Galilean Journey*, p. 101.

59. No Latino popular religious symbol is more indicative of this fundamental belief than that of Our Lady of Guadalupe, which lies at the heart of

Mexican (and, increasingly, all Latino) Christianity. With the symbol and narrative of Guadalupe, the Galilean principle takes root in the Americas and becomes the basis for a mestizo Christianity that survives the conquest, a Christianity that maintains the Galilean principle alive in the face of the dominant frontier Christianity of both the North and South. In the Guadalupan narrative, the Virgin appears to a poor indigenous man, Juan Diego (a "Galilean"), on a Nahua sacred site ("Galilee"), dedicated to the worship of the Mother Goddess Tonantzín. She asks Juan Diego to be her messenger to the Spanish bishop ("high priest") in Mexico ("Jerusalem"), requesting of the bishop that he build a temple to the Virgin on Tepeyac. The bishop refuses to believe Juan Diego, since the latter is a mere Indian. After repeated attempts, and a miraculous sign from the Virgin, Juan Diego succeeds in converting the bishop, whereupon the temple is built on Tepeyac. The literature on Guadalupe is extensive. Among historiographical studies, see especially: Jacques Lafaye, *Quetzalcóatl and Guadalupe: The Formation of Mexican National Consciousness, 1531–1813* (Chicago: University of Chicago Press, 1976); Richard Nebel, *Santa María Tonantzín, Virgen de Guadalupe: Continuidad y transformación religiosa en México* (México, DF: Fondo de Cultura Económica, 1995); and Stafford Poole, *Our Lady of Guadalupe: The Origins and Sources of a Mexican National Symbol, 1531–1797* (Tucson: University of Arizona Press, 1995). Among theological interpretations, see especially Virgilio Elizondo, *La Morenita: Evangelizer of the Americas* (San Antonio: Mexican American Cultural Center, 1980); idem, *Guadalupe: Mother of the New Creation* (Maryknoll, N.Y.: Orbis Books, 1997); and Jeanette Rodríguez, *Our Lady of Guadalupe: Faith and Empowerment among Mexican American Women* (Austin: University of Texas Press, 1994).

9

"Blowing the Dynamite of the Church": Catholic Radicalism from a Catholic Radicalist Perspective

Michael J. Baxter, C.S.C.

In the wake of their momentous encounter in December 1932, Peter Maurin subjected Dorothy Day to a pedagogical program that he dubbed "indoctrination," which, from Day's account, consisted of Maurin coming over to her apartment and expounding to her on God, the Church, the Church Fathers, the saints, the poor, hospitality, liberalism, capitalism, fascism, communism, personalism, distributism, anarchism, Aquinas, Catherine of Siena, Chesterton, Belloc, Maritain, Berdyaev, Kropotkin, and so on, until she had heard enough for one day and sent him away.[1] Maurin liked to compose and recite "easy essays"—clever, laconic commentaries on the Church and the world—and it is likely that one of the first easy essays he recited in Day's presence (her memory was not so clear on this)[2] was entitled "The Dynamite of the Church," which goes as follows:

> Writing about the Catholic Church,
> a radical writer says:
> "Rome will have to do more
> than to play a waiting game;
> she will have to use
> some of the dynamite
> inherent in her message."
> To blow the dynamite
> of a message
> is the only way
> to make the message dynamic.
> If the Catholic Church

> is not today
> the dominant social dynamic force,
> it is because Catholic scholars
> have taken the dynamite
> of the Church,
> have wrapped it up
> in nice phraseology,
> placed it in an hermetic container
> and sat on the lid.
> It is about time
> to blow the lid off
> so the Catholic Church
> may again become
> the dominant social dynamic force.[3]

The notion of the Church as "dynamic" and having "dynamite" in its possession is worth lingering over for a moment. Both words are derived from the Greek *dynamis*, meaning power or might. It appears many times in the Septuagint (the Greek translation of the Hebrew Old Testament) in reference to the mighty acts of God, and in the New Testament in reference to Jesus, who also is an agent of God's power and might, when he casts out demons and heals the sick, and commissions his disciples to do the same. After the resurrection, the apostles bear witness to Christ "with great power," especially Paul, who delivers the gospel "not with persuasive words of wisdom, but with a demonstration of spirit and power" (1 Cor 2:4). This same power will prevail at the end of time, when Christ destroys all other sovereignties and powers and hands over the Kingdom to God the Father (1 Cor 15:24).[4]

Peter Maurin's point is this: God unleashed a power, a *dynamis*, in the life, death, and resurrection of Christ, which was to be shared by his followers in their spreading of the Gospel message, but Catholic scholars have taken this dynamic message, cordoned it off, kept it under wraps, and rendered it socially impotent. They have done so in the way that scholars know best, by means of "nice phraseology."

In its own quipping way, the essay points to the fact that in the world of Catholic scholarship in the thirties, theology and social theory functioned as separate, unrelated disciplines. I elaborate on this separation in the first section of this article. In the second section, I draw on writings of Maurin and Day to show that they did not separate theology from social theory, but espoused a social theory suffused with theological terms and categories. In the third section, I argue that many Catholic scholars today fail to appreciate this integration because they continue to work under an assumed separation between theology and social theory, a separation that privileges the ethical agenda of the nation-state and unfairly marginalizes the radicalist ethical vision of the Catholic Worker. In the fourth and final section, I briefly describe the difficulty in presenting the Catholic Worker from its own radicalist perspective given the disciplinary lines that currently separate theology from social theory, and the nature of the task that is immediately before us.

THEOLOGY, HERMETICALLY SEALED

Maurin's description of theology "in an hermetic container" was not a critique of any particular Catholic scholar, but of how all Catholic scholars—or almost all—collectively went about their work. It was a critique of discourse, that is, of the paradigms, institutions, disciplines, practices, rules, regulations, and unexamined assumptions making up the frame of reference out of which a group of scholars works.[5] The questions and problems taken up by a given group of scholars emerge within this frame of reference, but the frame of reference itself often goes unquestioned, unproblematized. In his essay, Peter Maurin contends that the discourse or frame of reference of Catholic scholarship unwisely treats theology and social theory as if they constitute two separate fields of inquiry, and inaccurately views theology as asocial and social theory as having little to do with theology.

Peter Maurin was right. If we look at the theoretical paradigm dominating the discourse of Catholic scholarship in these years, we see that it divided all fields of knowledge according to two fundamentally distinct realms: the natural and the supernatural. Derived from a misreading of Aquinas, this neo-scholastic paradigm held that the natural desires of the human person—the desire to meet one's physical needs, to live in society, to marry and raise children, to produce and consume goods, to establish forms of governments that enable such natural activities to be performed in accord with justice and the common good—that these natural desires can be fulfilled without the aid of the supernatural life of Christ in the Church. In this view, there were two separate realms or tiers of human existence, the natural and the supernatural, and it was possible to confine the study of society, economics, and politics to one of those two realms, the natural.[6] Hence the separation between theology and social theory.

Any critique of discourse entails a critique of institutions; in this instance, a critique of the standard institutional arrangement in U.S.

Catholic higher education in the pre-conciliar era. With few exceptions, Catholic colleges and universities placed philosophy at the center of the curriculum as the discipline that would organize and place into proper perspective knowledge gained from all other academic fields, the arts, the natural sciences, and the newly emergent social sciences. Theology, by contrast, had virtually no place in the standard curriculum. It was studied in the seminaries, which were organizationally separate from the colleges and usually free-standing institutions. Dogma, christology, moral theology, sacramental theology, mystical theology, and scripture, were reserved for the training of future priests. What religious instruction was available at the colleges was catechetical in nature, and did not relate directly to the knowledge pursued and produced at the colleges and universities. This institutional arrangement reinforced the idea that the study of politics, economics, and society deals with natural activities and should be governed by philosophy, not theology.[7]

Admittedly, the situation was not as clear cut as this account implies, but I believe the picture I have painted, big brush and all, is accurate as regards Catholic social theory in the early twentieth century. John Ryan, for example, the most prominent Catholic social theorist of this era, wrote almost nothing on sin and grace, the sacraments, christology, soteriology, eschatology, or scripture.[8] The same is true of Moorhouse F. X. Millar, a colleague of Ryan's, whose extensive writings in philosophy and political theory propose no more than a marginal role for theology.[9] The same is true of the many lesser known social theorists whose journal articles about political, economic, and social matters are by and large devoid of substantive theological reasoning and argumentation. And the same is true, with qualifications, of the most influential Catholic social theorist of this century, John Courtney Murray.

How to read Murray is a hotly contested and complex matter these days, too complex to give a full account of here, so let me sum up my reading of him in a nutshell. Murray was more ready and able than his predecessors to import theological terms and categories into his social theory,[10] but he did so in such a way that his theology effaced itself as it moved into the realm of the natural and the social. In *We Hold These Truths*, he invokes the incarnation, but only to say that it established a spiritual, not temporal, order.[11] This spiritual/temporal distinction dictates (and mutes) the significance of other theological terms and categories. Thus he refers to redemption, but only to note in passing that the Western constitutional tradition may be seen as redemptive in a terrestrial sense.[12] He mentions providence, but only to suggest that it was operative at the U.S. founding.[13] He even brings up the Sermon on the

Mount, but only to insist that its precepts, or any other precepts drawn directly from scripture, have no direct bearing on the morality of public policy.[14] In each case, Murray's use of theological terms and categories only serves to reinforce the premise of the primacy of the spiritual order, a premise that serves to reinforce the existence of another order set aside solely for temporal affairs—the affairs of politics, the state, civil law, public discourse—wherein the language of faith and revelation yields to the language of reason and natural law. The overall effect is to lend support to the presiding contention of *We Hold These Truths*, that this spiritual/temporal distinction received full-fledged endorsement by the U.S. founders and was granted legal recognition in the First Amendment of the Constitution of the United States.

It is important to note the connection between the neo-scholastic division of the natural from the supernatural and the exigencies of liberal democratic political order in the United States of America. Murray set out to provide a basis for a "public philosophy" that would appeal to all parties in a religiously pluralistic setting; this meant a philosophy not grounded in the beliefs and practices of any specific ecclesial body, a philosophy not referring to the ultimate ends of human existence;[15] and the neo-scholastic natural law, autonomous from the supernatural and accessible by means of reason alone, was perfectly suited to this task.[16]

The problem with natural law conceived apart from its supernatural end is that it perpetuates the myth of the modern liberal state as a religiously neutral institutional arrangement. In fact, this is a debased, unnatural law that should rather be understood as a rival to true religion (in the Augustinian sense), and its emergence in the seventeenth and eighteenth centuries dissipated the authority of the Church not only among the networks of social and political power but also within its own membership.[17] Furthermore, when natural law is not ordered to its supernatural end, it lacks the linguistic and conceptual resources needed to challenge existing configurations of political power from a perspective other than the realm of "the political." In this sense, the neo-scholastic enclosure of the natural within an autonomous sphere precluded a fundamental theological critique of the modern liberal state.

Thus while Murray was an accomplished theologian, theology had little direct and substantive effect on his political theory. The same is true of Catholic social theory in general. It is remarkably bereft of references to Christ, the sacraments, scripture, the saints, and other tradition-specific theological terms and categories that do not easily conform to the discursive protocols of the modern liberal state.

This is what Peter Maurin put his finger on in "Blowing the Dynamite of the Church." What we need to put our finger on is that much the same is true of Catholic social theory today. But before commenting on the contemporary scene, I want to take up the Catholic Worker from its own non-state-centered, theologically informed, radicalist perspective.

THE DYNAMITE OF THE CHURCH

The social theory to which Maurin referred in his essay was dynamic because it possessed an explosive ingredient: Jesus Christ. The image of dynamite jolts the listener/reader into imagining Christ and the Church in temporal rather than in purely spiritual terms. This is not to say that Maurin denied that the Church's mission is "spiritual"; no Catholic intellectual of that era would have denied that; but, for Maurin, "spiritual" signified specific practices and a specific form of social life. In contrast to standard Catholic social theory, his social theory was, in a word, ecclesial.

Consider, for example, his three-pronged vision of a society based on cult, culture, and cultivation. Together with culture and cultivation he lists as an indispensable element "cult," the practice of the worship of God (and he had a specifically Catholic form of worship in mind).[18] Consider his designation of parishes and dioceses as sites for the practice of hospitality; not the "muni," not state-run shelters, but the Church.[19] Consider his view of St. Francis as one who lived the kind of life that could spark social reconstruction, not personal piety or ecclesiastical reform alone, but the reconstruction of *society*.[20] For Peter Maurin, society is not built on a "pure nature"; rather, society flows out of a "nature" ordered to and fulfilled by Christ in the Church, a nature that is, to paraphrase both Father John J. Hugo and the English theologian John Milbank, "supernaturalized."[21]

This supernaturalism permeates the writings of Dorothy Day, particularly *The Long Loneliness*. Think of the scene at the outset: "Confession"—the practice of bringing one's sins into the light of day, also writing about "all the things which had brought [her] to God," about how she "found faith" and "became a member of the Mystical Body of Christ."[22] Think of the scene in the postscript: people sitting, talking, dividing up loaves and fishes, welcoming the poor into houses with expanding walls, knowing God and each other in a Eucharistic banquet joining heaven and earth.[23] Confession, then communion—here we have the story of a practicing Catholic who like Augustine (whom she cites in depicting her own task as a writer)[24] feels compelled to tell how God has taken possession of her life.

This supernaturalist perspective is written into the structure of the overall narrative of *The Long Loneliness*, as it moves from the second to the third part. Dorothy Day's time on Staten Island with Forster Batterham, walking the beach, reading, cooking, eating together, sleeping together, bearing a child—this consoling time of "natural happiness" draws her into an overflowing supernatural love. With Forster she had a child she loved and he made the physical world come alive, awakening in her a flood of gratitude. But, she writes, "the final object of this love and gratitude was God. No human creature could receive or contain so vast a flood of love and joy as I often felt after the birth of my child. With this came the need to worship, to adore."[25] Natural happiness could not satisfy. It expands one's desire beyond what the natural itself can ever fulfill. Nature, in other words, produces a lack. It is like salt on the tongue, leaving us thirsting for something more; not for more salt, but for the water that alone quenches our thirst.[26] So the story moves on, painfully, to the baptism of her daughter, to the break-up with Forster, to her own baptism, and at length, to her life at the Worker—the story of natural love transformed into the love of the cross.

A theology of the supernatural comes in Day's account of the Retreat. She describes Fr. Pacifique Roy as talking "of nature and the supernatural, how God became man that man might become God, how we were under the obligation of putting off the old man and putting on Christ." This, he said, is done by "acting always for the 'supernatural motive,'" by "supernaturalizing all our actions every day."[27] Fr. John J. Hugo, director of the Catholic Worker retreats, stressed that as Christians "we have been given a share in the divine life; we have been raised to a supernatural level."[28] "Grace is a share in the divine life . . . ," he said, "and the law of this supernatural life is love, a love which demands renunciation."[29] Significantly, she wrote this chapter shortly after the promulgation of *Humani generis* (1950), the encyclical that defended the neo-scholastic notion of "pure nature" as necessary to preserve the integrity of nature and the gratuity of grace. This pronouncement called into question the *nouvelle theologie* of Henri de Lubac and others for arguing that the notion of a purely natural end was a distortion of Aquinas' belief that the human person has a *natural* desire for God and thus a single, supernatural end. Given this context, it is significant that Day alludes to the controversy, mentions de Lubac favorably,[30] and offers a brief formulation of her own supernaturalist theology: "Body and soul constitute human nature," she writes. "The body is no less good than the soul. In mortifying the natural we must not injure the body or the soul. We are not to destroy it but to transform it, as iron is transformed in the fire."[31] This is clearly a defense of Hugo against his critics, and also perhaps her own homespun attempt to allay official suspicion.

All of which goes to show that Day's integrated understanding of the natural/supernatural relation ran counter to the neo-scholastic two-tier paradigm that dominated the discourse of Catholic scholarship during the preconciliar era. She envisioned society not as enclosed within an autonomous "natural" realm of human activity, but as radically open and dynamically oriented toward the supernatural. Two scholars associated with the Worker, Virgil Michel, O.S.B. and Paul Hanly Furfey, articulated this perspective in books, academic journals, and articles in popular periodicals including *The Catholic Worker*: Michel, by rooting all social regeneration in the liturgy;[32] Furfey, by showing that all true society flows from participation in the inner life of the Trinity.[33] But it was Day who was able to articulate it in terms of specific practices that make up a supernaturalized life. Her thick descriptions of feeding the hungry, clothing the naked, giving hospitality to the stranger, instructing the ignorant (that is, picketing), growing food on the land (or trying to), and so on—all showed that Peter Maurin's "new society within the shell of the old" where "it is easier for people to be good"[34] was thoroughly realizable in the here and now, through the power of the Holy Spirit and the intercession of the saints.

But this "new society" never figured into the work of Catholic social theorists. It did not register as a "society" as they understood the term. It was "spiritual" rather than "temporal," "supernatural" rather than "natural," "ecclesial" rather than "social." It embodied "charity" rather than "justice." These are false oppositions, of course, produced by the separation of theology and social theory that dominated Catholic scholarly discourse in the preconciliar era, but the effect, as Peter Maurin saw so clearly, was to confine the power or *dynamis* of Christ to an asocial sphere where it lay dormant.

The situation is not fundamentally different now. Even though the Catholic Worker has received plenty of scholarly attention lately—something that Catholic Workers should fear because, as Stanley Hauerwas had observed, academics study religious movements that are dead or that they are trying to kill—it remains marginalized in the discourse of Catholic social ethicists. Some social ethicists exclude it willingly; others, against their best intentions; but in any case, the problem

is not so much with the ethicists themselves as with the discursive structure of their field, which still posits a division between theology and
social theory.

PUBLIC THEOLOGY AS IDEOLOGY

Permit me to make a sweeping generalization about Catholic social
ethics that is too complex to explain fully or defend here, but that needs
to be made anyway: Catholic social ethics today continues to posit a
separation between theology and social theory and it does so in two
ways: first, by extending John Courtney Murray's project of providing
the nation with a "public philosophy" (or now, a "public theology") to
which all in a pluralistic society can appeal; and second, by reinforcing
that project with a theoretical paradigm quite distinct from the neo-
scholastic one that shaped Murray, a paradigm inherited from Max
Weber.

The genealogy of this Weberian paradigm is long and complex, trac-
ing from Ernst Troeltsch, to H. Richard and Reinhold Niebuhr, and to
James Gustafson, whose influence in the field of Catholic social ethicists
today is pervasive.[35] For our purposes, we should note that this paradigm is structured along the lines of an antinomy between religion and
politics, each of which performs a distinct ethical function.[36] Religion,
for Weber, furnishes an ideal vision that forms the basis for an "ethic of
ultimate ends," while politics determines how ethical ideals may be
approximated in a world of conflict and violence, thus functioning as an
"ethic of means." These two ethical functions complement each other,
Weber maintains, but they operate within distinct life-spheres governed
by distinct laws. It is the task, indeed the "vocation," of the politician,
working within the domain of the state, to ensure that ethical means be
appropriate to real-life circumstances. The politician must ensure that
the harsh realities of necessary means be segregated from the lofty vision
of ultimate ends, thus avoiding irresponsible attempts to put religious
ideals such as, say, the Sermon on the Mount into practice in the "real
world" of politics—which is, as Weber himself acknowledges, a world
of ethical compromise. It is this religion/politics antinomy, along with
the dualism between ends and means, that has given rise to the litany of
antinomies that shape the discourse of social ethics in the Troeltsch-
Niebuhr-Gustafson tradition: ideal/real, absolute/relative, individual/social,
sect/church, love/justice, Christ/culture, kingdom/history, and so on. My
point in identifying this paradigm, along with that of Murray, is to

emphasize that in the field of Catholic social ethics they have combined to form the distorted lens through which the Catholic Worker is read.

This distortion is evident in the readings of the Catholic Worker offered by two very different thinkers, George Weigel and Charles Curran. In *Tranquillitas Ordinis* George Weigel, a neoconservative, presents what he calls "The John Courtney Murray Project" over the course of 150 pages and then pauses to deliver an overtly hostile critique of, among others, Dorothy Day and the Catholic Worker.[37] "Given the Weberian choice between an 'ethics of responsibility' and an 'ethics of absolute ends,'" he writes, "Dorothy Day unhesitatingly chose the latter." There is no problem with this in itself for Weigel; the problem is that "Dorothy Day and the Catholic Worker did not heed Weber's advice to eschew politics. The movement may have rejected 'politics as a vocation,' but it eagerly embraced politics as an avocation." This was especially the case regarding its approach to Soviet communism, which was "distorted by the apocalyptic horizon and its failure to distinguish relative evils." As regards Day herself, Weigel grants that her religious intuitions were sincere and intense, but this does not detract from her shortcomings as an absolutist unwilling to make the compromises and prudential judgments necessary in the political arena. She should have avoided politics altogether. Thus Weigel assures us that "Dorothy Day's life and witness remains a powerful sign in modern American Catholicism," but finally, "the enduring truth of [her] life rests . . . not in her political judgments, but in her faith."[38]

A surprisingly similar reading of the Catholic Worker has been offered by the liberal Catholic moral theologian and social ethicist Charles Curran. In *American Catholic Social Ethics*, Curran focuses on one of the Catholic Worker's leading theological spokesmen, Paul Hanly Furfey.[39] The primary positive feature of Furfey's "radicalism," says Curran, is that it is "prophetic" and thus has "the ability to see the problems." Whereas "Catholic liberals at times might tend to overlook some problems . . . , the Catholic radical possesses a methodological approach which makes one sensitive to the real problems facing our society." And yet, while the methodology of Catholic radicalism serves to make "Catholics and others in our society aware of the dangers of conformism," it is deeply flawed, as Curran sees it, in that it has not been "effective in helping the lot of the poor and oppressed in our society." The problem here is that it has a "one-sided emphasis on the change of the heart of the person with comparatively little or no stress on the need for the change of institutions or of structures."[40] Thus, while the work of Dorothy Day and the Catholic Worker has been "awe-inspiring and of great spiritual beauty," their program "has not been effective. They have concentrated only on the derelicts and have done little or nothing to help the poor of the ghetto change the conditions in which they live."[41] Nevertheless, Curran affords Day and the Worker a limited place within his "catholic and universal church," to wit: "within the total church there must always be room for a radical Christian witness. Individual Christians, but not the whole church, can be and are called to a radical vocation and witness within the church."[42]

Notice here the similarities between Weigel's and Curran's reading of the Worker. Both find it lacking in responsibility when it comes to institutional change. Both appeal to criteria of effectiveness. Both extol the Worker for its inspiring example, but its significance is restricted to the realm of individual witness. Both are indebted to the Weberian paradigm of politics. Differences in tone and emphasis notwithstanding, the readings of the Catholic Worker offered by Weigel and Curran are equally condescending and misleading.

And this is true, I would submit, of a host of social ethicists dedicated to developing a "public philosophy" or a "public theology," whose considerable differences give way to a common reading of the Catholic Worker's ecclesiology as "sectarian." This is a key word in the lexicon of Catholic social ethics done in the Troeltsch-Niebuhr-Gustafson lineage. It is invoked as a way to dismiss the claim that Christian discipleship entails a form of life that is embedded in the beliefs and practices of the Church and therefore cannot serve as the basis for universal, supra-ecclesial ethical principles that are then applied in making public policy.[43] In this dismissal, it is possible to detect the lineaments of the kind of Weberian critique of the Catholic Worker offered by Weigel and Curran, namely, that gospel ideals do not pertain to politics and must therefore be translated from ends into means, from absolute into relative terms, so as to have a more direct bearing in the world of pragmatic policy making. But such a translation reproduces the former neo-scholastic separation of theology and social theory that Peter Maurin criticized in his "easy essay." It also runs counter to the consistent claim of Maurin and Day that true society is rooted in the supernatural life of Christ and cannot be abstracted from the beliefs and practices of the Church. Most important, this "public theology" approach fails to take seriously a contention that has been central to the life of the Catholic Worker from the beginning, namely, that the modern nation-state is a fundamentally unjust and corrupt set of institutions whose primary function is to preserve the interests of the ruling class, by coercive and violent means if necessary—and there will always come a time when it is necessary.

Those working out of the Murray tradition of "public theology" find this assessment of the modern nation-state to be intolerably negative. And indeed it certainly is negative—but Day would add that this is for good reason. After all, she was formed politically by the Old Left during and after the Great War. This was the era of the Committee on Public Information, the suppression of journals such as *The Masses*, the Palmer Raids, the shut down of the Wobblies, and the Red Scare of the twenties. The history of state-sponsored political repression was very much intertwined with Dorothy Day's personal history (as is especially clear from the first part of her autobiography),[44] and it left her forever wary of the claims of the state, as she herself indicates with the title of the chapter in *The Long Loneliness* on anarchist politics: "War is the health of the state."[45]

The title comes from a phrase in an essay written by Randolph Bourne as the Great War was drawing to a close.[46] It was well known among the Old Left in the years after the war, and it is worth reviewing at length because it obviously reflects Day's worldview. The essay decries the way in which a nation's population during war is transformed into a single herd that conforms to the aims and purposes of the state. In times of war, Bourne observes, the state realizes its "ideal," which is "that within its territory its power and influence should be universal." It makes a claim on "all the members of the body politic," for "it is precisely in war that the urgency for union seems greatest, and the necessity for universality seems most unquestioned. The State is the organization of the herd," Bourne continues, and "war sends the current of purpose and activity flowing down to the lowest level of the herd, and to its most remote branches." Thus the state becomes "the inexorable arbiter and determinant of men's businesses and attitudes and opinions."[47] As an open supporter of the International Workers of the World (I.W.W.) or "Wobblies," an anarchist union that was subjected to intense governmental scrutiny and repression during and after the war, Bourne was concerned with the ways in which control is exercised over the population by means of the police, courts, prisons, and other state-sponsored institutions. But he is particularly insightful about the subtle mechanisms by which conformity is ensured through a complex network of symbols, attitudes, and customs that produce what he calls "State-feeling" or "State-enthusiasm."[48] Old symbols are taken out and dusted off. Old slogans are brought back into circulation. "Public opinion, as expressed in the newspapers, and the pulpits and the schools, becomes one solid block. And 'loyalty,' or rather war orthodoxy, becomes the sole test for all professions, techniques, occupations."[49] This is true in the academy, when the "herd-instinct" becomes the "herd-intellect,"[50] and also in the churches, "when Christian preachers lose their pulpits for taking more or less in literal terms the Sermon on the Mount."[51] The mechanisms that produce this "State-feeling" are so subtle, so well dispersed, reaching each cell in the body politic, that conforming to it feels natural and right, so much so that it feels natural and right to kill for it.

By using Bourne's provocative aphorism as a chapter title in her autobiography, at a time when the nation was in the throes of the cold war, Day reminded her readers that the Catholic Worker is "radical" in two related senses. It is radical in the sense that it addresses the roots of social reconstruction by grounding it in the person and work of Christ, and also in the sense that it refuses to conform to the order—or disorder—imposed by the modern nation-state. This second sense of radicalism is crucial for reading the Catholic Worker from its own radicalist perspective, for it challenges public theology's state-centered understanding of politics by disclosing the possibility of reading "public theology" as ideology, that is, as a constellation of ideas that legitimate the dominant power relations of capitalist order by depicting particular forms of social and political life as natural or universal.[52]

One way to begin reading "public theology" as ideology would be to examine the word "public," which is supposed to signify the inclusive nature of the workings of liberal democracy in the United States. From the perspective of the Catholic Worker, the mechanisms of the state have never really been "public" for much of the population—the ones who live in shelters and S.R.O.'s, who work the fields or sweep the floors at McDonald's, who live a pay check away from eviction, who are not counted in the census, who live in constant economic depression. Similar criticisms could be made of notions like "freedom," "justice," "the common good," "civil society," and "the limited state," words or phrases that conceal the dehumanizing world of those who live on the bottom fifth of "our society." Public theologians, of course, respond that this is the situation that they seek to reform, which would seem to be a worthy task; but this kind of reformist agenda only serves to reinforce the assumption that the only effective mechanism for implementing justice in the modern world is the modern state. It is this assumption that Dorothy Day, with the help of Robert Ludlow, rejects in her chapter on the state and Christian anarchism, in favor of a localist understanding of government and politics grounded in the power of the cross.[53]

The power of the cross moved Dorothy Day beyond the pale of the Old Left, where religion was seen only as part of the ideological superstructure that kept capitalism running smoothly. In her journey from natural happiness to supernatural love, she discovered another kind of religion, with a social program at least as radical as any she had encountered among the Marxists, socialists, and anarchists of her youth. Having been singed by "the dynamite of the Church," she could pose the startling question, in the first issue of the New York paper, "Is it not possible to be radical and not atheist?" The question pointed to a crucial flaw in the standard critique of religion put forth by radicals of the Old Left, namely, that it was a critique of *bourgeois* religion, religion that conforms to norms established by the social relations of capitalist production, religion that is designed to legitimate the workings of the state and market. That critique failed to consider the possibility of another religion, one founded on a Lord who preached love of enemies and good news to the poor, who healed the sick and welcomed the outcast, who made the rulers of this world tremble, and who bestows upon His followers the power to do the same. This is the religion that was proclaimed by Day in the first issue of *The Catholic Worker* and, as has been amply demonstrated by Catholic Workers ever since, it was—and is—a genuinely radical religion.

But this theological claim that can only be explicated from a radicalist perspective. Given the present configuration of the field of Catholic social ethics, this requires distinguishing the radicalist perspective of the Catholic Worker from the bourgeois perspective of public theology and unmasking public theology as a discourse that legitimates the nation-state. It requires a demolition of public theology using "the dynamite of the Church."

No More Playing a Waiting Game

Unmasking public theology as ideology is a theoretical task, a scholarly task, and one would expect that one place where such a task might be accomplished is the Catholic college or university. But here we run into a problem. The theoretical paradigms and institutional structures shaping Catholic colleges and universities today continue to separate theology from social theory and therefore militate against a supernaturalized social theory such as that embodied in the Worker. It is by no means a coincidence, therefore, that these Catholic schools all too often function as production sites of capitalist theory and training centers for capitalist practice. At times, the ethos of these schools is so drenched in late-twentieth-century capitalist culture as to lead one to conclude, in darker moments, that the shepherding being done at these schools is the kind that raises sheep not for the Church, but for the market.[54]

But resisting capitalism is a problem we face not only in our schools. It is a problem for everyone everywhere, as some Leftist theorists of hegemony began to recognize earlier this century. One of the first such theorists in this country is mentioned in *The Long Loneliness*, very briefly. He was the brother-in-law of Forster Batterham (Day's English, anarchist common-law husband), and when Day first met him, he was "writing the first of his strange books."[55] This was Kenneth Burke, the Marxist literary critic who informed the radical left of the thirties that revolution is a cultural as well as an economic struggle, and that (in the words of Frank Lentricchia) "a revolutionary culture must situate itself firmly on the terrain of its capitalist antagonist, must not attempt a dramatic leap beyond capitalism in one explosive, rupturing moment of release, must work its way through capitalism's language of domination by working cunningly within it, using, appropriating, even speaking through its key mechanism's of repression."[56] If the point provides a helpful corrective to Peter Maurin's image of dynamite (perhaps the image of termites is more appropriate), it only heightens the urgency of the message of Peter Maurin's "easy essay".

Catholic scholars will have to do more than play a waiting game.[57]

Notes

1. Dorothy Day, *The Long Loneliness* (San Francisco: Harper and Row, 1981), 169–74. Idem, *Loaves and Fishes* (New York: Harper and Row), pp. 3–9, 14–16.

2. Day, *Long Loneliness*, p. 172.

3. Peter Maurin, *Easy Essays* (Chicago: Franciscan Herald Press, 1977), p. 3. In this volume the essay is given a different title: "Blowing the Dynamite."

4. In both passages cited the word used is *dynamis*, but this word is not often used to refer to evil powers. See Walter Wink, *The Powers, vol. 1, Naming the Powers: The Language of Power in the New Testament* (Philadelphia: Fortress, 1984), pp. 161–62.

5. For a general understanding of the notion of discourse, see Paul Bove, "Discourse," in *Critical Terms for Literary Study*, ed. Frank Lentricchia and Thomas McLaughlin (Chicago: University of Chicago Press, 1995), pp. 50–65.

6. For a brief but helpful summary of this neo-scholastic understanding of the natural and the supernatural and the corrective to it proffered by Henri de Lubac, see Paul McPartlan, *Sacrament of Salvation* (Edinburgh: T & T Clark, 1995), pp. 45–60. See also Stephen Duffy, *The Graced Horizon: Nature and Grace in Modern Catholic Thought* (Collegeville, Minn.: Michael Glazier, 1992), pp. 50–84; and Fergus Kerr, *Immortal Longings* (Notre Dame, Ind.: University of Notre Dame Press, 1997), pp. 159–84.

7. For a general description of this institutional arrangement, see Michael J. Baxter, C.S.C., "In Service to the Nation: A Critical Analysis of the Formation of the Americanist Tradition in Catholic Social Ethics" (Ph.D. diss., Duke University, 1996), pp. 123–47.

8. Charles Curran, *American Catholic Social Ethics* (Notre Dame, Ind.: University of Notre Dame Press, 1982), pp. 84–87.

9. For a more extensive account of Millar, see Baxter, "In Service to the Nation," pp. 323–53.

10. Murray's dedication to serious theological concerns, particularly those articulated by the *nouvelle theologie*, has been convincingly shown in Joseph A. Komonchak, "John Courtney Murray and the Redemption of History: Natural Law and Theology," in *John Courtney Murray and the Growth of Tradition*, ed. J. Leon Hooper and Todd David Whitmore (Kansas City, Mo.: Sheed and Ward, 1996), pp. 60–81.

11. John Courtney Murray, S.J., *We Hold These Truths* (New York: Sheed and Ward, 1960), pp. 202–204.

12. Ibid., p. 155.

13. Ibid., pp. 30, 67, 68.

14. Ibid., 275ff.

15. Ibid., pp. 54, 73.

16. This summary raises the possibility of developing a philosophy that does make adequate reference to ultimate ends, a philosophy that points beyond itself and thus acknowledges its own insufficiency in providing a full account of society and politics. Such a task clearly goes beyond the purposes of this paper, but it is important at least to acknowledge that the radicalist position I am setting forth calls for the developing of precisely this kind of philosophy.

17. For an account of how the rise of the liberal state subverted the authority of the Church by confining it to the private sphere of "religion" (understood in the modern sense), see William T. Cavanaugh, "'A Fire Strong Enough to Consume the House': The Wars of Religion and the Rise of the State," *Modern Theology* 11 (October 1995): 377–420.

18. Day, *Long Loneliness*, p. 171.

19. Peter Maurin, *Easy Essays*, pp. 8–12.

20. Ibid., pp. 37–38.

21. As regards John Milbank, I refer to his admittedly crude characterization of the French theological movement the *nouvelle theologie* as "supernaturalizing the natural," as presented in *Theology and Social Theory* (Cambridge, Mass.: Blackwell, 1991), pp. 206–55.

22. Dorothy Day, *Long Loneliness*, pp. 9–12, 10.

23. Ibid., pp. 285–86.

24. Ibid., pp. 10–11.

25. Ibid., p. 135.

26. Henri de Lubac, *The Mystery of the Supernatural*, trans. Rosemary Sheed with an introduction by David Schindler (New York: Crossroad, 1998), p. 31.

27. Day, *Long Loneliness*, p. 247.

28. Ibid., p. 256.

29. Ibid., p. 257.

30. Ibid., p. 258.

31. Ibid., p. 257.

32. Michael J. Baxter, C.S.C., "Reintroducing Virgil Michel: Towards a Counter-Tradition of Catholic Social Ethics in the United States," *Communio* 24 (fall 1997): 499–528.

33. The clearest presentation of this theology is found in Paul Hanly Furfey, *Fire on the Earth* (New York: Macmillan, 1936).

34. Day, *Long Loneliness*, p. 170.

35. Again, this argument is too complex to put forth here, but it may be helpful at least to list some of the more important texts to be included in this genealogy: Ernst Troeltsch, *The Social Teaching of the Christian Churches*, trans Olive Wyon, with an introduction by H. Richard Niebuhr (New York: The Macmillan, 1931; repr., Chicago: University of Chicago, 1976). H. Richard Niebuhr, "Ernst Troeltsch's Philosophy of Religion" (Ph.D. diss, Yale University, 1924). Idem, *Christ and Culture* (New York: Harper and Row, 1951). James Gustafson, "The Sectarian Temptation: Reflections on Theology, the Church, and the University," *Proceedings of the Catholic Theological Society of America* 40 (1985): 83–94.

36. This position is explicated in Max Weber, "The Profession and Vocation of Politics," in *Weber: Political Writings*, ed. Peter Lassman and Ronald Speirs and trans. Ronald Speirs, Cambridge Texts in the History of Political Thought (Cambridge: Cambridge University Press, 1994), pp. 309–69, see especially 357–69. My characterization of Weber draws closely on a brief but illuminating summary of Weber in Frederick C. Bauerschmidt, "The Politics of the Little Way: Dorothy Day Reads Therese of Lisieux," in *American Catholic Traditions: Resources for Renewal*, ed. Sandra Yocum Mize and William Portier (Maryknoll, N.Y.: Orbis, 1997), p. 78.

37. George Weigel, *Tranquillitas Ordinis* (New York: Oxford, 1987), pp. 148–73.

38. Weigel, *Tranquillitas*, pp. 152–53.

39. Charles Curran, *American Catholic Social Ethics* (Notre Dame: University of Notre Dame Press, 1982), pp. 130–71. For another account of the importance of Furfey in the Catholic Worker Movement, see Mel Piehl, *Breaking Bread* (Philadelphia: Temple University Press, 1982), pp. 126–28.

40. Curran, *American Catholic Social Ethics*, pp. 166–67.

41. Ibid., p. 170.

42. Ibid., p. 169.

43. The most frequent target of this critique is Stanley Hauerwas. For a critique of Hauerwas and Hauerwas' response, see James Gustafson, "The Sectarian Temptation," pp. 83–94 and Stanley M. Hauerwas, "introduction," in *Christian Existence Today: Essays on Church, World, and Living In Between* (Durham, N.C.: Labyrinth Press, 1988), pp. 1–21.

44. Day, *Long Loneliness*, pp. 44–109.

45. Ibid., pp. 263–73.

46. Randolph Bourne, "The State," in *War and the Intellectuals: Collected Essays, 1915–1919*, ed. and with an introduction by Carl Resek (New York: Harper and Row, 1964), pp. 65–104, see especially 69, 71.

47. Ibid., p. 69.

48. Ibid., pp. 77, 78.

49. Ibid., p. 70.

50. Randolph S. Bourne, "The War and the Intellectuals," in *War and the Intellectuals*, pp. 3–14, 7.

51. Bourne, "The State," p. 71.

52. Ideology can be understood in a multitude of ways, as has been noted by Terry Eagleton in *Ideology: An Introduction* (London: Verso, 1991), pp. 1–3. Here I am combining several of these possible uses, though not, I hope, in a self-contradictory way.

53. Ludlow's argument that government need not be confined to the domain of the modern state can be found in Day, *Long Loneliness*, p. 268. For an illuminating account of Day's localist politics, including the influence on Day of Simone Weil's *The Need for Roots*, see Robert Coles, *Dorothy Day: A Radical Devotion* (Reading, Mass.: Addison-Wesley, 1987), pp. 89–109, especially 105–07.

54. I have taken and adapted this metaphor from Kenneth Burke, as presented in Frank Lentricchia, *Criticism and Social Change* (Chicago: University of Chicago Press, 1983), p. 88.

55. Day, *Long Loneliness*, p. 114.

56. Frank Lentricchia, *Criticism and Social Change*, p. 24.

57. This paper was originally presented at a conference on Dorothy Day and the Catholic Worker at Marquette University, October 10, 1997. I am grateful to Frederick C. Bauerschmidt, William T. Cavanaugh, Michael Dauphinais, Michael Garvey, Stanley Hauerwas, and Thomas Hibbs for reading and commenting on subsequent drafts of this essay.

10

Pledging Allegiance: Reflections on Discipleship and the Church after Rwanda

Michael L. Budde

> There are lots of things which one can be "at the same time,"
> and it is true particularly of all insignificant things that one
> can be a number of them "at the same time." One can be both
> this and that, and at the same time a dilettante violinist, mem-
> ber of a lodge . . . etc. The significant thing has precisely this
> characteristic, that just in proportion as it is significant it is
> less possible for a man [sic] to be that *and* at the same time
> something else.
>
> —Soren Kierkegaard, *Attack upon Christendom*

The central question of ecclesiology is one of ultimate loyalty: to whom or what do we belong, pledge allegiance, recognize as that commitment to which all others must bend or bow? From Paul and Constantine, Augustine and Luther, to the moderns and postmoderns alike, the question remains brutal in its simplicity: to whom do we belong? God or Caesar? God or Mammon? Christ or the world?

Such an either/or formulation is supposed to be the province of Protestant naysayers, or sectarian and small-minded simplifiers. It is certainly supposed to be out of bounds for Catholic theologians, whose mainstream of intellectual tradition throbs with both/and affirmations. In our tradition, grace builds upon nature, affirms the goodness found in all human cultures and efforts; faith and reason complement one another, church and state exist in separate-but-complementary spheres, and on and on.

The problem with such easy compatibility is that in many cases it is wrong. It often has as much to do with the life and message of Jesus as a GM Pontiac has with real Native Americans—nothing except a claimed, mostly imaginary, continuity of name. This sort of theology displaces the priorities, loyalties, and allegiances of Jesus—which the state and economic elites of his time correctly recognized as subversive, and for which they murdered him—with safer, more comfortable ones. Being a disciple of Jesus, to which all of us are called, was and is meant to be a *primary, ultimate, pivotal* vocation. By its very nature it cannot share allegiances with lesser goods and commitments. When it does, it is discipleship no longer, and whatever displaces it becomes a matter of idolatry.

Few people inside the churches seem eager to admit it, but in matters of human allegiance, loyalty, and priorities, Christianity is a nearly complete, unabashed failure. It has had little discernible impact in making the Sermon on the Mount (Pope John Paul II's "magna charta of Gospel morality")[1] remotely relevant in Christian life and lifestyles; it has provided no alternative sense of community capable of withstanding the absolutist claims of state, movement, and market; and it can offer nothing but an awkward, embarrassed silence in response to the scandal of Christians slaughtering Christians (not to mention everybody else) in "just" wars blessed by hierarchs on all sides in slavish obedience to presumably more important loyalties.

The failures are so huge, the contradictions with the gospel so enormous, that they don't even register as subjects of concern in the churches. When forced to confront our hypocrisy and our obedience to other sources of meaning, we wring our hands, lament the sinfulness of the human condition, and pray for a human solidarity that would terrify us if it ever came to pass. And the institutions of death grind on in our world, with good Christians serving them efficiently, responsibly, and in ways indistinguishable from those who reject the premise that Jesus of Nazareth incarnated God's way for his people on earth.

The twentieth century provides too many examples of Christian failure to consider any other conclusion. World wars, wars of national liberation and colonial conquest, unspeakable genocides—all of these and more testify to the irrelevance of Christianity as a category having any purchase on human loyalties or obligations. When states say "kill," Christians kill. When ethnic leaders say "die," Christians die. When the market says some must starve," Christians let some—too many—starve. Those whose Christian convictions and sensibilities move them to deny human sacrifice to the human-made gods of nationalism, those who refuse to bless systems of economic exploitation—these stand out as irritating, awkward exceptions whose witness exposes the timidity of the mainstream, a mainstream that elevates to a superhuman status those Christian exemplars it cannot hide or obscure.

In this chapter, I wish to reflect on matters of discipleship and allegiance in light of one of this century's most recent, world-class failures of Christianity—the genocidal undertakings in Rwanda during the spring of 1994. The choice of a "Third World" example should give no comfort to white, European, or American Christians, each of whose communities have perpetrated genocidal campaigns of their own over the past few centuries. Rwanda is the most recent example of what can happen *in extremis* when Christian formation is shallow and weak, easily bent to the purposes of groups who worship secular power instead of Yahweh. It offers startling lessons to Christians everywhere regarding a Christianity so diluted that it mixes easily and effortlessly with those human allegiances that demand killing and exploitation as their due. If Rwandan Christians deduced that Christians could kill one another (and everyone else) in the service of "more important" obligations, that is a lesson they learned from the white European churches. Rwanda merely reflects back to the universal church its own version of Christianity armed, mobilized and murderous.

"THE MOST CATHOLIC COUNTRY IN AFRICA"

Rwanda is a country small in area, densely populated, and long regarded as perhaps the "most Catholic country in Africa." By the 1990s, more than 60 percent of the population was considered Catholic (another 25 percent was Protestant), and Church institutions were primary national players in matters of education, employment, international development assistance, and other areas. As a social and cultural force, since the nineteenth century the Church helped develop, disseminate, and deepen several benchmark categories of Rwandan nationalist and ethnic identity—categories with horrific implications, as displayed in the 1994 genocide.

Along with the European colonizers of Rwanda, Church leaders initially helped develop the notion that Rwandese society was built upon qualitatively dissimilar tribes, with primary significance assigned to the differences separating the intellectually and culturally "superior" Tutsi and the "simpler," less intelligent Hutu. Scholarly debate continues on whether the two groups represent different cultural-ethnic groups (evidence to the contrary—that they speak the same language, for example—is plentiful); it is not disputed, however, that the terms "Tutsi" and

"Hutu" first meant "rich" and "poor" before becoming designations for discrete "tribes." This dichotomy, which undergirded the German (and later Belgian) policy of privileging local Tutsi elites to control the majority of the population (which was and is Hutu), dictated economic, educational, and ecclesial strategy for the colonial administration. Further,

> the result of this heavy bombardment with highly value-laden stereotypes for some sixty years ended by inflating the Tutsi cultural ego inordinately and crushing Hutu feelings until they coalesced into an aggressively resentful inferiority complex.[2]

The contemporary power of Catholicism in Rwanda belies the rapidity of its rise to hegemony. Indeed, until the 1920s the Church saw only slow growth, its mission disdained by Rwanda's elite and its few converts drawn mostly from poor and powerless groups. A massive wave of conversions began in 1927, as large numbers of the Tutsi elite began responding—not to the gospel, which was not new, but to the new leadership opportunities provided them by the takeover of Rwanda by Belgium (which assumed control of the colony from Germany under a League of Nations mandate after World War I). For their part, "many priests were delighted to see the country's elite suddenly flock to them rather than the social outcasts who used to be their clientele."

> Before 1927 the church had lacked a firm grounding in Rwandese social reality, but by 1932 it had become its main social institution, presiding over hundreds of thousands of converts, including the King himself.[3]

This hierarchical, quasi-Thomistic social ordering of superior and inferior groups did not prevent Catholicism from growing among the lower-class Hutu (in fact, the preferential access to education the church afforded to the Tutsi after 1927 led a disproportionate number of Hutu to enter Catholic seminaries as their only way to attain higher education). By the 1940s and 1950s, this Hutu presence in the church (encouraged by the developments in "social Catholicism" in Belgium and elsewhere in Europe) laid the base for a Hutu "counter-elite in the Church, and for greater sympathy for the numerically superior but oppressed Hutu.[4] By the time the Hutu majority overthrew their Tutsi overlords in 1959, leading the country into political independence in 1961, the Church had repositioned itself as supportive of Hutu power and majoritarian democracy. This deft changing of sides was made possible by the long-time Catholic conviction that Christian goals could be advanced by supporting the ends, means, and ideologies of almost any group claiming "legitimate" political authority. In the era of Hutu political control, therefore, the Church would remain as important in Rwanda as it had under Tutsi domination.[5]

> If there was a link between the two versions of the myth [first Tutsi, then Hutu leadership] it was the Catholic church. It had admired the Tutsi and helped them rule, but now it admired the Hutu and helped them rule. In both cases, this was perceived (and abundantly explained) as being the work of divine providence and a great step forward in the building of a Christian society in Rwanda.[6]

The Catholic Church in Rwanda established close ties with the dominant Hutu party, the MRND; indeed, the Archbishop of Kigali (the capitol), Vincent Nsengiyumva, was an active member of the party's central committee until forced by the Vatican to resign the political post in 1989.[7] Thus, in the same century, the Catholic Church stressed the compatible loyalties of Christian and Tutsi identities, and then again Christian and Hutu claims to allegiance; it emphasized the continuities between the gospel and Tutsi "tribal" virtues, and between the gospel and Hutu "tribal virtues." So closely was the gospel associated with the surrounding culture that the Church absorbed that culture and its mythologies—with all their negative aspects—into itself (a point made by Linden[8]). Having sown a political strategy of multiple, "harmonious" loyalties—in this case, Christian and political/ethnic loyalties—the Church in Rwanda reaped a genocidal harvest when those loyalties diverged in early 1994.

THE FAILURE OF CHRISTIAN FORMATION

A complicated set of political intrigues—an expatriate Tutsi military force, splits in the ruling coalition between Hutu zealots (for whom "Hutu Power" was their obsession and agenda) and Hutus willing to tolerate Rwanda's Tutsi minority—converged in the assassination of Hutu president Juvenal Habyarimana in early April, 1994. The most likely perpetrators were among the Hutu Power faction, which upon the president's death immediately began implementing a preplanned campaign of mass extermination targeting all Tutsis, "part-Tutsi" Rwandans, moderate Hutus, and anyone (including Hutus) who might attempt to shelter or assist Tutsis fleeing the slaughter.

What happened over the brief span of two months is probably unlike any genocide in modern memory. Roughly 800,000 men, women, and children were killed—either by the Rwandan army, armed vigilante groups (especially the notorious Interahamwe), and ordinary citizens. Hutus who had lived peacefully alongside—and frequently intermarried with—Tutsis eagerly turned them in to the armed groups, or killed them on their own initiative. With "hate radio" broadcasts urging Hutus to finish their "work" more quickly and thoroughly, the carnage (much of it using the low-tech tools of common agriculture, especially the machete) may have involved significantly more perpetrators per capita than the Nazi, Khmer Rouge, or Armenian extermination campaigns.

According to Amnesty International, some of the largest slaughters were connected to churches. Christian Tutsis fled to the Christian Churches seeking protection, where they were massacred by the thousands by Christian Hutus (nearly 50,000 were killed in a single nightmarish incident in a church compound southwest of the capital).[9] While many priests and nuns—mostly for being Tutsi—died with their congregations, in many cases priests and nuns were charged with having abetted or willingly participated in the selection and killing of Tutsis seeking protection, including many children.

The question of allegiance—Christian or tribal—played itself out in bloody fashion across Rwanda. African Rights, a London-based human rights group, documented allegations against two Hutu nuns who, the group contends, "willingly and enthusiastically help[ed] a mob that slaughtered thousands of Rwandan Tutsis seeking sanctuary in the nuns' convent at Sovu in southern Rwanda."[10] One nun, according to the report, ordered the Tutsi to march out to a waiting mob of Hutu soldiers and militia members, even shoving small children out the door. The other nun went even further, according to survivors, in supplying the perpetrators with gasoline to burn the Tutsis alive.

The nuns, now living with and protected by Benedictine and Church authorities in Belgium, deny the charges. They do concede, however, that they did hand the Tutsis over to their killers, but only after receiving threats to the nuns and assurances that the Tutsis would not be harmed.[11] These nuns' responses contrast starkly with that evidenced during a 1997 attack by Hutu militiamen on a business and accounting school in Rwanda's Gisienyi province. There, when confronted with militia demands to separate students into Hutu and Tutsi groups, the school's leader—a Belgian nun—and her students refused, preferring to die with their Tutsi colleagues. Twenty-two people died in this more recent attack, but in this case no one accuses the Church of facilitating mass murder.[12]

As a force impacting behavior, Christianity—especially the Catholic Church—must be judged a massive, abysmal failure in the Rwandan case. By making Christianity compatible with non-Christian identities, by subordinating the life of discipleship to obedience to legitimate authority (and to the Hutu perpetrators, the army and militia *did* constitute legitimate authority, given the circumstances and the political ideologies in play at the time), the Catholic Church in Rwanda brought disgrace upon itself and on Christianity worldwide. The killers exterminated more than one-tenth of the country's population, generated several hundred thousand refugees, and may have enlisted more than 100,000 direct perpetrators from a Hutu population of roughly six million; one observer estimates that a majority of Rwandan Hutus may have provided "moral support and approbation" to the massacres. Overall, "although . . . there were admirable acts of courage among individual Christians, the church hierarchies were at best useless and at worst accomplices in the genocide."[13]

Perhaps the final insult to the victims and the worldwide Christian community comes from the dogged refusal of Church leaders to take responsibility for their role in the genocide. Those Church groups (including foreign missionaries like the White Fathers) closest to the Hutu regime and its international allies in Belgium and France, continue to blame most of the killings on the Tutsi armed force that came to power via military victory after the April–May 1994 genocide.[14] Cases of clergy participation in the genocidal campaign are dismissed as Tutsi propaganda[15] or anti-Church polemic.

Pope John Paul II avoided discussing the Church's role in the Rwandan genocide for nearly two years (deliberately avoiding available opportunities like his Nairobi appeal for peace in Rwanda and Burundi in September, 1995).[16] When he finally confronted the topic in March 1996, he maintained that the Church as such could not be held responsible for the crimes of its members, be they clergy or laity, and instead praised those Catholics who acted as "true witnesses of the love of Christ and models of Christian life" during the massacres.[17] In this he continued Church efforts at postgenocidal image repair that pointed to the 192 clergy killed in Rwanda as being martyrs for the faith.

As Prunier notes, however, "There were few cases of priests being killed trying to defend their charges"; the majority of clergy were killed for being Tutsi.[18] Neither the Pope nor Rwandan Church officials took notice of the nearly universal failure of the Church to create a sense of Christian identity strong enough to resist the imperial claims of clan and state. Indeed, such an admission would represent an indictment of the basic ecclesiology of the Catholic mainstream, and not just in Rwanda; in trying to be both Christian *and* loyal tribal members/citizens, the Church in Rwanda demonstrated how trivial, feeble, and inconsequential Christian identity can be. Kirkegaard's claim quoted at the beginning of this chapter—that multiple loyalties necessarily involve inconsequential associations—is vindicated, in a fashion he would have loathed but nevertheless understood.

While the Rwandan Protestant churches didn't do much better than the Catholics, the leaders of the former confessed their guilt and failings at high levels of church leadership. In contrast to the Protestant and Catholic communities,

> The only faith which provided a bulwark against barbarity for its adherents was Islam. There are many testimonies to the protection members of the Muslim community gave each other and their refusal to divide themselves ethnically. This solidarity comes from the fact that "being Muslim" in Rwanda, where Muslims are a very small (1.2%) proportion of the population, is not simply a choice dictated by religion; it is a global [i.e., comprehensive, all-encompassing, primary] identity choice. Muslims are often socially marginal people [in Rwanda] and this reinforces a strong sense of community identification which supersedes ethnic tags, something the majority Christians have not been able to achieve.[19]

FREEDOM OF CHRIST AS FREEDOM FROM MISPLACED RESPONSIBILITIES

A journey through the Rwandan case might seem to some an odd frame for discussing the importance of Christian allegiances. But we need to see, beyond the particularities of colonial manipulation and local exterminations, matters of great importance to the entire Church. The grand, atrocious failures of the Church in Rwanda (and in other places like Hitler's Germany and the former Yugoslavia) are not evidence of rapid, unexpected developments; rather they are the consequence of ecclesial accommodation and the minimization of the gospel over the preceding decades. Among other things, Rwanda should remind Christians everywhere that every blending of cross and flag today—no matter how innocuous or benign—serves as an installment payment on a future war in which the church sins as a guilty participant or an impotent but complicit bystander.

Despite decades of efforts to inculturate the gospel in Africa, Asia, and the Americas in ways that free the message from its European trappings, one aspect of the European Christian synthesis has remained unchallenged throughout mainstream Catholicism—namely, the Constantinian bargain that hamstrings the gospel with the "responsibilities" of statecraft. We need to be clear here: whatever else states do, states always—*always*—dispense death, in the name of order, justice, self-defense, glory, ambition, and more. When Christians accept responsibility for the healthy, efficient operations of state or imperial power, they must *necessarily* devalue, debase, and degrade their allegiance to the body of Christ and the Kingdom of God. That we think nothing of situations where Christians kill one another in the name of nationalism or patriotism in wartime suggests just how far we have fallen from seeing commitment to the body of Christ as something real in the world.

Since the third century some Christians have attempted to put the sword in Jesus' hand, to avoid his prohibition on domination and death dealing in order to make for smoother relations between Christians and the institutions built upon those non-Christian means. Constantinianism represents the triumph of this urge, and the castration of Christian identity as a bulwark against exploitation and killing follows as night follows day.

Rwanda, like the other massive failures of the Church in our century, stands for the trivialization of Christianity—no longer a distinctive worldview, polity, or praxis, merely a quaint add-on compatible with capitalism, militarism, and racism. This sort of Christianity—the broad mainstream of the post-Constantinian era—has nothing left with which to resist the bloody imperatives of empire, clan, class, or state. Such a Christianity is nothing more than "twaddle" in Kierkegaard's colorful phrase.[20]

Capturing a sense of what the Church ought to be requires us to develop a positive appreciation for what I call "Christian freeloading." Like apostles without possessions, like the birds of the air, Jesus expects his followers to benefit from some things they don't produce (Mk 6:7–8; Lk 12:24–31), in order for them to produce the one thing no other group is called to—namely, experiments in prefiguring and exemplifying what Jesus called the Kingdom of God. The Church, as those who follow Jesus today, is called to explore new possibilities of human community that are *not* built upon an order entailing the right to kill or command death on their behalf.

Neither Jesus nor his disciples nor the first several generations of Christians conceived of their mission as helping Caesar run the empire better, more humanely, or more responsibly. Whatever the nature of political power,[21] Jesus and his disciples had more ambitious goals than control of or partnership with the empire. That Christians "benefit" in some way from the order-through-death constructed by political power does not make that order the "responsibility" of Christians—although state apologists since Roman times have attempted to make that argument. Origen's second-century rejoinder to Celsus stands as valid today: just by being what God wants it to be, the Church contributes to the world around it; and it need not serve the empire on the empire's terms in order to act "responsibly."[22]

It is not a question of whether the Church's withdrawal of allegiance from competing loyalties like states, empires, and clans will be the end of such powers—they or some similar death-centered forms of social control will likely endure until the second coming. And I am not persuaded that such institutions will be dramatically or automatically more unjust, oppressive, or deadly should some number of Christians withdraw their allegiance and active participation; indeed, if the ledgers of "Christianized" states, cultures, leaders, and followers include their victims as well as their accomplishments, the payoffs from such mixed loyalties is not obvious. The proponents of power-wielding Christianity in fact *do* attempt such an accounting in arguing for the net gain realized through Christian participation in these death-based forms of power. Unfortunately for them, in the New Testament that sort of reasoning is more typical of Caiaphas than Jesus; the former's utilitarian calculus, driven by political responsibility rather than the ways of God, stands as the epitome of realpolitik: "You do not seem to have grasped the situation at all; you fail to see that it is to your advantage that one should die for the people, rather than that the whole nation should perish" (Jn 11:49–50).

To advocate a return to the idea of Church as a unique experiment in divine love ordering a human polity requires us to refuse the rituals of obedience and allegiance that states and similar institutions demand. What separates the Church as a prefiguring of the Kingdom of God from all earthly kingdoms—be they monarchies, juntas, liberal democracies, or tribal hegemonies—is the stubborn insistence of the God who chooses to convene a people who renounce even "legitimate" death-dealing as constitutive of their life together. With fidelity to Christ and the discipleship to which he calls believers as our highest loyalty, "obligations" that require us to kill or dominate in service to lesser loyalties are simply null and void.

To persons socialized in the ether of nationalism and group self-love (state, tribe, clan, gang), such a refusal smacks of ingratitude, treason, and irresponsibility. How can Christians make the world a better place, how can they advance the causes of social justice and liberation, unless they participate as loyal citizens seeking to use power for good purposes? Forget that the Christians responsible for mass death in Rwanda—and in the Crusades, Germany, Vietnam, and elsewhere—believed themselves using power for good purposes. Even when using Caesar's power for more benign expressions of good—feeding the hungry, housing the homeless, and the like—strings are always attached. The strings tie the Church to the self-preservation and health of the state, which always presupposes the right to kill (inside and outside its borders) on its own behalf. If you want to use Caesar's tools, you must commit to doing more than praying for Caesar's health—you must be willing to kill (or hire killers) on Caesar's behalf. Lobbying, voting, legislating, and the like all stand as endorsements, legitimations, and blessings of state-based power. Christians might have an easier time seeing the stakes if the tradeoffs were put more starkly: for instance, how many foreign deaths are acceptable for the defense of Social Security? How many of other people's children may be sacrificed to protect aid to indigent children in this country? The tradeoffs are never so obvious or so simplistic, but states do offer a roundabout version of the choice to Christians and others: if you want the "good" state (or clan or imperial) programs, you must commit yourself to protecting the state from challenges to its health (or, at the extreme, you must be willing to kill existing state actors in order to construct a new regime willing to deliver more of the "good" programs, providing you're committed to defending its survival/health too). In the world of states, empires, power-wielding clans, and the like, the "good" programs are options, add-ons, luxuries; the essential elements are those of coercion, control, and power that preserve the state itself. Whatever the regime type, in a crisis welfare programs will be abolished long before the police, the army, and the prisons.

For most of us, our ability to think of ways to act on behalf of the poor or oppressed in ways that do *not* entail complicity with state-based structures has been stunted by the long centuries of Constantinian captivity. The Catholic Worker movement, various strains of the Anabaptist tradition, the experiences of the early Church—all of these and more remind us that such thought and practice is possible but underdeveloped. They remain underdeveloped due to the prioritizing of Christian thought and attention directed toward doing God's work via sword and rifle, army and police, master and slave.

Before engaging in these experiments in Christian community as our primary loyalty and means of caring for the world, and if we are to have and be a church worthy of the name, we must first of all recognize our situation(s) in the world. For Christians in the "advanced" capitalist countries, our situation is not one of the Church confronting paganism, or a non- or pre-Christian culture, but of a culture of debased Christianity. We are burdened with the legacy of a cheapened, mass-produced, minimalist Christianity—a counterfeit, if you will—that has swamped any more authentic version, and that makes it impossible for people to understand what Christianity should really be.

Recognizing our situation places an imperative of critique upon us. We must, as Christians, begin refusing all the old concordats with inferior goods: with nationalism (and "patriotism," many people's more benign term for state- and nation-worship), with the market god; with lifestyles of prosperity, power, and prestige; with conventional wisdom about self-interest, "family values," and more. We have few templates for what Christian discipleship should look like in our time and place, so pervasive is the diluted version, although the gospel stories of Jesus give us a powerful place to stand and begin such a reformation. But until we begin weaning ourselves from the cheapened variety, we will lack the appetite for a God-centered practice closer to the genuine article as exemplified by Jesus.

We need to admit, with Kierkegaard, that too much of Christian life and practice has been mostly an exercise in "playing Christianity,"[23] a child's game that imitates the sights and sounds of the authentic but is utterly lacking in risk, transformation, and substance. Moving beyond Christianity as child's play requires getting our priorities and loyalties straight. Unless we do, massive betrayals of Christian principles—as in Rwanda—will certainly happen again in our lifetime, and no corner of the Church universal should assume the next betrayal will not be its own.

NOTES

1. Pope John Paul II (1993). *Veritatis Splendor*, no. 15. (Available at www.vatican.va/holy_father/phf_en.htm).

2. Gerard Prunier (1995), *The Rwanda Crisis* (New York: Columbia University Press), p. 9.

3. Ibid., pp. 31–32.

4. Saskia Van Hoyweghen (1996), "The Disintegration of the Catholic Church of Rwanda: A Study of the Fragmentation of Political and Religious Authority," *African Affairs* 95:381.

5. Ibid., pp. 382–83.

6. Prunier, *The Rwanda Crisis*, pp. 80–81.

7. Ibid., p. 83.

8. Ian Linden (1977), *Church and Revolution in Rwanda*, (Manchester: Manchester University Press), p. 8.

9. Amnesty International (1994), *Rwanda: Mass murder by government supporters and troops in April and May 1994* (available at www.amnesty.org. aipub/1994/AFR/471194.AFR.txt), pp 6–10.

10. Associated Press (1997), "2 Nuns Are Accused of Rwanda Genocide," *Chicago Tribune*, April 20, p. 1.

11. Ibid., p. 2.

12. Luke Odhiambo (1997), "Two Catholic priests, nun among 31 killed in Rwanda," *AfricaNews Online*, May 19, p. 1 (available at www.africanews. org/east/rwanda/19970516_feat2.html).

13. Prunier, *The Rwanda Crisis*, pp. 242, 250.

14. For example, Prunier, *The Rwanda Crisis*, pp. 250–51.

15. Charles Masters (1995), "Priest accused of genocide," *Electronic Telegraph*, July 31, p. 1 (available at www.telegraph.co.uk:80/et?/ac=00012 . . . tmo=33a9b8ab&pg=/et/95/7/31/wrwand31.html).

16. See Reuter News Service (1995) "Pope Urges End to Bloodshed in Rwanda and Burundi." September 19, p. 1.

17. Reuter News Service (1996). "Pope Urges Catholics to Answer for Rwanda Killings." March 20, pp. 1–2.

18. Prunier, *The Rwanda Crisis*, p. 251.

19. Ibid., p. 252.

20. Soren Kierkegaard (1854–55/1968), *Attack upon "Christendom."* (Princeton, N.J.: Princeton University Press), p. 34.

21. See Jacques Ellul (1980), "Anarchism and Christianity," *Katallagete* (fall) for a particularly provocative scriptural analysis.

22. Contra Celsus; see Glenn E. Hinson (1986), *Understandings of the Church* (New York: Fortress Press), pp. 63–66.

23. Kierkegaard, *Attack upon Christendom*, p. 121.

Contributors

MICHAEL J. BAXTER, C.S.C., is an Assistant Professor of Theology at the University of Notre Dame.

ROBERT W. BRIMLOW is an Associate Professor of Philosophy at St. John Fisher College.

WALTER BRUEGGEMANN is the McPheeder Professor of Old Testament at Columbia Theological Seminary.

MICHAEL L. BUDDE is an Associate Professor of Political Science at DePaul University.

CURT CADORETTE is the John Henry Newman Associate Professor of Roman Catholic Studies at the University of Rochester.

RODNEY CLAPP is Editorial Director of Brazos Press.

ROBERTO GOIZUETA is Professor of Theology at Boston College.

STANLEY HAUERWAS is the Gilbert T. Rowe Professor of Theological Ethics at Duke University .

MARIANNE SAWICKI is an author of several books and articles on the historical recovery of information about Jesus and his earliest followers.

MICHAEL WARREN is Professor of Theology and Religious Studies at St. John's University.

Index